W9-BSF-850

# Bake and Freeze Desserts

# Bake *and* Freeze Desserts

130 Do-Ahead Cakes, Pies, Cookies, Brownies, Bars, Ice Creams, Terrines, and Sorbets

Elinor Klivans

William Morrow and Company, Inc.
*New York*

It is the policy of William Morrow and Company, Inc., and its imprints and affiliates, recognizing the importance of preserving what has been written, to print the books we publish on acid-free paper, and we exert our best efforts to that end.

Library of Congress Cataloging-in-Publication Data

Klivans, Elinor.
Bake and freeze desserts : 130 do-ahead cakes, pies, cookies, brownies, bars, ice creams, terrines, and sorbets / Elinor Klivans.
p. cm.
Includes bibliographical references and index.
ISBN 0-688-12347-3
1. Desserts. 2. Make-ahead cookery. 3. Cookery (Frozen foods) I. Title.
TX773.K574 1994
641.8'6—dc20 94-7762
CIP

Printed in the United States of America

First Edition

1 2 3 4 5 6 7 8 9 10

BOOK DESIGN BY RICHARD ORIOLO

To Jeffrey, Laura, and Peter,

who think I can do anything and
make me believe I can.

# Contents

# Acknowledgments

I want to thank the many people who worked so hard to help me write this book.

Judith Weber, my agent and worthy adviser.

Harriet Bell, my editor, who expertly guided this book through every step of the publishing process. How lucky I was.

Susan Derecskey, my compassionate copyeditor, who is a master at organizing a cookbook and making sure that everyone will understand and enjoy what I have written.

My husband, Jeff, who lived through and tasted every success and disaster.

My children Laura and Peter, who took time from their busy and faraway lives to proofread my recipes and cheer me on.

My mother, Selma Wishnatzki, who started me on my way; and my produce shipper father, Lester, who brings me wonderful fruit for baking.

Deb Martin, whose common sense opinions and good taste made this a better book.

Helen Hall, whose ideas I value and trust; and Reg Hall, my resident chemist.

Barbara Fairchild and Kristine Kidd, who published my first dessert article in *Bon Appétit* magazine.

I want to thank the companies who supplied information and the business people who returned calls night and day and offered their expertise: Richard Stier of Libra Laboratories, Bob Zedik and The Chocolate Manufacturers and Confectionery Association, The International Ice Cream Association, Allen Clark of Taylor Thermometers, the helpful experts answering the Saran Wrap consumer line, Amana Refrigeration Inc., Frigidare Company, Sub-Zero Freezer Co., Inc., and everyone at the General Electric Company consumer answer phone who were there 24 hours a day patiently finding the answers to my questions.

Finally, a giant thank you to my supporters and encouragers: Paula Collins, Maureen Egan, Lisa Ekus, Carole and Woody Emanuel, Betty and Joe Fleming, Kat and Howard Grossman, Heather Harland, Mom and Dad Klivans, Susan Lasky, Susie Lavenson, Rosie and Larry Levitan, Carolyn and Keith May, Dale Mudge, Jane Sommer, Erv Shames, Fern Tsao; and the family, friends, and teachers who shared their treasured recipes and advice with me.

# Bake and Freeze Desserts

# Introduction

When I was growing up, I used to watch and help my mother bake. Together we baked cakes and pies for birthdays and holidays; cookies to share at school; cakes heaped with fresh fruit, which my father, a produce shipper, brought home by the crate; and homey family desserts. As I waited to lick the bowl and beaters, my mother would share her baking wisdom with me—use fresh ingredients, bake with butter, don't make desserts too sweet, be gentle with batters and doughs, keep everything clean, and never use anything that falls on the floor. I'm sure my mother had some baking failures, but I don't remember any. She taught me that baking was easy and fun. Now baking is my life, this is what I do.

When I was first married, I spent leisurely weekends baking and trying out new recipes. I would spend an entire Saturday making six fillings and toppings for Danish pastry or a fancy cake encased in a chocolate cage. Those days are long gone, but I learned many techniques from those complicated recipes that I still use every day as a professional baker.

Then our children were born, and spending thirty minutes by myself in the kitchen was a rare luxury. Baking had to fit in with the requirements of a hectic household. That's when I really began to bake and freeze. Given a few minutes alone, I would rush to bake a batch of cookies or cake layers or put together an ice cream pie for the freezer.

The children grew older, and I began teaching classes in Miami cooking schools. Cooking was turning into a job. As I prepared the basic components for a class ahead of time, I put them in the freezer until I needed them. A dessert like Chocolate Thunder, a spectacular cake assembled from Fudge Bars and Chocolate Truffle Sauce, takes just minutes to put together when you have the elements already frozen.

In 1981 we moved to Maine, and a couple of years later I began baking the desserts at Peter Ott's restaurant in Camden. Baking in a restaurant was a surefire way to master techniques because I practiced them over and over and gained a thorough understanding of each one. After making meringues a hundred times, I've seen what happens when I add sugar too fast, bake at too high a temperature, or forget to line the baking sheet. I've seen exactly what happens when I whip egg whites in a bowl that is not clean and grease-free. Other times, when I do everything right, I achieve perfect results. I've also learned how to recycle a dessert when I make a mistake: Chocolate Blackout Cake became a successful deep dish cake when I dropped it on the counter one afternoon. On the other hand, there's no way to save a bitter chocolate cake when you forget to add the sugar. That's when it's time to give up and start over again.

I soon realized that working in a busy restaurant kitchen meant I would have to prepare various mixtures ahead and freeze them. At first, I just kept some basics in the freezer, Frozen Pantry items like Pound Cake, Lemon Curd, and praline. Soon I started to prepare complete desserts ahead of time and freeze them ready for serving. From big chocolate layer cakes to frozen terrines to Apple Crisp, I worked on recipes until I had a repertoire of such desserts. When they were served, they looked and tasted just as good as the day they were baked. My secret goal was to have some time off without anyone knowing I was away. The ideas carried over to my baking at home, and instead of making desserts just hours ahead, I prepare them weeks or even months in advance, at my convenience. It's nice to know there's a cake or pie sitting in the freezer ready to be served as a last-minute dessert.

This approach to desserts fits right into the demands of everyone's busy life. If you love to bake but don't have the time these days, *Bake and Freeze Desserts* will show you how to plan and prepare ahead. You don't have to have a big freezer to get started, just the one that is part of your refrigerator will do. And when you do have time to spare, you can skip the freezing step and serve the dessert freshly made, except for such desserts as ice cream pies and the like, which must be frozen at least overnight.

Over the years I've learned a lot about what works and what doesn't. I've made plenty of mistakes. This book is filled with my successes.

# Techniques

Successful baking depends on three things: good technique, quality ingredients, and the right tool for the task. None of the techniques, ingredients, or equipment in this book is hard to master, difficult to find, or unlikely to be in your kitchen. Here, to begin, are some of the techniques commonly used in home baking.

## Creaming Fats and Sugar

The purpose of creaming fat and sugar is to beat in air and form a smooth mixture that will combine easily with other ingredients. Thorough creaming creates air cells, which expand and help lighten a cake or cookies during baking. Most of the sugar crystals do not dissolve during creaming, and their rough texture helps hold in the air. To achieve a smooth fluffy mixture, the butter, margarine, or vegetable shortening should be at room temperature, 65° to 75°F. Cakes usually require a longer creaming time than cookies. When sugar and fat are creamed for cookies, the purpose is more to form a smooth mixture than to beat in air.

## Beating Eggs

When eggs are beaten, they form a foam that is filled with air cells. If the mixture is baked, the heat expands the air cells, which help leaven and lighten it. Mixtures that are not baked, like mousses, acquire much of their light texture from the air cells in beaten eggs.

Whole eggs and egg yolks are beaten until their color lightens and they thicken. Sometimes, the eggs or yolks are warmed first so that they whip faster and achieve greater volume. When eggs are beaten with sugar, the mixture becomes more dense and the foam more stable. Usually this sugar and egg mixture is beaten to the ribbon stage, that is, if you lift up some of the thickened mixture and let it fall back in the bowl, a thin, flat ribbon pattern will form.

When egg whites are beaten, they form a delicate foam. Because acid helps to stabilize egg white foams, cream of tartar, an acid, is usually beaten in. Egg whites will not whip properly if they come in contact with fat. As long as the whites do not contain any trace of yolk, and the mixing bowl and utensils are clean and absolutely free of fat, there should be no problem.

Properly beaten egg whites are shiny and will form a soft point or peak if you dip a spoon in the egg white and lift it out. At the soft peak stage, the moving beaters form smooth curving lines. Egg whites at the soft peak stage look creamy; they combine smoothly and easily with other mixtures. It is preferable to underbeat egg whites slightly than to overbeat them. Overbeaten egg whites look lumpy and dull and form big clumps if you try to fold them into another mixture.

I beat egg whites with an electric mixer on low speed until the cream of tartar is dissolved. Then I increase the speed to medium and beat until the soft peaks form. I find it's easier to check the egg whites and control the results on medium rather than high speed.

Adding sugar to beaten egg whites stabilizes the foam, and the mixture can sit for a while before being used. After sugar is added to egg whites, the mixture thickens; it can even be baked into a crisp meringue. When adding sugar, begin just as the whites reach the soft peak stage. Add it slowly so the whites have time to absorb it. Adding one tablespoon of sugar every thirty seconds is a good interval. Adding a hot sugar syrup stabilizes the whites even more than granulated sugar. The syrup heats the whites, causing some of the protein to coagulate, so that the air cells are less likely to burst. Egg whites beaten with sugar form firm peaks if you dip in a spoon and lift it out.

## Whipping Cream

The bowl, beaters, and whipping cream should be cold. Add flavorings, such as powdered sugar, vanilla extract, or coffee, to the cream in the mixing bowl, then begin beating the cream. Powdered sugar, which contains cornstarch, stabilizes the cream slightly so that it can be held for about 2 hours before it is served. If the cream is beaten with a stand mixer, beat the cream at medium speed, but if it is beaten with a handheld mixer, beat at high speed. Slowly move a handheld mixer around the mixing bowl as you beat the cream so that it all beats evenly.

Beat the cream either to the soft peak stage or the firm peak stage. At the soft peak stage, the movement of the beaters traces smooth lines in the cream, and if you dip a spoon in the cream and lift it out, the cream forms a point that falls over at its tip. The texture of the whipped cream is like a thick, fluffy sauce. At the firm peak stage, the movement of the beaters forms a teardrop shape in the cream, and if you dip a spoon in the cream and lift it out, the cream forms a point that stands straight up and remains that way. To check the stage of the whipped cream, I prefer to watch the pattern that the movement of the beaters makes in the cream. Once you beat some cream and watch the patterns form, it will be easy to judge. If the whipped cream is not to be used immediately, cover and refrigerate it. Give the whipped cream a quick stir with a spoon just before serving.

## Folding

When a light mixture is combined with a heavy mixture, the two are usually folded together gently so as not to push the air out of the lighter mixture and break up the air cells. I whisk a little of the lighter mixture into the heavier one to lighten the heavier mixture, then I use a large rubber spatula to fold in the rest. Use the spatula to dig down to the bottom of the bowl and bring the two mixtures up and over each other. Use a large bowl and turn the bowl as you fold so that the mixtures blend quickly.

## Cooking Sugar Syrups

Hot sugar syrups are used for some of these desserts. Italian meringue, which is the base for several frostings and some of the mousse recipes in this book, requires a sugar syrup cooked to a specific temperature. Cooking sugar syrups properly so that crystals do not form requires some patience and an awareness of a few standard procedures. Let the sugar dissolve in the water over low heat before allowing the mixture to boil. Before it boils it can be stirred gently to help the sugar dissolve, but after the mixture boils it should not be stirred. As soon as the sugar dissolves, clip a candy thermometer onto the inside of the pan so that you will know when the sugar reaches the correct temperature. The boiling mixture sometimes throws some sugar crystals on to the side of the pan; these should be wiped off with a brush dipped in water. Corn syrup helps prevent this crystallization, so I usually cook sugar syrups with a small amount of corn syrup.

I use caramelized sugar for nut pralines, caramel syrups, and caramel sauces. Caramelizing sugar is simply a process of melting the sugar and heating it to an amber (dark golden brown) color. A good thing about cooking caramel is that the sugar is heated to such a high temperature, above 310°F., that the sugar actually breaks down and crystals do not form. Chef Jorant, at the La Varenne cooking school, calls it "cooking the sugar past the stage of crystallization." It doesn't matter if you stir the sugar at any stage or dissolve it after it boils, the final caramelized sugar will still be smooth. Just remember to melt and caramelize all of the sugar so there are no hard lumps and to be careful that the hot caramel does not splash on you. Use a wooden spoon to stir the mixture. Melt and caramelize the sugar slowly and evenly so that spots of sugar do not blacken and burn. The only time I ruin caramel is when I burn it by trying to do other things at the same time. When the caramel becomes an amber color, remove it from the heat immediately.

## Melting Chocolate

Chocolate burns at a low temperature. The ideal temperature for melting chocolate is around 100°F. Chocolate melts smoothly if gentle heat is used to melt it slowly and if there are no sudden bursts of heat, such as steam from a double boiler. Cutting chocolate into small pieces, about ½ inch in size, helps it to melt evenly. White chocolate should be melted in a nonreactive container. Pyrex glass or stainless steel containers are nonreactive; aluminum is not.

When I melt chocolate without other ingredients, I melt it in a 175°F. oven for 8 to 10 minutes. The chocolate is not being heated to 175°F. since it is removed from the oven when it melts, not when it reaches 175°F. If the chocolate is left in the oven for a few additional seconds, the gentle heat will not harm it. I find I am able to melt slightly larger pieces of chocolate in the oven than I can in a double boiler, so a one-ounce piece of unsweetened chocolate, for example, does not need to be chopped first.

When I melt chocolate with other ingredients, such as butter, I do it in a double boiler so that I can stir the ingredients into a smooth mixture as the chocolate melts. Keep the water in the double boiler hot or barely simmering, below boiling so that steam doesn't form.

After chocolate is melted, water can be mixed with it, as in the Chocolate Fudge Frosting for the Chocolate Blackout Cake (page 120), but when the chocolate and water are combined, they must be at approximately the same temperature. Chocolate dislikes sudden temperature changes.

## Peeling, Toasting, and Grinding Nuts

Toasting nuts improves their flavor. When almonds, pine nuts, and hazelnuts are toasted, the flavor actually changes. When I toast nuts, I spread them out in a single layer on a baking sheet and bake them in an oven preheated to 325°F. Walnuts and pecans take 8 to 10 minutes, pine nuts about 8 minutes until they are golden. Blanched sliced or slivered almonds take about 12 minutes until golden, and blanched whole almonds and hazelnuts about 15 minutes. Just before the nuts are ready, you'll smell a pleasant aroma of toasting nuts.

Since hazelnuts must have their skins removed before they are used for baking, try to buy blanched (peeled) hazelnuts. To blanch hazelnuts, fill a saucepan with enough water to cover the hazelnuts and bring it to a boil. Add the hazelnuts and boil for 5 minutes. Drain the hazelnuts, immerse them in cold water for several minutes to cool, drain again, and peel the nuts with a small sharp knife. The skin will come off easily, and they will dry out later as they toast. If the hazelnuts are not toasted immediately, dry them with a clean dish towel and refrigerate or freeze them.

I chop nuts by hand with a large sharp knife which gives me control over the size of the pieces. Finely chopped nuts should be ⅛ inch in size and coarsely chopped nuts between ¼ inch and ⅜ inch in size. When I need ground nuts, I grind them in a food processor fitted with the steel blade. Processing the nuts with some of the sugar or flour from the recipe allows you to finely grind the nuts without their forming a paste. In the recipe for Gianduia Ice Cream (page 230), I want the hazelnuts ground very fine, so I process them with some of the liquid ice cream mixture from the recipe.

## Preparing Baking Pans

When pans need to be greased, I use the same shortening to grease the pan that I use in the recipe. I grease pie crust pans with vegetable shortening, cake pans with butter, and the pan for an oil-based cake like Coffee Chocolate Chip Coffee Cake (page 89) with oil. Any flavor that might be added to the dessert from the fat used to grease the pan will match the taste of the fat used in the dessert. Butter burns at a lower temperature than vegetable shortening or oil, but I have never had any problem.

I line some pans with aluminum foil, parchment, or wax paper and this is indicated in the individual recipes.

## Kitchen Temperature

Kitchen temperatures affect recipes, and I keep this in mind when I bake. On a hot summer day, when the temperature in my kitchen can climb above 80°F., preparing a pie crust or beating an Italian meringue, even to lukewarm, can be a challenge. When making pie crust or Tart Pastry Crust dough on a hot day, chill the shortening and the flour mixture in the freezer for 30 minutes. For a recipe that requires long beating I stop the mixer halfway through and put the bowl in the freezer for about ten minutes to cool down the mixture. A cold winter morning, when my kitchen can be as cool as 60°F., is ideal pie crust making weather, but butter will take longer to soften and creaming mixtures may take additional time.

# Equipment

You would probably be surprised at all the equipment I don't have in my kitchen. My two work horses are a heavy-duty KitchenAid electric mixer and a Cuisinart food processor. They sit on opposite sides of my kitchen counter so that they are always ready to go to work. I baked for many years without these appliances, but they certainly make preparation faster and baking easier.

The equipment listed here is what I use daily and what I used for testing the recipes in this book. It includes my personal opinion and experience. The best advice I could ever give is to choose quality equipment and to use the proper tool for the job.

## Baking Pans

The baking pan measurements given are the inside measurements of the pan.

**Baking Sheets** Heavy aluminum is a good choice for baking sheets since it conducts heat evenly. Heavyweight baking sheets will not warp or bend after repeated use. Precise measurements are not crucial, but baking sheets should not be so large that they touch the oven walls. This would prevent proper air circulation, and the oven would not heat evenly. Allow at least an inch of air space between the sides of the baking sheet and the oven walls. I use the general term baking sheet for both cookie sheets and jelly-roll pans.

Cookie sheets usually have open sides so that cookies slide easily off the pan and a rim at one or both ends to grasp. Sizes suitable for home ovens range from about 15 × 12 inches to about 17 × 14 inches.

Jelly-roll pans are baking sheets with a one-inch rim around all sides; they are used for baking cookies, thin cakes, and bars. They range in size from about 15½ × 10½ inches to about 17 × 12 inches.

**Cake Pans** When I got married, someone gave me several lightweight round cake pans with 1¼-inch-high sides. I felt obliged to use them, and for years I baked cakes with humped, overbrowned tops. Finally, after a cake overflowed out of the pan and all over the oven, I went out and bought heavy aluminum 9- and 10-inch layer pans with 2-inch-high sides. I wish I had done it sooner, but it taught me a good lesson.

Rectangular and square cake pans should be heavyweight aluminum, preferably with a nonstick coating and with 2-inch-high sides.

Whenever springform pans are appropriate for a dessert I use them. Mousses and ice cream pies are removed easily from the pan and keep a perfect shape. I prefer no-rust Hillware brand aluminum springform pans, which have 3-inch-high sides and a sturdy clip mechanism. The sides should be at least 2¾ inches high. Since they remove easily, nonstick coatings are unnecessary.

I use an aluminum nonstick tube pan 10 × 4½ inches with a 16-cup capacity and a permanently fixed bottom, but a smaller tube pan with as little as a 14-cup capacity will work fine for the recipes in this book. Even if a pan has a nonstick coating, I line the bottom with parchment or wax paper. The nonstick coating helps release the cake sides smoothly but not always the bottom.

**Loaf Pans** Loaf pans come in two standard shapes with numerous small measurement differences. The standard loaf pan has about 7 cups capacity and measures about 9 × 5 × 3 inches; the long narrow loaf pan, sometimes called a terrine pan or terrine mold, has a capacity of 7 to 8 cups and ranges in size from 12 × 4 × 2¾ inches to the slightly larger 12¾ × 4¼ × 2½ inches. I prefer the long narrow loaf pan for my desserts. I use metal loaf pans with sharp corners that produce cakes and frozen terrines with attractive, even edges.

**Pie and Tart Pans** I use 10-inch heavy aluminum pie pans for baking pies. These pans allow for a generous amount of filling, and the pies are large enough to be cut into 8 generous slices. I have 4 pie pans so I can store several pans in the freezer filled with unbaked pie crusts. Eleven-inch black steel tart pans with a removable bottom are my choice for baking tarts. Black steel retains the heat efficiently and helps the crust brown even more quickly than aluminum, but the pans must be thoroughly dried after washing or they will rust.

## Electric Mixer

My heavy-duty KitchenAid mixer with its 5-quart bowl performs every mixing job I require. It's my best friend in the kitchen, and I recommend it if you are buying an electric mixer. It is a considerable investment, however, and other countertop mixers will work fine in any of my recipes. Handheld mixers are especially good for whipping small amounts and can perform most beating jobs. When using less powerful electric mixers, plan on slightly longer beating times and increase the speed a notch. Most double recipes of batters are too large to mix with handheld mixers; they should be mixed in separate batches.

## Food Processor

It makes sense to buy a machine with a large capacity and a powerful motor, which can handle small and large jobs.

## Freezer

It has been only ten years since I bought my first upright freezer. For many years I used a side-by-side refrigerator/freezer combination. But there is no question that a freestanding freezer, which will be opened infrequently and has its own temperature control, maintains a more constant, colder temperature than a refrigerator/freezer combination and is preferable for storing frozen foods. If you lack space for a full freezer, a compact under-the-counter freezer is often a good solution.

## Ice Cream Machine

I use a Simac Il Gelataio Super and a Simac Il Gelataio SC. The Il Gelataio Super is a large machine with its own refrigeration unit, which I use in the restaurant. It produces about 1½ to 2 quarts of ice cream or sorbet and can churn batch after batch. It is, however, a major investment, and it is heavy and bulky to store. At home I use the SC, which costs about a fifth as much as the larger machine. The SC has a freezing chamber with a nonstick lining that you chill in the freezer before filling it with the ice cream mixture; it has a small electric motor to churn the ice cream. It produces about 1 quart of ice cream; it is the most reliable machine that I have found for home use.

## Oven

Oven temperatures vary about 10°F. within the oven with the upper third and rear of the oven usually being the warmest places. If your oven thermometer and oven thermostat differ by more than 10°F., or if your baked goods suddenly begin burning or underbaking during their normal baking period, the oven should be recalibrated.

When baking in a standard oven, reverse desserts front to back and from lower rack to upper rack during the baking to ensure even browning, and be careful to avoid overloading the oven so the air can circulate properly.

My oven bakes with either convection or standard heat. Since most household ovens are standard ovens, I tested all of these recipes using my oven as a standard oven. However, I do recommend baking with convection heat if you have it. The heat is even throughout the oven, and desserts seldom need to be rearranged for even browning. For convection baking, follow the baking instructions for a recipe but lower the oven temperature by 50°F., i.e., if the recipe says 350°F., bake the cake or whatever at 300°F. Some manufacturers claim baking times are shorter in a convection oven, but I find baking times to be the same as in a standard oven.

## Saucepans

I use stainless steel saucepans, which do not react with acidic foods. The pans have either a copper-clad or aluminum-clad bottom to help conduct heat evenly. The small saucepan holds 1 quart; the medium 2 quarts; and my 2 large saucepans hold 3 and 4 quarts, respectively.

My 2-quart saucepan has an insert to convert it into a double boiler. If you don't have a double boiler, heat a small amount of water in a 4-quart saucepan and place a 2-quart saucepan filled with whatever needs to be melted over the 4-quart saucepan. The rim of the smaller saucepan must rest on the rim of the larger saucepan. A copper- or aluminum-clad bottom on the top saucepan diffuses the heat evenly and reduces the chance of overheating the ingredients. It is easy to see the water in the saucepan below and prevent it from boiling or producing steam, which could burn a delicate ingredient like chocolate.

## Scale

A scale with a removable bin on the top, rather than a flat top, is practical for kitchen use. The bin holds whatever food must be weighted without its rolling off.

## Thermometers

I use four kinds of thermometers — oven, freezer, food, and candy. Once a week, I put the oven thermometer in the oven when preheating it to check the accuracy of the oven thermostat. I leave a freezer thermometer in the freezer and adjust the freezer control to maintain a freezer temperature between 0° and 8°F. To measure temperatures of custards or melted chocolate,

I use an instant-read food thermometer that goes from 0° to 220°F. An instant-read food thermometer is also useful for checking the temperature of such ingredients as soft butter or hot milk. This kind of thermometer actually registers the temperature within 10 to 15 seconds, fast but not quite instant. Wear an oven mitt on the hand holding the thermometer for protection from heat or steam. I use the candy thermometer to measure the higher temperatures needed for testing sugar syrups. My mercury candy thermometer has a stainless steel back, clips onto the side of the pan, is easy to read, and gives a slightly more accurate reading than an instant-read thermometer. It registers temperature within 20 to 30 seconds. I use Taylor thermometers; they are high quality and readily available.

## Utensils

Less is better in my kitchen, so I steer away from gadgets. The following utensils and gadgets are the ones I consider essential.

**Cardboard Cake Circles** Cookshops sell these corrugated paper circles in several sizes. They provide a good flat surface for holding a cake and are useful for freezing a cake. If a dessert has a high butter content that might be absorbed by the cardboard, use a moisture-resistant coated cake circle or wrap a cardboard circle with aluminum foil. Moisture-resistant and other cardboard cake circles can be ordered from Maid of Scandinavia (page 245).

**Cooling Racks** I cool most desserts in their pans, but for the few that require cooling racks, such as sticky cakes that must be removed from their pan while still warm, I use a rectangular cooling rack with thin crosswoven wires, which support a cake without digging into it. Unlike round racks, rectangular racks hold almost any size cake or a large number of cookies. When I cool a cake in its pan, I still place it on a cooling rack so that air circulates around the pan and the cake cools evenly.

**Graters and Peelers** I use a four-sided box grater for grating citrus zest and chocolate. This type of grater rests securely on the counter. The tiny teardrop holes are the best for grating zest. A stainless steel vegetable peeler with a 2½-inch swivel blade that is an extension of the handle is a good tool for making chocolate curls and removing large strips of zest from citrus fruit.

**Knives** I use a small sharp paring knife with a 4½-inch blade to loosen desserts from their pans. A large chef's knife with an 8-inch blade is good for cutting large cakes and firm desserts like ice cream pies. A serrated bread knife with an 8-inch blade splits cake layers evenly.

**Measuring Spoons and Cups** Have two sets of measuring spoons, one for dry ingredients and one for wet. For accurate measuring, use dry measuring cups to measure dry ingredients and liquid measuring cups to measure liquid ingredients. It may sound obvious, but it makes a difference when measuring. Measure dry ingredients by filling the cup and leveling the top with a thin metal spatula. For liquids, use cups with clear markings and place the cup on a flat surface when measuring. Three measuring cups in 1-, 2-, and 4-cup sizes are a good assortment to have.

**Mixing Bowls** When I refer to small mixing bowls, I mean a 2- to 3-cup capacity; medium, a 6-cup capacity; and large, 2- to 5-quart capacity. Pyrex bowls are heatproof and chip resistant, and I have been using the same set for over 20 years. Stainless steel bowls are easy to clean, will not react with ingredients, and are virtually unbreakable. I do not recommend plastic mixing bowls because they can absorb odors and fat.

**Mixing Spoons** Have at least 1 wooden spoon to use when cooking sugar to a high temperature. Since wood is a poor conductor of heat, a wooden spoon will not draw heat from a mixture, nor will it melt the spoon. For general mixing, I have several heatproof plastic mixing spoons which do not absorb odors as wooden spoons might.

**Paper Liners** Parchment paper, which usually comes in rolls, is the most practical liner for baking pans. Wax paper can be used to line cake pans since the paper is covered by the batter, but it is not suitable for lining cookie sheets since it will smoke and burn where it is not covered by the cookies. In some recipes where the liner must cover the sides and bottom of the pan and mold smoothly to the pan and for meringues, I use aluminum foil.

**Pastry Bags and Pastry Tips** I use Ateco cloth pastry bags with a plastic-coated lining that makes them easy to clean. Dry the pastry bags on a sunny windowsill to prevent them from developing a musty odor. A 16-inch pastry bag is a good all-purpose size. Ateco also makes good quality pastry tips that do not rust easily. A large star tip like the Ateco #5 and round tips with ⅜- and ½-inch openings are the ones I use most often. I prefer 2-inch-long pastry tips to the 1-inch-long size.

**Pastry Brush** Buy a good quality pastry brush that will not drop its bristles into your desserts. A 1-inch-wide brush with 2-inch-long bristles is a useful size.

**Rolling Pins and Rolling Surfaces** I prefer a fixed rolling pin, without ball bearings, but with handles. For a rolling surface, I use a freestanding white Corning Counter Saver with hard rubber feet. The surface remains cool; it measures a substantial 18 × 16 inches; it is lightweight; and it can be washed in the kitchen sink. When I'm not using it for rolling, it doubles as an extra cutting surface. I bought it at a local kitchen design center.

**Spatulas** I use rubber spatulas with wooden handles to scrape bowls clean and fold mixtures together. I have a long narrow metal spatula with a 9 × 1-inch blade for frosting cakes, smoothing glazes, and smoothing the top of batters before they are baked. An offset spatula, which looks like a pancake turner with a long blade, is useful for sliding desserts onto a platter or cookies off a baking sheet. My offset spatula has a 9-inch-long blade that is 2½ inches wide. Its long length allows me to slide it under the entire bottom of many desserts, such as ice cream pies, to loosen them from their pan.

**Strainers and Sifters** I use a fine mesh strainer to strain food and sift dry ingredients. It has a 7-inch diameter and holds about 4 cups of dry ingredients. It is easy to clean and does a fine job of straining lumps from dry ingredients, removing overcooked bits from custards, and removing small seeds from fruit. When I want to remove every last seed, I clean the strainer and strain the fruit a second time. I sift dry ingredients through the strainer onto a large piece of wax paper to save cleaning a bowl.

**Turntables** When I frost or decorate a cake, I place the cake on the kind of plastic turntable normally used for storing spices. It's much less expensive than a professional cake-decorating turntable.

**Whisks** Stainless steel sauce whisks are invaluable for whisking out a few lumps and for smoothing out thick mixtures like pastry cream or chilled sauces. Since I prefer to beat egg whites and whipped cream with an electric mixer, I seldom use a balloon whisk, which has a round bottom and more wires than a sauce whisk.

# Ingredients

All of the ingredients in this book have met the "Camden, Maine, Ingredient Test." Since I didn't want to use ingredients that would be difficult to find, I limited myself to ingredients that I could buy in our small town. I figured that if I could buy it in Camden (population 5,000), it should be available almost anywhere. There is a list of mail order sources at the end of the book in case you find it necessary to order an ingredient or equipment.

## Butter, Shortening, and Oils

Unsalted butter is used in all of the recipes, and corn oil margarine with salt in the few recipes that call for margarine; I store both in the freezer to keep them fresh. I occasionally use Crisco vegetable shortening and corn or canola oil. Room temperature butter, margarine, or vegetable shortening should be at 65° to 75°F.; check it once with a food thermometer to see exactly how it looks and feels at this temperature.

## Chocolate

Chocolate comes from cocoa beans. The beans are roasted and cracked open to remove the nibs or kernels. These are ground, producing chocolate liquor, which also contains cocoa butter (or cocoa fat). Unsweetened chocolate is pure chocolate liquor; semisweet and bittersweet chocolate have sugar added; and milk chocolate has sugar and milk solids added. Some additional cocoa butter is added to all of these chocolates.

Manufacturers guard their chocolate formulas carefully. If you could compare the percentage of chocolate in different products, it would be easy to decide which one to buy, but such a comparison is not easy to make. European chocolate companies refer to the cocoa butter (cocoa fat) content when they list the percentage of chocolate in their product while U.S. government standards use the chocolate liquor content in setting requirements for chocolate manufacture in the United States. For this and other reasons, most U.S. chocolate manufacturers will not quote the percentage of chocolate in their products.

According to the requirements set by the Food and Drug Administration (FDA), unsweetened chocolate (chocolate liquor) must have a 50 to 58 percent cocoa butter content. Other chocolates have chocolate liquor requirements. Semisweet chocolate must have a 15 to 35 percent chocolate liquor content, bittersweet chocolate must have at least 35 percent. Milk chocolate must have a 10 percent chocolate liquor content and also contain milk solids. Unsweetened cocoa powder must contain from 10 to 22 percent cocoa butter. White chocolate is not classified as chocolate by the Food and Drug Administration because it does not contain chocolate liquor, only cocoa butter; there are no official requirements.

A good way to choose a good quality baking chocolate is to taste different brands. If a chocolate tastes good in your mouth, it will taste good in your desserts. When you taste chocolate, let it melt in your mouth and notice the taste of the chocolate. Pay attention to whether the dominant taste is sugar or chocolate and whether the chocolate actually tastes of chocolate. Less expensive or lower quality chocolate may have a waxy or chemical taste and may contain little real chocolate; taste one of these less expensive chocolates and you will see the difference. Taste at least two brands of chocolate at a time to compare the flavors. Since I use top quality semisweet chocolate with a high chocolate content, I am comfortable using semisweet and bittersweet chocolate interchangeably in dessert recipes. I do steer away from using some of the European bittersweet chocolates that have an unusually high cocoa butter content, sometimes over 60 percent, as a substitute for semisweet chocolate.

As Harold McGee says, white chocolate is not "a rare albino roast," but a product containing cocoa butter, milk solids, and sugar. Since the FDA doesn't consider white chocolate to be chocolate, it is labeled as white confectionery coating. Many "white confectionery coatings" contain no cocoa butter, so be sure to check the package to see that what you're buying contains cocoa butter.

Unsweetened cocoa powder is chocolate liquor with most of the cocoa butter removed. When cocoa powder is treated with an alkaline solution, it is called Dutch process cocoa powder. I prefer Dutch process cocoa which has a slightly sweeter flavor and darker color than nonalkalized cocoa powder.

After I open chocolate, I wrap it tightly in plastic wrap then in aluminum foil and store it in a cool dry place. If handled properly, unsweetened, semisweet, and bittersweet chocolate will keep for up to a year. Since milk chocolate and white chocolate contain milk solids, they are more perishable than dark chocolate. I store milk chocolate for up to 3 months in a cool dry place. White chocolate, lacking chocolate liquor, is even more perishable; I freeze it if I am storing it for more than a few weeks. Before freezing a large block of chocolate, break it into manageable 1- and 2-pound pieces, and wrap each piece tightly in plastic wrap then heavy aluminum foil. Defrost the wrapped chocolate in a cool place to prevent "sweating" when the chocolate defrosts.

I store unsweetened cocoa powder for up to 2 years in a tightly covered tin in a cool dark pantry.

The following are the chocolates I prefer and the ones I used to test the recipes:

- Unsweetened chocolate: Baker's, Nestlé, and Guittard
- Semisweet chocolate: Nestlé, Dove Bar, Hershey's Dark, and Callebaut
- Bittersweet chocolate: Guittard, Lindt, and Callebaut
- Semisweet chocolate chips: Nestlé and Guittard
- Milk chocolate: Dove Bar and Callebaut
- White chocolate: Callebaut
- Unsweetened cocoa powder: Droste or Hershey's European Style, both are Dutch process

## Citrus and Citrus Zest

Use fresh citrus juice for all of the recipes. Citrus zest is the colored part of the rind of the fruit without any of the bitter white pith. Before grating the zest, wash the fruit and dry it.

## Cream and Milk

Heavy whipping cream contains from 36 to 40 percent butterfat. Cartons may be labeled heavy whipping cream or heavy cream. I use the term heavy whipping cream. I use heavy whipping cream for whipped cream, chocolate whipped cream, and whipped cream combined with Lemon or Orange Curd. For other recipes light whipping cream, which has less fat, works fine.

Light whipping cream contains from 30 to 36 percent butterfat. Cartons may be labeled light whipping cream or whipping cream, which is the term I use.

Half-and-half contains at least 10.5 percent butterfat.

Whole milk contains 4 percent butterfat; low fat has 1 to 2 percent butterfat; skim milk is considered fat free. I have noted if a recipe requires a particular kind of milk.

## Eggs

Cold, large eggs are used in my recipes. Cold eggs are easier to separate, and bacteria are less likely to multiply in an egg that is kept cold. I've never noticed a significant difference between whipping egg whites cold or at room temperature, so I whip them cold.

If you have egg whites left over from a recipe, freeze them for up to 3 months. Put them in a clean greasefree plastic freezer container, leaving at least 1 inch of air space, press plastic wrap onto the surface of the egg whites, and cover tightly. Label the container with the date and the number of egg whites in the container. Defrost the covered egg whites overnight in the refrigerator. I do not recommend freezing or storing leftover egg yolks. Either use them immediately or discard them. Fortunately, eggs are one of the less expensive baking ingredients.

Although salmonella bacteria have been found in only a small percentage of the millions of eggs sold in our country, I still take precautions with eggs. Salmonella is killed at 160°F. I cook all custards, including those for ice cream, at least to this temperature, and I use an instant-read food thermometer to check. Before adding egg yolks to uncooked mousse desserts, I heat the yolks with other ingredients from the recipe just to 160°F. The only dessert in this book that contains uncooked egg yolks is the Key Largo Lemon Crunch Pie (page 192). Salmonella bacteria are unlikely to grow or survive in the high-acid environment of lemon juice. Egg whites, which contain little protein, are unfriendly to salmonella, and I use cold raw egg whites in some of my recipes. There is much debate about this issue; the final decision will have to be up to you whether or not to prepare a specific dessert.

## Flavorings and Spices

Always use pure vanilla extract. It would be better to omit vanilla than to use an artificial substitute. I tested the recipes with either McCormick or Durkee vanilla extract, which are both readily available. When flavoring desserts with almond extract, be stingy. Adding too much almond extract will give the dessert a chemical taste.

I use decaffeinated, freeze-dried instant coffee granules to add coffee flavoring to desserts.

Use fresh spices and store them tightly covered. Storage times and conditions for different spices vary; a simple way to see if a spice is fresh is to taste it. If the spice is stale, it will add little or no taste to a dessert. Even with the amount of baking that I do, it is hard for me to finish a can of ground nutmeg before it loses its flavor, so I buy whole nutmeg and use a small nutmeg grater to grate fresh nutmeg whenever I need it. Although I used supermarket cinnamon to test the recipes, extra fancy China Tunghing cinnamon is an exceptionally strong, sweet cinnamon that is worth trying. It is available from Penzey's Spice House Ltd. (page 245).

## Flour

I tested the recipes using either unbleached all-purpose flour or cake flour. Cake flour contains less gluten than all-purpose flour. If you could see gluten strands under a microscope, they would look like a bunch of tangled, stretchy rubber bands. A higher gluten flour adds a tougher structure to baked goods, which is desirable in a bread dough but not in a tender cake. Some of the recipes, like pie crust, use a combination of all-purpose flour and cake flour to balance the gluten content and achieve a tender pastry. Pie pastry prepared completely with cake flour would be too tender to form flaky layers and would crumble and fall apart. Store flour, tightly covered, and keep it dry.

## Leavening Agents

Air, steam, yeast, baking soda, and baking powder leaven baked goods. Air is beaten into batters, and the liquid in batters produces steam during baking. When activated in some way, yeast, baking soda, and baking powder produce carbon dioxide gas cells in a batter or dough. The gas cells are like tiny bubbles or air pockets that lighten the batter or dough.

Yeast, the slowpoke leavening, is activated by moisture and warmth; it produces carbon dioxide gas cells slowly. If yeast is fresh when purchased, it will stay active for 3 to 6 months. Yeast in packets is marked with an expiration date. I use granulated yeast and store it, tightly covered, in the refrigerator.

Baking soda, or sodium bicarbonate, is an alkaline leavening that is activated when it is combined with an acid ingredient like sour cream, molasses, or buttermilk. If kept dry, baking soda can be stored indefinitely.

Baking powder contains baking soda (alkaline) plus an acid ingredient; it is activated when combined with a liquid. Double-acting baking powders contain two acid ingredients, one activated by liquid and one activated by heat. I use double-acting baking powder. Store baking powder, tightly covered, and do not use it past the expiration date on the can.

## Nuts

I use blanched almonds (without skins), unblanched almonds (with skins), pecans, walnuts, hazelnuts, unsalted roasted cashew nuts, unsalted roasted pistachio nuts, pine nuts, and chestnuts in the recipes. Generally, the new crop of nuts appears in supermarkets from September to December; this is a good time to buy a year's supply. Store the nuts in the freezer in a tightly sealed heavy duty freezer bag or plastic freezer container. Fresh nuts can be stored for a month in the refrigerator, but the freezer is best for longer storage.

## Sugars

Three types of sugar are used in the recipes: granulated sugar, brown sugar, and powdered sugar. Brown sugar contains molasses, and light brown sugar has less molasses than dark brown sugar. Powdered sugar, or confectioner's sugar, is granulated sugar that has been ground to a powder. Cornstarch is added to prevent caking, but it's still a good idea to sift powdered sugar before using it to remove any lumps. Store all sugar tightly covered and in a dry place; brown sugar should be stored in a tightly sealed plastic bag to preserve its moisture.

# How to Freeze Desserts

After a dessert is prepared, it must be packaged properly and frozen quickly so that its quality will be retained during storage in the freezer. If you follow the freezing guidelines in this chapter, your desserts will taste delicious when you defrost and serve them.

## How Desserts Freeze

A basic understanding of how food freezes will help you to do the best job of freezing desserts. For a dessert to freeze properly, it must be thoroughly cooled or chilled first. It will freeze faster with less condensation and, therefore, taste better when defrosted. As food freezes, the water (moisture) in the food freezes in the form of ice crystals. Small ice crystals preserve a smooth, fine texture while large crystals create a coarse, unpleasant texture. Large ice crystals can also rupture the cell walls of food and cause moisture to flow out of the food as it defrosts. It is these large ice crystals and broken cell walls that create a mushy texture and cause juices to flow out of frozen fruit during defrosting.

Freezing food quickly and maintaining it as close as possible to 0°F. produce small ice crystals. When ice cream melts and refreezes, the very small ice crystals melt and refreeze on larger ice crystals, which then become larger still; this gives the ice cream a disagreeable grainy texture.

Freeze desserts in the coldest spot of the freezer, usually the bottom rear shelf. To locate the coldest spot, use a freezer thermometer. Leave the dessert overnight to freeze solid. Once it is frozen, the dessert can be moved to another place inside the freezer. Do not put desserts on the door shelves, where the greatest temperature fluctuations occur.

The most important factor to consider when deciding whether or not a dessert is suitable for freezing is its water (moisture) content. Lower moisture content means fewer ice crystals form; thus there are fewer ice crystals to interfere with creamy texture and to rupture cell walls. Desserts with a lower moisture content can be stored for a longer time in the freezer than those with a high moisture content. Cakes and cookies freeze easily because of their low moisture content. Fruit desserts with a high water content need to be adapted in some way for freezing; they are usually stored in the freezer for a shorter period of time. Freezing fruit desserts unbaked and then baking them while still frozen is a good way to adapt them. Of course, desserts that are baked while still frozen will need extra baking time.

Generally, dense-textured desserts containing little moisture, such as cakes without frosting, store well for longer periods, while moist and light-textured desserts, such as ice creams and terrines, store best for shorter periods. Most desserts that have a stable structure and are good keepers when not frozen are good choices for freezing. A sturdy pound cake that can be kept unfrozen for about 5 days freezes well. Such desserts as a cake with an egg white–based frosting or a pie with a soft meringue, are fragile on the other hand, best prepared and served the same day; they do not freeze well. Custards made without cornstarch or flour thickening are also fragile; their delicate structure can be damaged by freezing.

## Choosing the Right Desserts to Freeze

**Cakes** Since the dry heat of baking removes some moisture from cakes, they form fewer ice crystals and freeze well. Baked pound and loaf cakes, crumb-topped cakes, gingerbread, and upside-down cakes can be successfully frozen. Layers for cakes can be frozen either before or after they are filled and frosted. When baking cake layers, I make several batches at a time and store extra layers in the freezer. Another advantage to freezing cake layers is that partially defrosted cake layers are easier to split, handle, and frost.

**Fillings and Frostings** When choosing frostings and fillings consider two important points. Frostings and fillings that freeze well are fairly dense—again not too much liquid—and they contain fat, usually in the form of butter or heavy cream. Fat globules perform the good role of keeping ice crystals in frozen food separated; this prevents small ice crystals from joining with other ice crystals to form disruptive large ice crystals. Fat helps keep filling and frosting textures smooth and creamy throughout the freezing and defrosting stages. Buttercream frostings, cream cheese frostings, mousse fillings, and chocolate or white chocolate glazes all freeze well. They contain butter, heavy cream, or chocolate, or a combination. For a mousse filling to freeze successfully, the finished mousse should consist of at least one-third whipped cream by volume. Adding chocolate or butter will create a richer, denser mousse that is even better adapted to freezing. Buttercreams and chocolate glazes make excellent coverings for frozen cakes.

Plain whipped cream is a good example of a frosting with too much water content, so I frost cakes with whipped cream after I defrost them. Adding chocolate to whipped cream increases the fat content and boosts its freezing capabilities.

**Sauces** Butterscotch, caramel, chocolate-based sauces, and cooked and uncooked fruit sauces freeze well. Some of these sauces may separate upon defrosting, but blending them with a whisk or a vigorous stirring will bring them back. Pastry creams thickened with cornstarch or flour can be frozen.

**Pies and Tarts** Freeze pie and tart crusts unbaked because they taste better when freshly baked with the dessert.

The most important consideration when deciding if a pie or tart is suitable for freezing is again water content, i.e., the fruit juices or liquid remaining in a pie or tart after it is baked. When the water in the fruit in a fresh fruit pie freezes and expands, it can break the cell walls of the fruit. Then as the fruit defrosts, it becomes limp. In addition, when fresh fruit pies bake, they release a large amount of juice, which soaks into the crust and makes it soggy.

The two ways I deal with excess moisture in fruit pies are to add ingredients that absorb some of the moisture or to freeze the dessert unbaked. The Maple Apple–Walnut Crunch Pie (page 155) is a moist pie that is frozen after baking, but oatmeal absorbs just the right amount of liquid from the apples as the pie bakes. My Prizewinning Blueberry Crumb Pie (page 162) is frozen unbaked, and the fruit juice is not released until the pie is baked. Both of these pies taste just as good after a month of freezing as the day they were prepared. Blueberry, raspberry, blackberry, and cranberry pies lend themselves well to freezing. Assemble these pies and freeze them unbaked so that the moisture remains in the frozen berry until the pie is baked. When you want to serve the pie, bake it frozen. Frozen pies usually require an additional 10 to 15 minutes baking time.

Toss raw apples and pears with sugar and lemon juice to preserve them better and prevent the fruit from browning during freezer storage. I prefer to bake peaches and cherries in cakes rather than in frozen fruit pies if I'm going to freeze the dessert. Nut- and coconut-based pies and tarts are excellent choices for baking and freezing.

Custard- and pudding-type pies do not freeze well because the crusts become soggy and some custards do not freeze well. But a frozen crust can be baked and then filled with cooked pudding or pastry cream. A traditional lemon meringue pie has far too much moisture to bake and freeze successfully, but a Lemon Cream Pie (page 163) made with dense Lemon Curd will taste delicious after freezing.

**Cookies and Bars** In my experience all cookies and bars freeze exceptionally well, so I freeze them after baking and remove them from the freezer as I need them. An exception is the Apricot-Pecan Butter Strudel (page 62), which is frozen unbaked in individual strips. Even when kept in an airtight container, many cookies and bars lose their fresh-baked flavor after a few days storage at room temperature; freezing preserves them in a just-baked condition.

**Terrines and Mousse Pies** As with mousse fillings, frozen mousse desserts should contain whipped cream to help them remain creamy when frozen. The frozen mousse desserts in this book contain either chocolate, praline, or a cooked fruit cream folded into the whipped cream. Adding chocolate produces a creamier mousse because it incorporates more fat. The praline in the Pistachio Praline Mousse (page 188) helps keep the mousse smooth by lowering its freezing point. In the Lemon Meringue Terrine (page 184), cooked lemon cream is combined with whipped cream to produce a mousse that remains creamy when frozen. A mousse prepared only with plain whipped cream and uncooked fruit would develop a granular texture when frozen.

**Meringues** Crisp meringues freeze extremely well. Meringues can be frozen without fillings for up to 2 months. I serve meringues combined with a mousse, as in the Lemon Meringue Terrine (page 184), within a week. When the meringues are combined with a buttercream, as in the Toasted Hazelnut–Chocolate Chip Meringue Cake (page 86), the dessert can be frozen for a month because buttercream has less moisture than a mousse. Soft meringue has a fragile texture and lacks fat; it does not freeze well.

**Ice Cream Desserts** Obviously, ice cream desserts freeze well, but there are still some considerations to be aware of. Homemade ice creams and sorbets, which lack the preservatives and stabilizers of commercial ice cream, are best when served within ten days. The longer ice cream is stored in your freezer, the larger the ice crystals will become, and these larger ice crystals reduce the creamy texture of ice cream. The denser the texture of the ice cream or sorbet, the better it will store in the freezer. Beating less air into ice cream and sorbet adds to their density, with fat contributing density to ice cream and thick fruit pulp contributing density to sorbet. Dense Chocolate Pudding Ice Cream (page 234) can be stored a few extra days if necessary.

While I love serving ice cream and cake together, I never freeze them together because frozen cake is too firm to enjoy and has little flavor. Ice cream pies made with crumb crusts and layered with crushed cookies, crushed toffee, brownie pieces, chocolate sauce, fruit curd, or crisp meringue pieces are a better way to go.

## Freezer Temperatures

Freezer temperatures should be kept as close as possible to 0°F. Most home freezers are built to maintain a temperature between 0°F. and 8°F., but the 0°F. is preferable. I keep a freezer thermometer in my freezer and adjust the freezer thermostat as needed. Usually freezer temperatures fluctuate because of warming during the defrost cycle of a self-defrosting freezer, opening the door frequently, or adding many unfrozen items to your freezer at the same time.

## Packaging Desserts for the Freezer

After the dessert is prepared and it is time to freeze it, proper packaging becomes vital. The goal when freezing desserts is to keep as much of the moisture as possible in the dessert. Since air in a freezer is dry, it will naturally pull moisture out of food. Poorly wrapped desserts allow dry freezer air to seep in and literally suck out the moisture. No matter how well you wrap, some moisture will be lost, but you want to keep this loss to a minimum for your desserts to remain at their best.

After making desserts with top quality ingredients, package them for freezing with good quality wrapping materials. Spend the extra few cents to buy the best supplies for the job—heavy-duty freezer bags, heavy aluminum foil, polycoated paper freezer wrap, plastic wrap, and rigid plastic freezer containers. Square or rectangular containers that can be stacked take up less room in the freezer. These heavyweight materials will protect your dessert better from air, moisture, and odors than lightweight packaging materials. Heavy aluminum foil is so easy to use that I prefer it to the polycoated freezer wrap that requires tape for sealing. Saran Wrap, made from polyvinylidene chloride, is the plastic wrap rated as having the best barrier against water and odor transmission. If you are freezing desserts for less than 2 weeks, other plastic wraps are fine, but for longer storage, Saran Wrap provides the best protection. Do not reuse plastic bags from the produce department.

I have found that different categories of desserts lend themselves to certain kinds of packaging. Cakes, pies, tarts, bombes, terrines, and pie crusts should all be well wrapped with plastic wrap, then with a layer of heavy aluminum foil. The plastic wrap fits smoothly against the dessert, forming a tighter seal than foil alone, and the heavy foil provides a strong barrier against moisture and resists punctures.

Cookies, brownies, bars, and small cakes should be individually wrapped in plastic wrap, then placed in a metal or rigid plastic container and covered tightly. If the cookies do not stick together, you can wrap several cookies together in the plastic wrap. Clean and dry coffee and shortening tins work fine.

Ice cream, sorbets, and sauces should be frozen in rigid plastic containers. Leave 1 inch of air space for expansion at the top and press a piece of plastic wrap onto the surface of the sauce or ice cream before you close the container. Waxed cartons, such as the ones for commercial ice cream, work also, but they are hard to find and are not designed to be washed and reused. Clean plastic containers with tight-fitting lids are easy to clean and reuse.

## Labeling Desserts

Every time I try to get away with putting something in the freezer and not labeling it, I eventually regret it. Inevitably, the dessert gets lost in freezerland. Take a few extra seconds to label your package with the date and contents. Masking tape or self-sticking labels are easy to use. There is usually a white area on plastic freezer bags to write information with a ballpoint pen or felt tip marker. I keep these supplies with my plastic containers. Since a cold moist surface is hard to apply a label to or to write on, label packages before the dessert goes in the freezer.

## Storage Times

The accompanying chart lists the maximum times that desserts can be stored in the freezer without losing quality.

## Defrosting Desserts

Properly defrosting desserts is as important as freezing them. Many of the desserts in this book are served frozen and require no defrosting. Pie crusts, frozen unbaked pies, and frozen unbaked strudel, are baked while frozen and also require no defrosting beforehand.

For the other desserts, following a few simple guidelines will preserve them in fine condition while they defrost. Keep desserts wrapped or in covered containers while you defrost them; the moisture that forms as the dessert defrosts will develop on the wrapping rather than on your dessert. If a dessert is going to be stored in the refrigerator, defrost it in the refrigerator. If a dessert is going to be stored at room temperature, defrost it at room temperature.

Once the dessert is defrosted, it is ready to serve. Each of the recipes gives specific storage and serving suggestions.

## Freezing Tips at a Glance

- Cool desserts before freezing them.
- Keep freezer temperature as close to 0°F. as possible.
- Use suitable materials for packaging and wrap packages well.
- Label desserts with date and contents.
- Store desserts inside the freezer, not on door shelves.
- Use desserts within specified time.
- Defrost desserts correctly.

## Storage Times

This chart lists the maximum times that desserts can be stored in the freezer without losing quality.

| Dessert Item | Storage Time |
|---|---|
| Baked crumb crusts | 1 month |
| Baked fruit desserts | 1 month |
| Bombes and parfaits | 2 weeks |
| Cakes with frosting | 1 month |
| Cakes without frosting | 3 months |
| Cookies and brownies | 3 months |
| Fruit curds | 2 months |
| Fruit sauces, cooked or uncooked | 1 month |
| Homemade ice creams and sorbets | 10 days |
| Ice cream pies | 2 weeks |
| Non-fruit sauces, cooked | 2 months |
| Nuts | 1 year |
| Pastry cream | 3 weeks |
| Pies or tarts without fruit | 2 months |
| Pralines | 3 months |
| Terrines and mousses | 3 weeks |
| Unbaked fruit pies | 1 month |
| Unbaked pie crusts and pastries | 2 months |

# The Frozen Pantry

Every few months I have a frozen pantry day, and in a surprisingly short time, I assemble pie crusts, cook praline, bake cake layers, shave chocolate curls, or prepare whatever I need. While I seldom have every one of these items in my freezer, I always have a selection ready and waiting.

It is so easy to bake a pie if the crust is already prepared, or to finish a cake if the layers have been previously baked or if a filling only needs defrosting. Besides the time factor, there's the feeling that with part of the dessert already done, finishing it will be "a piece of cake."

All of these preparations freeze and defrost well, and many of them actually improve from their stint in the freezer. Pie and tart crusts hold their shape better when baked while still frozen, and cake layers are easier to handle if cold or frozen. Frozen chocolate curls are easy to handle since they do not break or melt easily. Nut pralines are generally used in small quantities, so freezing praline allows you to remove exactly what you need and to keep the remainder for another dessert. Lemon and orange curd freeze into a semisolid state that whips up successfully with cream.

One of the first things I discovered while baking at Peter Ott's restaurant was how quickly a dessert could be assembled if I had several of the parts already prepared. Now when I do the recipes in this chapter, I make enough for several desserts. The list is not long, but it represents the "basics" that I use repeatedly in my desserts. With a sauce ready to warm, a cake ready to defrost, or a crust ready to fill, dessert making is a cinch.

## Good Advice

• This recipe uses butter for flavor and vegetable shortening for flakiness. Adding cake flour to all-purpose flour lowers the total gluten content and makes the crust tender. The butter and shortening must be cold so they form little fat pockets, which will form the flaky layers of the crust. Use ice water for the liquid so the cold shortening doesn't soften.

• If you are making this dough or the Tart Pastry Crust (page 35) in a warm kitchen on a hot summer day, chill the shortening and flour mixture in the freezer for 30 minutes.

• Since the pie crusts will be frozen when placed in the oven for baking, I use aluminum pie tins rather than glass or ceramic to prevent the possibility of a cold glass pie plate breaking when placed in a hot oven. I usually double this recipe and keep a well-wrapped unbaked pie crust in the freezer, ready to fill.

• Sprinkle leftover dough scraps with a little sugar or cinnamon sugar and bake them in a 400°F. oven until golden brown.

## Doubling the Recipe

Double the ingredients. For more than two pie crusts, make another batch of dough.

# Easy as Pie Crust

**Makes one 10-inch pie crust**

Some of the best cooks I know often confess to me that they can't make a good pie crust. I, too, was a failure at making pie crust until I began using the food processor. While it does make a good crust, using an electric mixer gives me even better results. It's fast, yet I can watch what is happening and have more control when mixing the dough, even though it takes less than two minutes.

**1 cup unbleached all-purpose flour**
**⅓ cup cake flour**
**½ teaspoon salt**
**1 tablespoon sugar**
**6 tablespoons (¾ stick) cold unsalted butter, cut in 4 pieces**
**2 tablespoons plus 2 teaspoons cold vegetable shortening**
**3½ to 4 tablespoons ice water**
**Sifted cake flour, for rolling pie crust**

1. Lightly grease a 10-inch pie pan with vegetable shortening or spray it with a vegetable oil spray.

2. Put the flours, salt, and sugar in the large bowl of an electric mixer and mix on low speed just to blend the ingredients, about 10 seconds. Stop the mixer, add the butter and shortening, and mix just until the butter and shortening pieces are the size of small lima beans, about 20 seconds. They will not all be the same size, and you will still see loose flour. Slowly add the water, 1 tablespoon at a time. Stop mixing as soon as the mixture begins to hold together, about 20 seconds. You may not need all of the water. The dough will form large clumps and pull away from the sides of the bowl but will not form a ball. Stop the mixer at any time and squeeze a small piece of dough to check if it holds together. Mixing the crust with a hand mixer will take about 30 seconds longer.

3. Turn the dough mixture out onto a lightly floured rolling surface. With the heel of your hand push the dough down and forward against the rolling surface. Fold the dough in half and repeat 6 times. The dough will be smooth. Form the dough into a round disk about 4 inches in diameter. It will be easier to roll into a circle if it is round and the edges are smooth, but don't handle it a lot just to get smooth edges or a perfect circle. Wrap the dough in plastic wrap and chill in the refrigerator for at least 20 minutes or overnight.

4. Remove the dough from the refrigerator and unwrap it. If the dough has become cold and hard, let it sit at room temperature until it is easy to roll, 5 to 10 minutes. Lightly flour the rolling surface and rolling pin. Roll the

dough from the center out into a circle about 4 inches wider than the bottom of the pie pan. Lift and turn the dough several times as you roll it to prevent it from sticking to the rolling surface, but don't flip it over. Dust the rolling surface and rolling pin with flour as necessary. Roll the dough circle over the rolling pin and unroll it onto an aluminum pie pan. Press the dough into the pie pan. Trim the edges evenly to ¾ inch over the edge of the pie pan. Press a ½-inch edge of dough under itself to form an even edge. Form a crimped edge by pressing the dough between your thumb and forefinger.

### To Freeze

Wrap the unbaked pie crust tightly with plastic wrap. Wrap any scraps in plastic wrap and place on the pastry. The pie crust scraps can be used to patch the crust or sprinkled with a little sugar and baked for a snack for the cook or the cook's helper when you bake the pie crust. Wrap with heavy aluminum foil, gently pressing the foil against the dough. Label with date and contents. Freeze up to 2 months. Once the pie crust is frozen, it can be stacked inside other pie crusts in the freezer.

# Cookie Crumb Crust

Cookie crumb crusts are so easy to prepare at the last minute that you don't really need to bake and freeze them ahead of time, but if you have the freezer space it is nice to have one or two on hand. I use graham crackers, chocolate wafers, and chocolate sandwich cookies. After trying many brands, my favorites are Sunshine Graham Crackers or crumbs, Nabisco Famous Chocolate Wafers, and Nabisco Oreos. Oreos make a sweeter, crisper crumb crust and require less melted butter than the others because the frosting helps the crumbs cling together; chocolate wafers have a good chocolate flavor and less sweet taste.

### Graham Cracker Crumb Crust

For a 10-inch pie pan

**1½ cups graham cracker crumbs**
**¾ teaspoon ground cinnamon**
**5 tablespoons unsalted butter, melted**

For a 9-inch springform pan

**1¾ cups graham cracker crumbs**
**1 teaspoon ground cinnamon**
**6 tablespoons (¾ stick) unsalted butter, melted**

### Chocolate Wafer Cookie Crumb Crust

For a 10-inch pie pan

**1½ cups chocolate wafer cookie crumbs**
**3 tablespoons unsalted butter, melted**

For a 9-inch springform pan

**2 cups chocolate wafer crumbs (9-ounce package)**
**6 tablespoons (¾ stick) unsalted butter, melted**

### Oreo Cookie Crumb Crust

For a 10-inch pie pan

**2 cups Oreo cookie crumbs (about 3 cups Oreos)**
**2 tablespoons unsalted butter, melted**

For a 9-inch springform pan

**2¼ cups Oreo cookie crumbs (about 3⅓ cups Oreos)**
**2 tablespoons unsalted butter, melted**

1. Position a rack in the middle of the oven. Preheat the oven to 325°F. Butter the baking pan of your choice.

2. Put the cookie crumbs and cinnamon, if used, in a large bowl and mix together. Add the melted butter and stir the mixture until the crumbs are evenly moistened with the butter. Transfer the crumbs to the baking pan. Using your fingers, press the crumbs evenly over the bottom and sides. If using a springform pan, press the crumbs 1 inch up the sides of the pan.

### Good Advice

- Use a food processor to make the cookie crumbs. Start with a few on/off pulses to break up the cookies, then process until the cookies form crumbs. Or, put about eight cookies at a time between two sheets of wax paper and crush them with a rolling pin.
- Don't add sugar to crumb crusts; it gives the crust a gritty taste, and the cookies have enough sweetness.
- Press the crumbs evenly into the pan with your fingers. This is much faster than using a spoon and you can feel any thick areas that form.

### Doubling the Recipe

To prepare more than one crust, multiply the ingredients for as many crusts as you need, but don't overload the food processor.

### To Freeze

Press plastic wrap tightly onto the cooled crumb crust. Wrap with heavy aluminum foil, pressing the foil tightly around the edges of the pan. Freeze up to 1 month.

Check to see that the crust isn't too thick where the sides and bottom of the pan meet at an angle. Bake the crust for 6 minutes. Cool the crust thoroughly before filling or freezing it. Crumb crusts can be baked a day ahead, wrapped tightly with plastic wrap, and stored overnight at room temperature.

## Tart Pastry Crust

**Makes one 11-inch tart crust**

An all-butter pastry is used as a crust for most of my tarts, including nuts. Since butter is the only fat, this pastry is less flaky and not quite as tender as pie crust. After tasting the pure butter flavor of this pastry, I think you'll agree that it's worth giving up a little tenderness. The egg and sugar add even more flavor and a beautiful golden color to the pastry.

**1 cold large egg**
**2 tablespoons ice water**
**1¼ cups unbleached all-purpose flour**
**2 tablespoons sugar**
**¼ teaspoon salt**
**¼ pound (1 stick) cold unsalted butter, cut into 8 pieces**

1. Butter an 11-inch metal tart pan with a removable bottom.

2. Put the egg and water in a small bowl and mix with a fork just to break up the yolk. Put the flour, sugar, and salt in the large bowl of an electric mixer and mix on low speed just to blend the ingredients, about 10 seconds. Add the butter and mix until the butter pieces are the size of small lima beans, about 30 seconds. You will still see loose flour. With the mixer running slowly, add the egg mixture. Stop mixing as soon as the mixture begins to cling together and pull away from the sides of the bowl, about 15 seconds.

3. Turn the dough out onto a rolling surface. With the heel of your hand push the dough down and forward against the rolling surface. Fold the dough in half and repeat 6 times. The dough will look smooth and have a golden color. Form the dough into a round disk. Wrap in plastic wrap and refrigerate until firm, for at least 1 hour or overnight.

4. Remove the dough from the refrigerator and unwrap it. If the dough has become cold and hard, let it sit at room temperature until it is easy to roll, 5 to 10 minutes. Lightly flour the rolling surface and rolling pin. Roll the dough from the center out into a circle 3 inches wider than the bottom of the tart pan; for an 11-inch tart pan you will have a 14-inch circle. Lift and turn the dough several times as you roll it to prevent it from sticking to the rolling surface, but don't flip it over. Dust the rolling surface and rolling pin with more flour as necessary. Roll the dough circle over the rolling pin and unroll it into the tart pan. Gently press the dough into the pan and trim the edges to leave a ¾-inch overhang. Fold the overhang into the pan and press it against the pan to form slightly thickened sides.

### Good Advice

• The egg, water, and butter must be cold. Some small specks of butter should be visible after the dough is mixed. These tiny pieces of butter will add some flakiness to the pastry as it bakes.
• Folding the edges of the pastry into the sides of the tart pan makes pastry sides that are strong enough to hold the filling once the pan has been removed.
• Save the extra dough scraps for patching the pastry. Sometimes cracks form when the tart crust is baked before it is filled. Patch any cracks with raw dough before the final 5 minutes of baking.

### Doubling the Recipe

Double all of the ingredients. For more than two crusts make another batch of pastry.

### To Freeze

Wrap the unbaked butter pastry tightly with plastic wrap. Wrap any dough scraps in plastic wrap and place on the pastry. Wrap with heavy aluminum foil, gently pressing the aluminum foil against dough. Label with date and contents. Freeze up to 2 months. Once the tart pastry is frozen, other things may be placed on top of the pastry.

# Yellow Butter Cake Layers

More than sixty years ago, my grandmother Sophie baked this butter cake for her family of seven, and my mother has baked the same cake for our family for more than fifty years. I used to come home from school, smell this cake baking in the oven, and know we were in for a treat. Now, when I want to bake light, moist yellow cake layers for frosted cakes or upside-down cakes, or want plain cake to go with a cup of tea, I bake my grandmother's versatile butter cake.

For one 9-inch cake layer

**1½ cups cake flour**
**1¼ teaspoons baking powder**
**Pinch of salt**
**¼ pound (1 stick) soft unsalted butter**
**1 cup sugar**
**2 large eggs**
**1 teaspoon vanilla extract**
**½ cup whole milk**

For two 9-inch cake layers

**3 cups cake flour**
**2 teaspoons baking powder**
**⅛ teaspoon salt**
**½ pound (2 sticks) soft unsalted butter**
**2 cups sugar**
**4 large eggs**
**2 teaspoons vanilla extract**
**1 cup whole milk**

For one 10-inch cake layer

**1¾ cups plus 1 tablespoon cake flour**
**1¼ teaspoons baking powder**
**Pinch of salt**
**¼ pound plus 2 tablespoons (1¼ sticks) soft unsalted butter**
**1¼ cups sugar**
**2 large eggs plus 1 large yolk**
**1½ teaspoons vanilla extract**
**⅔ cup whole milk**

For two 10-inch layers

**3½ cups plus 2 tablespoons cake flour**
**2 teaspoons baking powder**
**⅛ teaspoon salt**
**½ pound plus 4 tablespoons (2½ sticks) soft unsalted butter**
**2½ cups sugar**
**4 large eggs plus 2 large yolks**
**1 tablespoon vanilla extract**
**1⅓ cups whole milk**

## Good Advice

- Thorough beating is important when creaming the butter and sugar and after adding the eggs to the cake batter; the beating develops the cake's structure. Adding the dry ingredients and milk is only a matter of combining them thoroughly into the batter and does not require long beating.
- To fill and frost frozen cake layers, defrost the layers until they are thawed just enough to cut easily. (Cold layers are easy to split and handle.) Fill and frost the layers and return the cake to the freezer. I have never noticed any flavor change from this partial defrosting of cake layers.
- Use layer pans with 1¾- to 2-inch-high sides. Line the bottoms of the pans with parchment or wax paper, and the cake will release easily from the pan.

## Doubling the Recipe

For more than two nine-inch or two ten-inch layers, prepare separate batches of batter. Two ten-inch layers are best prepared in a heavy-duty mixer with a five-quart bowl.

### To Freeze

Use a small sharp knife to loosen the sides of the cakes from the pan. Invert each layer onto a piece of plastic wrap. Carefully remove and discard the paper liner. Wrap each layer tightly with plastic wrap then with heavy aluminum foil. Label with date and contents. Freeze up to 3 months. Once the layers are frozen, they may be stacked in the freezer.

### To Serve

To use the cake plain, defrost the wrapped cake at room temperature 3 hours or overnight. Cut into wedges and serve with ice cream, fresh fruit, whipped cream, or plain with a cup of tea or coffee. Wrap leftover cake with plastic wrap and store at room temperature up to 3 days.

1. Position an oven rack in the middle of the oven. Preheat the oven to 350°F. Butter the bottom and sides of the baking pan or pans you are using. Line the bottom of each pan with parchment or wax paper and butter the paper.

2. Sift the flour, baking powder, and salt together and set aside. Put the butter in the large bowl of an electric mixer and mix on low speed for 15 seconds. Slowly add the sugar. Increase the speed to medium and beat the butter and sugar for 2 minutes, until the mixture is fluffy and lightens from a yellow to a cream color. Stop the mixer and scrape the sides of the bowl during this mixing. Add the eggs and yolks, if required, one at a time. Beat for 2 more minutes at medium speed, scraping the sides of the bowl again. Add the vanilla extract to the milk. Decrease the speed to low and add the flour mixture and the milk alternately, beginning and ending with the flour mixture (3 flour, 2 milk). Stop the mixer and scrape the sides of the bowl after the last addition of flour. The batter is ready when the final addition of flour is mixed completely into the batter. If any flour is clinging to the sides of the bowl, stir it into the batter.

3. Pour the batter into the prepared pan or pans and smooth the top of the batter. Bake for 30 to 35 minutes for 9-inch layers and 40 to 45 minutes for 10-inch layers. To test for doneness, gently press your fingers on the middle of the cake. It should feel firm. If it does, insert a toothpick into the center of the cake. When the toothpick comes out clean, the cake is done. Cool the cake in the baking pan on a wire cooling rack.

# Chocolate Butter Cake Layers

When I want a chocolate cake to fill, frost, or eat by itself, this is the cake that I bake. A dark, moist chocolate cake with fine-textured layers, it is easy to split into thin layers. Then the cake can be filled with such fillings as chocolate buttercream or chocolate mousse or covered with a chocolate frosting or shiny chocolate glaze.

For two 9-inch cake layers

**4 ounces unsweetened chocolate, in 1-ounce pieces**
**2 cups plus 2 tablespoons cake flour**
**1½ teaspoons baking powder**
**1 teaspoon baking soda**
**¾ teaspoon salt**
**¼ pound plus 2 tablespoons (1¼ sticks) soft unsalted butter**
**1¾ cups sugar**
**3 large eggs**
**1½ teaspoons vanilla extract**
**1¼ cups sour cream**
**⅔ cup water**

For one 10-inch layer

**3 ounces unsweetened chocolate, in 1-ounce pieces**
**1⅔ cups cake flour**
**1 teaspoon baking powder**
**¾ teaspoon baking soda**
**½ teaspoon salt**
**¼ pound (1 stick) soft unsalted butter**
**1⅓ cups sugar**
**2 large eggs**
**1 teaspoon vanilla extract**
**1 cup sour cream**
**½ cup water**

For two 10-inch layers

**6 ounces unsweetened chocolate, in 1-ounce pieces**
**3⅓ cups cake flour**
**2 teaspoons baking powder**
**1¼ teaspoons baking soda**
**¾ teaspoon salt**
**½ pound (2 sticks) soft unsalted butter**
**2⅔ cups sugar**
**4 large eggs**
**2 teaspoons vanilla extract**
**2 cups sour cream**
**1 cup water**

### Good Advice

• Unsweetened chocolate gives the cake a rich chocolate flavor.
• When melting chocolate without other ingredients, put it in an ovenproof container and melt it in the oven. It's simpler than melting chocolate over hot water. It also saves the extra pot of hot water and eliminates any worry about escaping steam overheating the chocolate.

### Doubling the Recipe

For more than two nine- or ten-inch layers, prepare separate batches. Two ten-inch layers are best prepared in a heavy-duty mixer with a five-quart bowl.

### To Freeze

Use a small sharp knife to loosen the sides of the cakes from the pan. Invert each layer onto a piece of plastic wrap. Carefully remove and discard the paper liner. Wrap the cake tightly with plastic wrap then with heavy aluminum foil. Label with date and contents. Freeze up to 3 months. After the layers are frozen, they may be stacked in the freezer.

## To Serve the Cake Plain

**Defrost the wrapped cake at room temperature at least 3 hours or overnight. Cut the cake into wedges and top with ice cream or whipped cream. Wrap leftover cake with plastic wrap and store at room temperature up to 3 days.**

1. Position an oven rack in the middle of the oven. Preheat the oven to 175°F. Butter the bottom and sides of the baking pan or pans. Line the bottom of each pan with parchment or wax paper and butter the paper.

2. Place the chocolate in an ovenproof container and melt it in the oven, about 8 minutes. As soon as the chocolate is melted, remove it from the oven and stir it smooth. Set the chocolate aside to cool slightly while you mix the cake. Increase the oven temperature to 350°F.

3. Sift the flour, baking powder, baking soda, and salt together and set aside. Put the butter in the large bowl of an electric mixer and mix on low speed for 15 seconds. Add the sugar and beat on medium speed for 2 minutes, until the mixture is fluffy and lightens from a yellow to a cream color. Decrease the speed to low and mix in the melted chocolate, just until it is combined with the other ingredients. Stop the mixer and scrape the sides of the bowl during this mixing. Increase the speed to medium and add the eggs, one at a time. Beat for 2 minutes at medium speed. Decrease the speed to low and add the vanilla extract and sour cream and mix just until the sour cream is incorporated. Add the flour mixture and the water alternately, beginning and ending with the flour mixture (3 flour, 2 water). Stop the mixer and scrape the sides of the bowl after the last addition of flour. The batter is ready when the final addition of flour is mixed completely into the batter. If any flour is clinging to the sides of the bowl, stir it into the batter.

4. Pour the batter into the prepared pan or pans and smooth the top of the batter. Bake 30 to 35 minutes for 9-inch layers and 40 to 45 minutes for 10-inch layers. To test for doneness, gently press your fingers on the middle of the cake. It should feel firm. If it does, insert a toothpick into the center of the cake. When the toothpick comes out clean, the cake is done. Cool the cake in the baking pan on a wire cooling rack.

# Pound Cake

**Makes 12 to 20 slices, depending on the length of the pan**

My idea of perfect pound cake is one that is not too sweet, is light but still moist, and has the taste of pure butter—just like this one.

**2 cups cake flour**
**½ teaspoon salt**
**1 teaspoon baking powder**
**½ pound (2 sticks) soft unsalted butter**
**1 cup plus 1 tablespoon sugar**
**4 large eggs**
**¼ cup whole milk**
**2 teaspoons vanilla extract**

1. Position an oven rack in the middle of the oven. Preheat the oven to 325°F. Butter the pan. Line the bottom of the pan with parchment or wax paper and butter the paper.

2. Sift the flour, salt, and baking powder together. Set aside. Put the butter in the large bowl of an electric mixer and mix on low speed for 15 seconds. Slowly add the sugar. Increase the speed to medium and beat the butter and sugar for 5 minutes, until the mixture lightens from a yellow to a cream color and looks fluffy. Stop the mixer and scrape the sides of the bowl once during the creaming. Decrease the speed to low and mix in ½ cup of the flour mixture, just until the flour is incorporated. Add the eggs, one at a time, beating each egg completely into the batter before adding another egg. The batter should look smooth before another egg is added. Return the mixer to medium speed and beat for 3 minutes. Stop the mixer and scrape the sides of the bowl again during this beating. Decrease the speed to low and slowly mix in the milk and vanilla. The batter may look slightly curdled. Add the remaining flour and mix just until all of the flour is incorporated. The batter will be smooth and thick. If any flour is clinging to the sides of the bowl, stir it into the batter.

3. Pour the batter into the baking pan. Scrape the sides of the bowl to remove all of the batter. Smooth the top of the batter. Bake the cake for about 1 hour. If the cake is baked in a standard loaf pan, the cake will probably need to bake an additional 5 minutes. To test for doneness, gently press your fingers on the middle of the cake. If it feels firm, insert a toothpick into the center of the cake. If the toothpick comes out clean, the cake is done. Cool the cake in the pan on a wire cooling rack.

## Good Advice

• Long, narrow loaf pans, the type used for terrines, make good baking containers. The cake slices easily and has an air of sophistication. A standard loaf pan size is about 9 × 5¼ inches (7 to 8 cups). Long, narrow pans vary in measurement; any one with a 7- to 8-*cup capacity is fine.

• With their high butter content and dense texture, pound cakes are good keepers.

## Doubling the Recipe

To prepare two cakes use ¾ teaspoon salt and 2 teaspoons baking powder and double the remaining ingredients. Bake the cake in two pans.

## To Freeze

Use a small sharp knife to loosen the sides of the cake from the pan. Invert the cake onto a piece of plastic wrap. Carefully remove and discard the paper liner. Wrap the cake tightly with plastic wrap then with heavy aluminum foil. Label with date and contents. Freeze up to 3 months.

## To Serve

Defrost the wrapped cake at room temperature at least 5 hours or overnight. Serve at room temperature. Store leftover cake, wrapped in plastic wrap, up to 5 days at room temperature.

# Shortcake

**Makes 8 to 9 shortcakes**

Every July at Peter Ott's restaurant we celebrate the local berry bounty with a strawberry festival and two separate dessert menus. A bright pink menu features old-fashioned strawberry desserts; the second menu is for diehard chocolate lovers. For about three weeks as we give our customers their fill of sweet native strawberries, my hands turn red, and I become somewhat of a strawberry celebrity.

Over the years I have developed a shortcake recipe worthy of all those juicy berries. Good shortcakes taste like luxurious biscuits. An egg gives these an appealing golden color; the melt-in-your-mouth texture comes from using cream as the liquid.

**⅔ cup plus up to 1 tablespoon cold whipping cream**
**1 cold large egg**
**1 teaspoon vanilla extract**
**2 cups unbleached all-purpose flour**
**1 tablespoon sugar**
**½ teaspoon salt**
**4 teaspoons baking powder**
**¼ pound (1 stick) cold unsalted butter, cut into 8 pieces**

1. Position an oven rack in the middle of the oven. Preheat the oven to 425°F. Have ready a large ungreased baking sheet.

2. Measure the ⅔ cup cream into a measuring cup and add the egg and vanilla. Stir the mixture with a fork until the egg breaks up and combines with the cream. Set aside. Sift the flour, sugar, salt, and baking powder into the large bowl of an electric mixer. Add the butter pieces and mix on low speed until they are approximately the size of small lima beans, about 30 seconds. Slowly add the cream mixture and mix until a soft dough forms. Stop the mixer and touch the dough; it should feel sticky and soft. Add up to 1 more tablespoon of cream to obtain a soft dough. Gather the dough into a soft ball.

3. Turn the ball of dough onto a lightly floured rolling surface and knead the dough about 10 strokes until it looks smooth and feels soft. Knead the dough by pressing down on it with the heel of your hand and folding it over on itself. Give the dough a quarter turn as you knead. Lightly flour the rolling surface and a rolling pin. Roll the dough into a ½-inch-thick circle and use a 2¾-inch biscuit cutter to cut it into circles. Gather the scraps together, roll them out ½ inch thick, and cut the remaining shortcakes. Make a final, not-quite-perfect shortcake by rolling the last few scraps into a ball and patting it into a 2¾-inch disk. Place the shortcakes on the baking sheet. Bake about 12 minutes, until the tops are golden brown. Cool the shortcakes on the baking sheet.

## Good Advice

• Cold butter makes flakier shortcakes. I prefer an electric mixer, but it can also be done by hand. The technique is similar to mixing pie crust. Cut the butter into the flour mixture, add the liquid ingredients, and stir until a soft dough forms. It should feel sticky—a soft dough makes a more delicate shortcake. If the dough is dry and firm, the shortcake will be also.

• Cutting shortcakes with a biscuit cutter gives them a sharp edge that helps them rise.

## Doubling the Recipe

Use ¾ teaspoon salt and 2 tablespoons baking powder. Double the remaining ingredients. Divide the dough in two portions before rolling it. For more than double the recipe, prepare another batch of dough.

## To Freeze

Put the bottoms of 2 shortcakes together and wrap the pair in plastic wrap. Put the wrapped shortcakes in a plastic freezer bag, a plastic freezer container, or a metal container and cover tightly. Label with date and contents. Freeze up to 2 months.

## To Serve

Defrost the wrapped shortcakes at room temperature. Unwrap them and warm in a 225°F. oven for 10 minutes. Serve warm or at room temperature.

Crème Pâtissière

# Pastry Cream

**Makes 2 cups**

Since pastry cream is so versatile, I always like to keep some on hand. It can, however, be stored in the refrigerator for only three days. Since this soft custard is thickened with starch, I thought it ought to be stable enough to stand up to freezing. So I prepared a classic pastry cream with flour as the thickening agent and some of the milk replaced with whipping cream. (Using whipping cream increases the fat content slightly, and this additional fat helps Pastry Cream freeze well.) After three weeks, I defrosted the Pastry Cream and tasted it—it was delicious. When I want something lighter, I fold in some whipped cream after defrosting the Pastry Cream. The French sometimes call this combination Crème Mousseline.

With a tart pan filled with Tart Pastry Crust (page 35) and a container of Pastry Cream in my freezer, I can whip up a Fresh Fruit Tart (page 180) in a matter of minutes. For a quick dessert I lighten Pastry Cream with an equal amount of whipped cream, spoon it into wine goblets, and top my Crème Mousseline with fresh berries.

**1½ cups whole milk**
**½ cup whipping cream**
**¾ cup sugar**
**¼ cup unbleached all-purpose flour**
**6 large egg yolks**
**1½ teaspoons vanilla extract**

1. Pour the milk and cream into a large heavy saucepan and heat the mixture over medium heat until it is hot and a few bubbles just begin to form, about 150°F. if measured with a food thermometer.

2. Put the sugar and flour in a large bowl and whisk them together. Mix in the egg yolks and whisk the mixture until it is smooth. Whisking constantly, slowly pour the hot milk mixture into the yolk mixture. Return the mixture to the saucepan and cook, stirring constantly, over medium heat until it begins to boil. You will see large bubbles. Stir the sauce often where the bottom and sides of the pan meet to prevent burning. Turn the heat down to low and cook for 1 minute, stirring constantly. Remove from the heat. Strain the custard into a large bowl. Stir in the vanilla. Press a piece of plastic wrap onto the custard and poke a few holes in the plastic wrap with the tip of a knife to let steam escape. Refrigerate the custard until it is cold.

### Good Advice

- After the pastry cream comes to a boil, cook it over low heat for another minute to ensure that the flour is cooked and the cream has no raw flour taste.
- Beating the hot milk mixture into the egg yolk mixture tempers the yolks so that they do not curdle.
- After defrosting frozen Pastry Cream, whisk it until it is smooth, about 15 seconds to remove any small lumps.

### Doubling the Recipe

Double the ingredients.

### To Freeze

Divide the Pastry Cream between 2 plastic freezer containers, leaving 1 inch of space in the top of each container. Press plastic wrap onto the surface of the Pastry Cream. Cover the containers tightly and freeze up to 3 weeks. This allows you to defrost as much Pastry Cream as you need since it is always possible to defrost both containers but not half of a large container.

### To Use

Defrost the Pastry Cream in the refrigerator at least 6 hours or overnight. Spoon the Pastry Cream into a medium bowl and whisk it smooth, about 15 seconds. The Pastry Cream is now ready to use. Store pastry cream in the refrigerator up to 3 days. To prevent spoilage, always keep the pastry cream chilled.

## Variations

Traditional pastry cream is flavored with vanilla extract, but there are many possible flavorings. Add any of the following to the custard with the vanilla extract: 1 tablespoon dark rum, 1 tablespoon Grand Marnier, or 2 tablespoons ground almond praline.

Crème Mousseline: Fold an equal amount of whipped cream into chilled Pastry Cream, for example, 1 cup of whipped cream into 1 cup of Pastry Cream.

# Lemon Curd

**Makes 1 1/2 cups**

Lemon curd is a thick, smooth lemon butter sauce, which originated in England. There it is often spread on muffins, buns, or the beloved English gingerbread. Whether in its pure state or whipped with heavy cream, it is the first ingredient I turn to for inspiration when creating a lemon dessert. I try to keep a container of Lemon Curd in my freezer at all times. It can quickly become a filling for a Lemon Cream Pie (page 163), be combined with vanilla ice cream for a Lemon Ripple Ice Cream Pie (page 211), or be spread into a baked Tart Pastry (page 35) for an instant lemon tart. I also prepare an orange-flavored variation that I combine with whipped cream and serve as a topping for Orange Poppy Seed Cake (page 148).

**6 tablespoons (3/4 stick) soft unsalted butter, cut into 6 pieces**
**1 cup sugar**
**1/3 cup fresh lemon juice (about 2 lemons)**
**2 large eggs**
**2 large egg yolks**
**1 teaspoon grated lemon zest**

Put the butter, sugar, lemon juice, eggs, and yolks in a medium nonreactive saucepan with a heavy bottom. Cook over low heat, stirring constantly, until the butter melts. Increase the heat to medium-low and cook, stirring constantly, until the mixture thickens, leaves a path on the back of a spoon, and measures 170°F. on a food thermometer. Stir the sauce often where the bottom and sides of the saucepan meet to prevent burning. Do not let the mixture boil. Strain the custard into a plastic freezer container, leaving at least 1 inch of space at the top. A few bits of cooked egg will probably remain in the strainer. Stir in the lemon zest. Press plastic wrap onto the surface of the Lemon Curd and chill it in the refrigerator. Lemon Curd will thicken further as it cools.

## Variation

**Orange Curd:** Use the following ingredients and follow the directions for preparing Lemon Curd: 1 tablespoon grated orange zest; 6 tablespoons (3/4 stick) unsalted butter, cut into 6 pieces; 3/4 cup sugar; 1/4 cup fresh orange juice (1 orange); 2 large eggs, and 3 large egg yolks. This makes about 1 1/8 cups.

### Good Advice

• For years I cooked Lemon Curd in a double boiler and carefully tempered the eggs with the hot lemon mixture before cooking them. My friend Helen Hall said that she found putting everything into one saucepan and cooking it over low heat worked just as well. It does, and it saves time on clean-up.

• Eggs thicken the sauce as it cooks, but because of the eggs the sauce must be heated slowly and never heated to the boiling point; that would curdle the sauce.

### Doubling the Recipe

Multiply the ingredients by two, three, or four to prepare a larger quantity and cook the mixture in a large saucepan. More than four times this recipe is difficult to cook properly. You will need almost twice the amount in this recipe for the Lemon Cream Pie (page 163).

### To Freeze

Cover the chilled curd tightly. Label with date and contents. Freeze up to 2 months.

### To Use

Spoon out the necessary amount of Lemon Curd or Orange Curd from the freezer container as needed and defrost it in the refrigerator for about 2 hours or overnight, until it is spreadable.

# Chocolate Truffle Sauce

**Makes about 2 cups**

Chocolate Truffle Sauce has many uses—a thick hot fudge sauce, a fudge filling, or a shiny glaze to top a pie or cover a cake. The first time I made this sauce, which takes only about five minutes to prepare, I knew I would be using it often. Not only is it versatile, but since the warm cream is poured over chopped chocolate, the chocolate doesn't need to be melted ahead of time. No kidding, this is easy! One of my favorite last-minute desserts is to top Fudge Bars (page 76) with ice cream and warm Chocolate Truffle Sauce. It's the best hot fudge brownie sundae you'll ever eat.

**¾ cup whipping cream**
**2 tablespoons unsalted butter, cut into 2 pieces**
**12 ounces semisweet chocolate chips or semisweet chocolate, chopped**
**1 teaspoon vanilla extract**

Put the cream and butter in a medium saucepan and heat over medium-low heat until the cream is hot and the butter is melted. The hot cream mixture will form tiny bubbles and measure about 175°F. on a food thermometer. Do not let the mixture boil. Remove the pan from the heat. Add the chocolate and let it melt in the hot cream mixture for about 30 seconds to soften. Add the vanilla and stir the sauce until it is smooth and all of the chocolate is melted.

### Good Advice

Heat the cream and butter mixture to a bare simmer; it will be just warm enough to melt the chocolate without burning.

### Doubling the Recipe

Double or triple the ingredients.

### To Freeze

Pour 1 cup of the sauce into each of 2 plastic freezer containers, leaving 1 inch of space at the top. Loosely cover and cool for 1 hour at room temperature. Press a piece of plastic wrap onto the top of the sauce and cover the container tightly. Label with date and contents. Freeze up to 2 months.

### To Serve

Remove from the freezer. Defrost in the covered container overnight in the refrigerator. Warm the sauce in a medium saucepan over low heat, stirring frequently. Use the sauce warm as hot fudge sauce or as directed in the recipes in this book. If you need the sauce in a hurry and don't have time to defrost it, run some hot water over the covered container and remove the frozen sauce from the container. Warm the sauce in a heatproof container placed over (but not touching) barely simmering water, stirring occasionally. Leftover sauce can be stored up to 2 weeks in the refrigerator.

## Good Advice

The sauce will freeze solid and cannot be divided when it is frozen. Divide the sauce into smaller portions before freezing it; defrost what you need.

## Doubling the Recipe

Double the ingredients and use a large saucepan to cook the sauce.

## To Freeze

Divide the sauce among 2 or 3 plastic freezer containers, leaving at least 1 inch of space at the top. Press a piece of plastic wrap onto the top of the chilled sauce and cover the container tightly. Label with date and contents. Freeze up to 2 months.

## To Serve

Defrost the sauce in the covered container overnight in the refrigerator. Stir the sauce until smooth and serve cold.

# Cold Chocolate Sauce

**Makes about 3 cups**

When I serve a chocolate sauce with a cake or a terrine, I use this one. It is made with unsweetened cocoa powder and flavored with coffee and rum. Cocoa powder makes a thinner chocolate sauce than chocolate, which gives you a fudge-type sauce. Toasted Hazelnut–Chocolate Chip Meringue Cake (page 86), Mocha Mud Ice Cream Pie (page 207), and Hazelnut, Chocolate, and Espresso Terrine (page 186) are all served with this dark, bittersweet sauce. The sauce has the consistency of whipping cream and is served cold.

**1½ cups half-and-half**
**6 tablespoons (¾ stick) unsalted butter**
**1 tablespoon light corn syrup**
**⅔ cup unsweetened Dutch process cocoa powder, sifted**
**1 cup sugar**
**2 teaspoons instant decaffeinated coffee granules**
**1 tablespoon dark rum**
**1 teaspoon vanilla extract**

Put the half-and-half, butter, corn syrup, cocoa, and sugar in a large saucepan. Stir over low heat until the butter is melted and the cocoa is combined with the other ingredients. Increase the heat to medium-low and cook for 3 minutes, stirring constantly. Stir the sauce often where the bottom and the sides of the saucepan meet. Do not let the sauce boil. Remove the saucepan from the heat and add the coffee, rum, and vanilla. Stir until the coffee is dissolved. Pour the sauce into a storage container and refrigerate, loosely covered with plastic wrap, until the sauce is cold. Cover tightly and store the sauce up to 2 weeks in the refrigerator or freeze.

## Good Advice

- If your hands are cold, run them under warm water and dry them. When the chocolate is ready, it will feel slightly sticky and soft. Dark chocolate will lose some of its shiny appearance. On a hot day Callebaut white chocolate may not need any warming; try shaving it without warming it.
- Depending on the temperature or the brand of chocolate, the shavings will vary in thickness and therefore weight, so I measure Chocolate Curls and Curves in cups.

## Doubling the Recipe

An 8-ounce block of chocolate or white chocolate will make 6 to 7 cups of chocolate shavings. There will be a small (about 1-ounce) piece of chocolate remaining that will be difficult to shave. Save this to use in other recipes.

## To Freeze

Spoon the cold chocolate shavings into a plastic freezer container. Gently press plastic wrap onto the chocolate and cover the container tightly. Label with date and contents. Freeze up to 3 months. Do not defrost the chocolate curls before using them, and they will be less likely to melt.

# Chocolate Curls and Curves

**Makes 4 cups**

These are thin shavings of dark or white chocolate for decorating desserts, especially cakes. I use a vegetable peeler to a shave a thick block of chocolate into coiled chocolate curls or open, petal-like chocolate curves. They resemble the thin wood shavings found in woodworking shops. Each one is different in size and shape, and this adds to the appeal.

The only tricky part is that the chocolate must be at a temperature where it is slightly soft but not melted; then the chocolate will roll off in smooth shavings as it is peeled. I have tried different ways to warm the chocolate: the pilot light of an oven, a barely heated oven, a sunny windowsill. Here's what I found most dependable: Hold the chocolate between the palms of your hands until it warms slightly. It is easy to feel the chocolate begin to soften, and there's no danger of overheating it.

**8 ounces semisweet, bittersweet, or white chocolate, in 1 piece about 1 to 1¼ inches thick and 3 inches square, Callebaut or Guittard preferred**

1. Have ready a baking sheet lined with wax paper.

2. Hold the chocolate between the palms of your hands and warm it with your hands for about 2 minutes. The chocolate will take longer to warm in a cold room. To shave the chocolate, hold the chocolate in 1 hand and use a stainless-steel vegetable peeler with a 2½-inch swivel blade to scrape curls and curves from the block of chocolate in a single layer onto the baking sheet. Scrape the peeler away from you. Scrape the vegetable peeler in 1½- to 2-inch-long strokes along the chocolate and make the shavings about 1 inch wide. Scrape along all sides of the chocolate. The shavings will vary in shape and size. Longer shavings will form curls, shorter ones, curves. You will not use all of the chocolate to prepare 4 cups of shavings, but a large piece of chocolate is easier to handle. If the shavings begin to flake and break, the chocolate is too hard and should be held between your hands again for about 45 seconds. Put the baking sheet in the freezer for about 30 minutes to firm the shavings.

# Nut Praline

Cooking powdered sugar and nuts to a caramel or combining nuts with caramelized granulated sugar gives you praline. Either method covers the nuts with a coating of caramelized sugar that becomes hard and crisp as it cools; it's like an easy nut brittle.

I use the quick powdered-sugar method when I want to grind praline to a powder or crush it into small pieces and the granulated-sugar method for praline powder and large pieces or wedges of praline. The powder is delicious mixed into ice cream, buttercream, or a mousse, and larger praline pieces make an attractive garnish for desserts. Almonds and toasted hazelnuts are the classic nuts to use, but pine nuts, roasted pistachios, pecans, and walnuts all make good praline. I prefer to make praline with one kind of nut rather than a combination so the flavor of that nut is apparent.

## Powdered Sugar Praline

**Makes 2 cups**

**2 cups powdered sugar**
**1 cup nuts, such as blanched slivered almonds, toasted skinned hazelnuts, roasted pistachios, pine nuts, pecans, or walnuts**

1. Lightly oil a metal baking sheet.

2. Warm a large heavy frying pan over medium heat. Add the sugar and nuts. Stir often with a wooden spoon to ensure the sugar melts evenly. As soon as the sugar begins melting, stir the mixture constantly. Cook until all of the sugar turns a dark golden color and the nuts are coated, about 8 minutes. Blanched nuts will turn golden. Immediately pour the praline onto the baking sheet and spread with the wooden spoon. This praline will not spread much. Be careful as the mixture is very hot. Cool the praline until it hardens and is cool to the touch.

3. Break the praline into 1-inch pieces. Crush the praline with a clean mallet, rolling pin, or meat pounder into ¼- to ⅜-inch pieces. To prepare praline powder, transfer the crushed praline to a food processor fitted with a metal blade and process just until the praline forms a powder. Overprocessing can turn the praline into a paste. Use the same day or freeze.

### Good Advice

- Caramelized sugar is very hot, about 330°F., so be careful not to splash any on yourself. The process of caramelizing sugar is easy—all you're doing is melting sugar and cooking it to a dark golden color. Stir the sugar with a wooden spoon to help it melt evenly and to prevent burning. When sugar cooks to the caramel stage it cooks past the stage of crystallization; you don't have to worry about the sugar crystallizing and turning grainy as it cools.
- If using pistachio nuts, rub off any loose skins and discard them before adding them to the sugar.
- If using pine nuts, stir them constantly as they burn easily.

### Doubling the Recipe

Double the ingredients.

### To Freeze

Put crushed or ground praline in a plastic freezer container. Press plastic wrap onto the praline. Cover the container tightly and freeze up to 3 months. Praline can be used directly from the freezer. Spoon out the amount needed and return the remaining praline to the freezer.

## Granulated Sugar Praline

**Makes 1 cup**

**½ cup granulated sugar**
**1 cup nuts, such as blanched slivered almonds, toasted skinned hazelnuts, roasted pistachios, pine nuts, pecans, or walnuts**

1. Lightly oil a metal baking sheet.

2. Put the sugar in a large heavy frying pan and cook over low heat. Stir occasionally with a wooden spoon to ensure the sugar melts evenly. Increase the heat to medium and cook the melted sugar to a light golden color. Add the nuts and cook until the mixture is a dark golden color, about 1 minute. Immediately pour the praline onto the baking sheet and spread with the wooden spoon. This praline will spread thinner than Powdered Sugar Praline. Be careful as the mixture is very hot. Cool the praline until it hardens and is cool to the touch.

3. Crush or process the praline as directed for Powdered Sugar Praline. This praline can also be broken into large wedges for use as a garnish. Freeze as directed for Powdered Sugar Praline.

# Glazed Nuts

**Makes about 1¼ cups**

Glazed nuts are used to embellish cakes, top sundaes, garnish a bombe, or decorate desserts. Plain toasted nuts soon soften after sitting on buttercream or whipped cream, but these nuts remain crunchy for days.

**1¼ cups sliced blanched almonds, chopped toasted hazelnuts, pecans, walnuts, or unsalted pistachio nuts**
**1 large egg white**
**1 tablespoon plus 2 teaspoons sugar**

1. Position a rack in middle of the oven and preheat the oven to 300°F. Have ready an ungreased nonstick baking sheet.

2. Check for any dark or wrinkled nuts and discard them. If using pistachio nuts rub off any loose skins and discard them. Put the egg white in a medium bowl. Add the nuts and stir until they are evenly coated with egg white. Sprinkle the sugar over the nuts and stir the mixture. Spread the nuts in a single layer on the baking sheet. Bake 5 minutes. Stir the nuts with a wooden spoon to loosen them from the baking sheet. Bake 5 more minutes and remove the nuts from oven. Immediately stir the nuts to loosen them from the baking sheet. Cool the nuts on the baking sheet. The nuts will become crisp as they cool.

### Good Advice

When still warm the nuts will be soft, but they become crisp as they cool. After topping a dessert with the nuts, sift powdered sugar over them for a pretty finish.

### Doubling the Recipe

Double or triple the ingredients.

### To Freeze

Place the cooled nuts in a plastic freezer container. Press plastic wrap on the nuts, cover the container tightly, and freeze up to 4 months. Remove as many nuts as needed from the container and return the remaining nuts to the freezer.

# Cookies, Small Cakes, *and* Brownies

We are a cookie family. If there is no other dessert in our house, there will always be some cookies in the freezer. My husband, Jeff, often conducts a cookie search in the freezer before dinner and arranges a stack of cookies for dessert. One day I looked at his cookie stack, and I saw cookies from three generations of my family's recipes. Our family history was in that pile of cookies: My Grandmother Sophie baking butter cookies in her Brooklyn kitchen, my mother pressing her face against a bakery window to look for her favorite Macaroon Tarts, and my Chocolate Acorns perpetuating my fondness for chocolate and carrying on the family cookie tradition.

Many cookies contain a large amount of sugar, and the bottoms often brown quickly before the rest of the cookie is baked through. To prevent this, bake cookies in the middle or upper third of the oven, use sturdy, heavyweight baking sheets, and check the cookies as they bake. When I bake a cookie with a large proportion of sugar like Mrs. Wilson's Chocolate Pecan Wafers, I add insulation to the baking sheet by lining it with heavy aluminum foil. Lining baking sheets with foil, or with parchment paper, also makes clean-up easy.

I usually cool cookies on the baking sheets since most cookies do not lose any of their crispness, and it's easier not to bother with a cooling rack if it isn't necessary. Some cookies, like strudel, require cooling on a rack. If strudel is left to cool on the baking sheet, any filling that may have leaked out during baking will harden and fasten the cooled strudel to the baking sheet or liner.

Everyone thinks I serve some sort of fancy dessert with dinner every night, but in reality we usually have several cookies, bars, or a piece of unfrosted cake with fresh fruit or ice cream. For company, I dress things up by presenting an assortment of cookies with homemade ice cream or sorbet. After all, we are a cookie family.

Individual desserts are very practical since you can serve one person or a crowd. You serve exactly what you need and avoid leftovers. My small cakes range from simple frosted cupcakes to tender shortcakes heaped with berries and whipped cream to chocolate-filled meringue hearts. (The meringues can be piped into other shapes as well.)

When I'm really pressed for time and want to make something sweet, fast, and easy to freeze, I turn to my recipes for bars. Bars are faster to prepare than cookies, which must be formed individually and often require several baking pans. Some of my favorites, like Fudge Bars prepared with a pound of chocolate, Pat's Toffee Bars covered in white chocolate, or crunchy and chewy Caramel Cashew Squares, can be quickly mixed, spread in a pan, and baked.

## Good Advice

Bake the cookies just until the edges are light brown. This cooks the butter enough to give the cookies their buttery taste. Pale butter cookies will have little flavor. You will need three baking sheets for these cookies. Bake two sheets, then the remaining sheet. Even if your oven has three racks, three sheets of cookies won't bake properly.

## Doubling the Recipe

This is a large recipe, so it is easier to mix separate batches of dough.

## To Freeze

Place the bottoms of 2 cookies together and wrap them in plastic wrap. Put the wrapped cookies in a metal or plastic freezer container and cover tightly. Freeze up to 3 months.

## To Serve

Remove as many cookies from the freezer as needed. Unwrap the cookies and place them on a plate. Cover with plastic wrap and defrost at room temperature. Serve within 3 days.

# Grandmother Sophie's Butter Cookies

**Makes about 54 cookies**

My Grandmother Sophie was a smart baker. She kept things simple and used quality ingredients. Only seven basic ingredients are required for these crisp, brown-edged butter cookies. They always remind me of the virtues of simplicity.

**¾ pound (3 sticks) soft unsalted butter**
**¼ teaspoon salt**
**1 cup sugar**
**3 large egg yolks**
**1 teaspoon vanilla extract**
**¼ teaspoon almond extract**
**3¼ to 3½ cups unbleached all-purpose flour**

1. Position 2 oven racks in the middle and upper third of the oven. Preheat the oven to 350°F. Have ready 3 ungreased baking sheets. The baking sheets can be lined with regular weight aluminum foil or parchment paper for easier clean-up.

2. Put the butter and salt in a large mixing bowl and mix with an electric mixer on low speed for 15 seconds. Add the sugar and beat on medium speed for 1 minute until smooth. Stop the mixer and scrape the sides of the bowl once during the mixing. Mix in the egg yolks, vanilla, and almond extract until the egg yolks are incorporated. Stop the mixer and scrape the bowl again. On low speed, add 3¼ cups of the flour and mix just until the flour is incorporated completely. The dough should feel soft and smooth but not sticky. Add up to ¼ cup more flour if necessary to achieve a soft dough.

3. To form a cookie, roll 1 tablespoon of dough between the palms of your hands into a 1-inch ball, and flatten the ball into a 1¾-inch circle. Place cookies 1 inch apart on the baking sheets. Set aside 1 baking sheet of cookies at room temperature and bake the other 2 sheets about 18 minutes, until the edges and bottoms of the cookies are light brown. Reverse the baking sheets after 9 minutes, front to back and top to bottom to ensure the cookies bake evenly. Bake the remaining sheet of cookies on the middle rack of the oven, reversing the baking sheet after 9 minutes. Cool the cookies on the baking sheets for 5 minutes. Transfer the cookies to a wire cooling rack to cool completely.

## Variation

Before baking, place a chocolate chip in the center of each cookie.

# Selma Cookies

**Makes 12 sandwich cookies, 2¾ inches in diameter**

When my mother, Selma, was a young woman in Brooklyn she always chose these cookies at the bakery, and my father soon dubbed them Selma Cookies. Selma Cookies are two crisp butter almond cookies sandwiched together with raspberry jam. The top cookie has a hole cut out of the center and is sprinkled with powdered sugar, so the bright jam shines through. The result: a beautiful red and white cookie sandwich.

Like mother, like daughter. I love these cookies too. We used to buy them in a bakery, but in our Maine village, it was bake them at home or do without. And bake I did—thin cookies, thick cookies, tasteless cookies, spread-all-over-the-place cookies—but none were good enough to be called a Selma Cookie. Finally, I called my mother. Why didn't I think of it a hundred cookies sooner? We decided to try adding almonds to a shortbread-type cookie, and it worked. These are the best Selma Cookies I've ever tasted, Selma through and through.

**2 cups unbleached all-purpose flour**
**½ teaspoon salt**
**½ pound (2 sticks) soft unsalted butter**
**¾ cup powdered sugar**
**1 teaspoon vanilla extract**
**½ teaspoon almond extract**
**½ teaspoon ground cinnamon**
**1 cup unblanched almonds, ground**
**¼ cup seedless raspberry jam**
**Powdered sugar, for dusting**

1. Position 2 racks in the middle and upper third of the oven. Preheat the oven to 325°F. Line 2 large baking sheets with parchment paper.

2. Sift the flour and salt together and set aside. Put the butter and powdered sugar in a large bowl. Beat with an electric mixer on medium speed for 30 seconds, until the mixture is smooth. Decrease the speed to low and mix in the vanilla, almond extract, and cinnamon. Mix in the ground almonds. Add the flour mixture and mix just until all the flour is incorporated completely and the dough holds together and comes away from the side of the bowl. Stop the mixer and scrape down the sides of the bowl once during the mixing. Form the dough into two 6-inch disks and wrap in plastic wrap. Refrigerate until the dough is cold and just firm enough to roll, about 40 minutes.

### Good Advice

Use almonds with skins, which intensify the almond flavor of the cookies.

### Doubling the Recipe

Double the ingredients.

### To Freeze

Wrap each cookie sandwich in plastic wrap. Be careful not to disturb the powdered sugar. Put the wrapped cookies in a metal or plastic freezer container and cover tightly. Freeze up to 3 months.

### To Serve

Remove as many cookies from the freezer as needed. Defrost the wrapped cookies at room temperature. Serve within 3 days.

3. Remove 1 disk of dough from the refrigerator. Lightly flour the rolling surface and rolling pin. Roll the dough ¼ inch thick. Use a metal spatula to loosen the circle of dough from the rolling surface. Use a metal cutter to cut out 2¾-inch circles. Place the cookies 1 inch apart on one of the prepared baking sheets. Gather together the dough scraps and roll and cut them to make 12 circles. Remove the second disk from the refrigerator and repeat the rolling process to form 12 more 2¾-inch circles. Cut a 1-inch circle from the center of 12 cookies and remove the circle from the cookie. The wide end of a pastry tube works well for cutting the circles. Place cookies 1 inch apart on the second baking sheet. The 1-inch circles can be baked with the cookies for snacks.

4. Bake the cookies 13 to 16 minutes, until they are golden, reversing the baking sheets after 8 minutes, front to back and top to bottom, to ensure the cookies bake evenly. Cool the cookies on the baking sheets for 5 minutes. Use a wide metal spatula to transfer the cookies to a wire cooling rack to cool completely. Leaving a ¼-inch edge, spread 1 teaspoon of raspberry jam evenly over each of the cookies without holes. Sift powdered sugar over the cookies with the holes and place them on top of the jam-covered cookies.

## Variation

These cookies are also delicious plain. Cut out any size cookie circles, but with no holes. Bake as directed. Dust all of the cooled cookies with powdered sugar.

# Chocolate Acorns

**Makes 44 to 48 cookies**

These crisp, dark, chocolate butter cookies are formed into acorn shapes before baking. After the cookies cool, the flat end is dipped in melted white chocolate, for a dark chocolate acorn with a white chocolate cap.

**2 cups plus 2 tablespoons unbleached all-purpose flour**
**6 tablespoons unsweetened Dutch process cocoa powder**
**½ teaspoon salt**
**½ pound (2 sticks) soft unsalted butter**
**¾ cup sugar**
**½ teaspoon instant decaffeinated coffee granules**
**2 teaspoons vanilla extract**
**4 ounces white chocolate, chopped, Callebaut preferred**

1. Position 2 oven racks in the middle and upper third of the oven. Preheat the oven to 325°F. Line 2 baking sheets with heavy aluminum foil. Butter the aluminum foil lightly.

2. Sift the flour, cocoa, and salt together and set aside. Put the butter in a large mixing bowl and mix with an electric mixer on low speed for 15 seconds. Increase the speed to medium, add the sugar, instant coffee, and vanilla, and beat for 1 minute. Slowly add the flour mixture. Mix until the flour mixture is blended completely into the dough and the dough holds together, about 45 seconds.

3. Roll about 2 teaspoons of the dough between the palms of your hands into a 1-inch ball, then a 1¾-inch cylinder. Press 1 end of the cylinder against your palm to flatten it and pinch the opposite end to a point. The cookie will now have an acorn or cone shape. Place cookies 1 inch apart on the baking sheets. Bake 20 minutes, reversing the baking sheets after 10 minutes, front to back and top to bottom, to ensure the cookies bake evenly. Cool the cookies on the baking sheet for 5 minutes. Transfer the cookies to a wire cooling rack to cool completely.

4. While the cookies cool, melt the white chocolate. Preheat the oven to 175°F. Place the white chocolate in a small nonreactive container and melt it in the oven, about 8 minutes. Remove it from the oven as soon as it is melted. Stir the white chocolate smooth.

5. Line a baking sheet with wax paper. Dip the flat end of each cookie in the melted white chocolate, covering about ½ inch of cookie. Place the dipped cookies on the baking sheet.

## Variation

Dip some or all of the cookies in melted semisweet chocolate rather than white chocolate.

### Good Advice

These cookies will spread only slightly during baking.

### Doubling the Recipe

Double the ingredients.

### To Freeze

Refrigerate or freeze the cookies until the white chocolate is firm. Wrap 2 or 3 cookies together in plastic wrap. Put the wrapped cookies in a metal or plastic freezer container and cover tightly. Freeze up to 3 months.

### To Serve

Remove as many cookies from the freezer as needed. Unwrap the cookies and place them on a plate. Cover with plastic wrap and defrost at room temperature. Serve within 3 days.

## Good Advice

The batter will become very firm before all the cookies are formed, but this does not affect the finished cookies. Use three baking sheets for the cookies, but put only two at a time in the oven.

## Doubling the Recipe

Double the ingredients.

## To Freeze

Place the bottoms of 2 cookies together and wrap them in plastic wrap. Put the wrapped cookies in a metal or plastic freezer container and cover tightly. Freeze up to 3 months.

## To Serve

Remove as many cookies from the freezer as needed and defrost the wrapped cookies at room temperature. Serve within 3 days.

# Mrs. Wilson's Chocolate Pecan Wafers

**Makes 36 cookies**

Eva Wilson's family has lived in Camden for so long that the street she lives on is called Wilson Street. One day I walked into her kitchen and smelled these cookies baking. She promptly offered me the recipe.

**3 ounces unsweetened chocolate, in 1-ounce pieces**
**½ cup vegetable shortening, at room temperature**
**½ teaspoon salt**
**1 teaspoon vanilla extract**
**1 cup sugar**
**2 large eggs**
**¾ cup unbleached all-purpose flour, sifted**
**¾ cup pecans, coarsely chopped**

1. Position 2 oven racks in the middle and upper third of the oven. Line 3 baking sheets with heavy aluminum foil. Preheat the oven to 175°F.

2. Put the chocolate in a small heatproof container. Melt the chocolate in the oven, about 8 minutes. Remove the chocolate from the oven as soon as it is melted and stir it smooth. Set the chocolate aside to cool slightly while you prepare the cookie batter. Increase the oven temperature to 350°F.

3. Put the vegetable shortening, salt, and vanilla in the large bowl of an electric mixer and mix on low speed just to blend the ingredients. Add the sugar and beat on medium speed for 2 minutes. The mixture will look grainy. Add the eggs, one at a time, then beat for 15 seconds. Decrease the speed to low and mix in the melted chocolate. Stop the mixer and scrape the sides of the bowl. Add the flour and mix just until no white specks of flour remain. Mix in the pecans.

4. Use 1 rounded teaspoon of batter for each cookie. Place the mounds of batter 2 inches apart on the prepared baking sheets. Use your fingers to gently flatten the top of each cookie. Bake about 10 minutes, reversing the baking sheets, top to bottom and back to front, after 5 minutes to ensure even baking. The cookies will spread into wafers as they bake and the tops will lose their shine. The cookies are done as soon as they are no longer shiny. The finished cookies will be about ⅜ inch thick. Bake the remaining sheet of cookies on the middle rack of the oven, for about 10 minutes, reversing it after 5 minutes. Cool the cookies on the baking sheet for 5 minutes. Use a wide metal spatula to transfer the cookies to a wire cooling rack to cool completely.

## Good Advice

Cut the dough circles with a round metal pastry cutter, rather than the rim of a glass or anything makeshift. These cutters are sharp and cut cleanly through dough, forming sharp edges that let the cookies puff properly as they bake.

## Doubling the Recipe

Double the ingredients.

## To Freeze

Place 2 or 3 cookies together and wrap in plastic wrap. Put the wrapped cookies in a metal or plastic freezer container and cover tightly. Freeze up to 3 months.

## To Serve

Remove as many cookies from the freezer as needed and defrost the wrapped cookies at room temperature. Serve within 2 days.

# Swedish Sandwich Puffs

**Makes about 52 sandwich cookies**

Since people know I like to bake, they often share their favorite recipes with me. One day, out of the blue, this cookie recipe arrived in the mail from one of my mother's friends, Hazel Melik. It's her treasured family recipe, and I felt honored to receive it. Swedish Sandwich Puffs are dainty, one-bite, melt-in-your-mouth cookies that look as if they take hours to prepare but happily don't.

### Cookie Puffs

**2 cups unbleached all-purpose flour**
**½ pound (2 sticks) cold, unsalted butter, cut into 16 pieces**
**5 to 6 tablespoons ice water**
**1 large egg white**
**2 tablespoons plus 2 teaspoons granulated sugar**

### Puff Filling

**4 tablespoons (½ stick) soft unsalted butter**
**¾ cup powdered sugar, sifted**
**1 teaspoon vanilla extract**

1. Preheat the oven to 450°F. Position 2 oven racks in the middle and upper third of the oven. Line 3 baking sheets with parchment paper.

## Prepare the cookies

2. Put the flour in the large bowl of an electric mixer. Add the butter pieces and mix on low speed just until the butter pieces are the size of small lima beans, about 45 seconds. They will not all be the same size, and you will still see loose flour. Slowly add the water, 1 tablespoon at a time. Stop mixing as soon as the mixture begins to hold together, about 30 seconds. Turn the dough mixture out onto a lightly floured rolling surface and divide the dough in half. With the heel of your hand push one of the dough pieces down and forward against the rolling surface. Fold the dough in half and repeat 8 to 10 times, until the dough looks smooth. Repeat with the second piece of dough. Form each piece of dough into a 4-inch disk and refrigerate 15 minutes, until the dough is cold and firm.

3. Remove 1 piece of dough from the refrigerator. Lightly flour the rolling surface and rolling pin. Roll the dough into a circle about 12 inches in diameter and ⅛ inch thick. Using a 1½-inch round pastry cutter, cut out circles and place them on the baking sheets ¾ inch apart. The cookies do not spread but actually shrink a little in diameter as they bake and puff. Repeat with the second piece of dough. Press the dough scraps together, roll, and cut in circles. Using a pastry brush lightly brush each cookie with egg white and sprinkle evenly with a pinch of sugar. One teaspoon of sugar will cover about 12 cookies. Bake 2 sheets at a time 9 to 11 minutes, reversing the sheets, top to bottom and back to front, after 5 minutes of baking.

The top and bottom of the cookies will be golden and the baked cookie will be ½ inch thick. Bake the remaining sheet of cookies on the middle rack of the oven for 9 to 11 minutes, reversing it after 5 minutes. Leave the cookies on the baking sheets placed on a wire cooling rack to cool completely.

## Fill the cookies

4. Put the 4 tablespoons of butter, powdered sugar, and vanilla in a small bowl and mix with an electric mixer on low speed or with a large spoon until smooth. Spread a thin layer of frosting, a scant ¼ teaspoon, on the bottom of half of the cookies. Press another cookie, bottom side down, onto each frosted cookie.

### Good Advice

Chunky preserves like cherry or strawberry or raspberry jam are good choices for the filling. Any of these will give the strudel a definite fruit flavor.

### Doubling the Recipe

Double the ingredients.

### To Freeze

Place 2 pieces of strudel together and wrap them in plastic wrap. Put the wrapped strudel in a metal or plastic container and cover tightly. Label with date and contents. Freeze up to 3 months.

### To Serve

Remove as many pieces of strudel from the freezer as needed and defrost the wrapped strudel at room temperature. Serve within 3 days.

# Grandmother Sophie's Nutty Fruit Strudel

**Makes 40 pieces**

This is the strudel my Grandmother Sophie baked many years ago. Whenever I bake it, I think of her and the wonderful baking legacy she left her family. The strudel is filled with jam or preserves, plumped raisins, and pecans. Vegetable oil produces a firm dough that bakes into a particularly crisp crust. Before baking, the filled strudel strip is rolled in a coating of bread crumbs, sugar, and cinnamon.

Strudel Pastry

**¾ cup corn or canola oil**
**¾ cup whole milk**
**1 teaspoon vanilla extract**
**1 tablespoon sugar**
**3¼ to 3½ cups unbleached all-purpose flour**
**¼ teaspoon baking soda, any lumps pressed out**

Strudel Filling

**1 cup raisins**
**1⅓ cups strawberry or raspberry jam or cherry preserves**
**1 cup pecans, coarsely chopped**

Crumb Coating

**⅓ cup fine dry bread crumbs**
**3 tablespoons sugar**
**1 teaspoon ground cinnamon**

1. Position an oven rack in the center of the oven. Preheat the oven to 350°F. Lightly oil a large baking sheet.

## Prepare the strudel pastry

2. Put the oil, milk, vanilla, and sugar in the large bowl of an electric mixer. Mix on low speed just to combine the ingredients. Add 2 cups of the flour and the baking soda and mix just until the flour is combined. Add 1¼ cups more flour and mix to a soft dough, about 30 seconds. Poke your finger several inches into the dough. It should be soft but should not stick to your fingers. Add up to ¼ cup more flour to achieve a soft dough that pulls cleanly away from the mixing bowl. The dough will look shiny from the oil and ragged, but will become smooth when it is rolled. Cover the dough and set it aside to rest 15 to 30 minutes.

## Fill the strudel

3. Put the raisins in a small bowl and cover with 1 cup boiling water. Let sit 15 minutes. Drain the raisins and pat with a clean dish towel to remove any excess water.

4. Divide the dough into 4 equal parts. Lightly flour the rolling surface and rolling pin. Roll 1 piece of the dough to a 12 × 7-inch rectangle ⅛ inch thick. Roll the dough into an even layer, with no thin spots, so the filling doesn't break through the crust as the strudel bakes. Leaving a ½-inch edge on all sides of the dough, spread ⅓ cup jam evenly over the dough. Sprinkle ¼ cup of the pecans and a quarter of the raisins evenly over the jam. Roll tightly to form a 12-inch-long roll. Pinch the edges tightly to seal them completely. The dough is firm and the seams of the strudel roll must be pinched tightly so they do not open during baking.

## Coat the strudel

5. Mix the bread crumbs, sugar, and cinnamon in a small bowl. Spread the mixture on a 15-inch long piece of wax paper. Roll the strudel in the crumbs.

6. Place the strudel, seam side down, on the baking sheet. Repeat with the remaining 3 pieces of dough and place the strudel strips 1 inch apart on the baking sheet. Bake 45 to 50 minutes. Reverse the baking sheets, top to bottom and front to back, after 25 minutes to ensure even browning. The crust will be light golden brown. Let the strudel cool on the baking sheet for 5 minutes. Using a long wide spatula, transfer the strudel to a wire cooling rack to cool completely. While the strudel is still warm, use a serrated knife to cut through the top crust at approximately 1-inch intervals. After the strudel cools completely, place it on a firm cutting surface and use a large, sharp knife to cut all the way through the cuts on the strudel.

# Apricot-Pecan Butter Strudel

**Makes 32 pieces**

My mom is a champion strudel maker, and this is the strudel that made her reputation. In this recipe I wanted to include all the little details that make her strudel special, so on one of her visits we had a marathon strudel baking session. Mom rolled dough, and I watched, measured, and asked questions. Then I rolled dough as she explained exactly what to do. When we finished, we had lots of strudel for the freezer.

My mother got this recipe years ago from her high school friend Pauline Tauber. The unique pastry is prepared with flour, butter, and ice cream. It is a silky smooth dough that is a pleasure to work with; it bakes into a crisp butter pastry. The strips of strudel are frozen without baking and are baked as needed.

### Good Advice

- When adding the ice cream to the warm butter, stir constantly to break up the ice cream as it melts. The dough can be prepared a day ahead of time and chilled overnight.
- Use golden raisins; they remain moist as the strudel bakes and blend well with the golden-colored filling. Roll the dough ⅛ inch thick, but don't worry if it's not exactly even.
- The finished strudel strip is rolled up in a piece of heavy aluminum foil. Do not use plastic wrap since the strudel is baked frozen and plastic wrap might stick to it.
- Bake the strudel until the crust is a rich golden brown. This enhances the buttery taste of the dough and ensures that the filling is cooked properly.

### Doubling the Recipe

Double all ingredients.

### To Freeze

Roll each strudel strip tightly in heavy aluminum foil. Label with date and contents. Freeze up to 3 months.

Strudel Dough

**½ pound (2 sticks) unsalted butter**
**1 cup (½ pint) vanilla ice cream, softened, not premium ice cream**
**2 cups unbleached all-purpose flour**

Apricot Strudel Filling

**½ cup apricot preserves**
**1⅓ cups golden raisins**
**1 cup pecans, coarsely chopped**

## Prepare the strudel dough

1. Put the butter in a medium saucepan and melt it slowly over low heat. Do not let the butter brown. Pour the warm butter into a large bowl. Add the ice cream and stir together until the ice cream is melted. The mixture will look lumpy. Add the flour and stir together until the flour is incorporated and a soft dough forms. Cover and refrigerate at least 2 hours or overnight. The chilled dough should feel firm to the touch.

## Fill the strudel

2. Remove the dough from the refrigerator and divide it into 4 pieces. Roll one of the pieces of dough between your hands into a smooth ball. Do this quickly so that the dough does not soften. Press the dough into a 1-inch-thick disk. Lightly flour a rolling surface and roll the dough to a 12 × 6-inch rectangle about ⅛ inch thick. Lift and turn the dough several times as you roll it so it doesn't stick to the rolling surface. The 12-inch side of the dough should be facing you. Leaving a ½-inch edge all around, spread 2 tablespoons of the apricot preserves evenly over the dough. Sprinkle evenly with ⅓ cup raisins and ¼ cup pecans. With the long side still facing you, roll up the strudel. Press the edges and seam together to seal tightly. Repeat with the 3 remaining pieces of dough.

### To Bake and Serve

Position an oven rack in the bottom third of the oven and preheat the oven to 375°F. Unwrap as many strudel strips as you want to bake. Line a baking sheet with the aluminum foil from the frozen strudel. Place the strudel, seam side down, on the baking sheet. If baking more than 1 strip of strudel, place the strips 2 inches apart. Bake 35 to 40 minutes, reversing the baking sheet front to back after 25 minutes to ensure even browning. The strudel crust should look golden brown. Cool 10 minutes on the baking sheet. Use a long wide metal spatula to transfer the strudel to a wire cooling rack to cool completely. Transfer to a cutting surface. Using a sharp knife and a slight sawing motion, cut each strip on the diagonal into 8 pieces. Wrap baked strudel with plastic wrap and store up to 3 days at room temperature.

### Variation

For the preserves in the filling, use a mixture of 6 tablespoons apricot preserves and 2 tablespoons orange marmalade.

### Good Advice

• Use a pastry cutter with a fluted edge to cut out the cookies. It's a simple way to give the cookies a fancy looking finish.

• The macaroon mixture is firm and doesn't lose its shape during baking.

### Doubling the Recipe

Double the ingredients.

### To Freeze

Wrap the cooled tarts individually in plastic wrap. Put the wrapped tarts in a metal or plastic freezer container and cover tightly. Label with date and contents. Freeze up to 3 months.

### To Serve

Remove as many tarts from the freezer as needed and defrost the wrapped tarts at room temperature. Serve with fresh fruit, after-dinner coffee, or afternoon tea. Serve within 3 days.

# Macaroon Tarts

**Makes fifteen 2½-inch tarts**

My memories of the Macaroon Tarts that were sold long ago by the now defunct Ebinger's bakeries in Brooklyn inspired this recipe. The tarts have a butter cookie base with a ring of chewy almond macaroon baked on the cookie. A spoonful of raspberry jam brightens the center of the tart. When I was a little girl, I would cut my Macaroon Tart in half, intending to save some for the next day, but somehow it never lasted that long.

Cookie Base

**1¼ cups unbleached all-purpose flour**
**½ teaspoon baking powder**
**¼ teaspoon salt**
**¼ pound (1 stick) soft unsalted butter**
**¼ cup powdered sugar, sifted**
**1 teaspoon vanilla extract**
**1 tablespoon whipping cream**

Macaroon Topping

**2½ cups blanched almonds**
**1 cup granulated sugar**
**1 tablespoon cornstarch**
**1 large egg**
**1 large egg white**
**½ teaspoon almond extract**

**1 large egg white, lightly beaten with a fork until slightly foamy**
**3 tablespoons raspberry jam with seeds**

1. Position a rack in the center of the oven. Preheat the oven to 350°F. Line a baking sheet with parchment paper.

## Prepare the cookie base

2. Sift the flour, baking powder, and salt together and set aside. Put the butter in the large bowl of an electric mixer and mix on low speed for 15 seconds. Add the powdered sugar and vanilla and mix on medium speed until smooth and creamy, about 30 seconds. Slowly add the flour mixture and beat until the flour is incorporated and the dough looks smooth and holds together, 1 minute. Add the cream and mix just until the cream is absorbed. Form the dough into a round disk about 6 inches in diameter. Wrap in plastic wrap and refrigerate 30 minutes.

3. On a lightly floured surface with a lightly floured rolling pin, roll the chilled dough into a 10-inch circle ¼-inch thick. Using a 2½-inch round pastry cutter, preferably with a fluted edge, cut out circles and place them

on the prepared baking sheet about 1 inch apart. The tarts will not spread as they bake. Gather together the dough scraps, roll them, and cut out more circles.

## Prepare the topping

4. Put the almonds in the workbowl of a food processor fitted with the metal blade. Process with 15 on/off bursts to chop the almonds, then process for 10 seconds. Add the granulated sugar and cornstarch and process until the almonds are finely ground, 1 minute. Add the egg, egg white, and almond extract and process until the mixture is smooth and holds together, about 30 seconds. The mixture will be a firm paste. Scrape the mixture into a bowl, cover, and refrigerate about 1 hour.

## Form the tarts

5. Lightly dust your hands with cornstarch and roll about 1½ tablespoons of the almond mixture between the palms of your hands into a 4½ × ½-inch rope. Form the almond rope into a circle. Leaving a ¼-inch edge, gently press it on the cookie base. Smooth the edges of the seam. Use a pastry brush to gently brush only the almond circle with the beaten egg white. Bake 10 minutes. Gently brush only the almond rope for a second time with the beaten egg white. Place about ½ teaspoon of raspberry jam in the hole in the center of each tart. Bake another 8 to 10 minutes until the tarts are golden. The almond mixture will puff as it bakes. Cool the tarts completely on the baking sheet.

# Toasted Almond Meringue Hearts with Chocolate Cream

**Makes 6 large filled meringue hearts**

These toasted almond meringues are formed into heart shapes and filled with a whipped chocolate cream for a Valentine's Day dessert. Each heart is enough for two sweethearts to share. But you don't have to wait for Valentine's Day—just pipe the meringues into circles instead of hearts and serve them anytime.

**1 recipe Toasted Almond Meringue mixture, unbaked (page 184)**
**1 recipe Chocolate Cream Filling (page 136)**
**Powdered sugar, for dusting**

1. Preheat the oven to 275°F. Line 2 large baking sheets with aluminum foil. Butter the aluminum foil and lightly coat it with powdered sugar. Using a heart-shaped metal cutter or paper heart shape, about 5 inches long and 4 inches wide, as a guide, mark 7 hearts with the tip of a dull butter knife on each baking sheet.

## Bake the meringues

2. Prepare the meringue mixture as directed. Fit a large pastry bag with a ⅜-inch plain tip and fill the pastry bag no more than two-thirds full with the meringue mixture. Pipe the meringue onto the marked hearts. The meringues will be ⅜ inch thick. Bake 65 to 75 minutes, until the meringues are crisp and dry. Remove the meringues from the oven. Gently place the metal cutter on the meringues and trim any rough edges with a small sharp knife while the meringues are still warm. Cool the meringues on the baking sheet. Use a wide metal spatula to remove the meringues from the baking sheet.

## Fill the Meringue Hearts

3. Prepare the chocolate cream as directed. Reserve the 6 most attractive meringue hearts to use for the top heart, and turn 6 meringues with their bottoms facing up. Crush the 2 least attractive meringues into fine crumbs and set aside to garnish the finished meringues. Using a thin metal spatula, immediately spread a generous half cup of chocolate cream over the 6 bottom meringues. Spread the chocolate cream slightly thicker toward the top of the heart. This tilts the top meringue and looks attractive. Place a top meringue, flat side down, on top of the chocolate cream. Press the meringue crumbs onto the sides of the hearts. The crumbs will adhere to the chocolate cream filling. Sift powdered sugar over the top of the hearts.

### Good Advice

- If the edges of the baked meringues need to be trimmed, do it while they are still warm.
- I use a metal heart-shaped cutter as a guide; it is 5 inches long and 4 inches wide.
- If a meringue breaks in half, use it for the bottom heart and glue it together with a little chocolate cream.

### Doubling the Recipe

Double the ingredients. Use four baking sheets.

### To Freeze the Meringues

Carefully layer the meringues in a shallow large plastic or metal container, placing wax paper between the layers. Put plastic wrap over the top layer. Cover tightly. Label with date and contents. Freeze up to 1 month. Do not defrost the meringues before using them.

### To Freeze the Hearts

Carefully wrap each meringue sandwich in plastic wrap. Place the hearts in a single layer in a metal or plastic freezer container. Do not crowd them in the container. Cover tightly and label with date and contents. Freeze up to 1 week.

### To Serve

Defrost the wrapped meringues in the refrigerator for 4 to 8 hours. Let the meringues sit at room temperature about 15 minutes before serving. Store the meringues up to 2 days in the refrigerator.

## Good Advice

- The galettes are baked in round porcelain ramekins (small soufflé cups) to give them a perfectly smooth and round shape. To prevent the bottoms from overbaking before the insides are done, place the ramekins on baking sheets.
- Since the galettes contain so much butter, they store exceptionally well—up to one week at room temperature.

## Doubling the Recipe

Prepare the dough in separate batches.

## To Freeze

Wrap each galette in plastic wrap. Put the wrapped galettes in a metal or plastic freezer container and cover tightly. Freeze up to 3 months.

## To Serve

Remove as many galettes from the freezer as needed. Defrost the wrapped galettes at room temperature. Galettes can be served plain or can also be served with strawberries and whipped cream. Wrap leftover galettes in plastic wrap and store up to 1 week at room temperature.

# Butter Galettes

**Makes eight 3-inch galettes**

Actually half-cake and half-cookie, Butter Galettes have the texture of a crisp, crumbly cookie and the taste of butter—pure butter. Usually, the cake is baked in one large round, but I prefer individual cakes, which have more crisp, buttery edges per cake. You can also defrost and serve only as many as you need. I often serve these little cakes with fresh strawberries and whipped cream.

**4 large egg yolks**
**2 tablespoons whipping cream**
**1 teaspoon fresh lemon juice**
**1 teaspoon vanilla extract**
**2 cups unbleached all-purpose flour**
**½ teaspoon salt**
**½ teaspoon baking powder**
**½ cup sugar**
**6 ounces (1½ sticks) cold unsalted butter, cut into 12 pieces**
**1 large egg yolk, lightly beaten, for brushing the top of the galettes**

1. Put the 4 egg yolks, cream, lemon juice, and vanilla in a small bowl and mix with a fork until blended. Sift the flour, salt, baking powder, and sugar into the large bowl of an electric mixer. On low speed, slowly add the egg mixture to the flour mixture. Mix until the mixture looks grainy and forms fine crumbs, about 25 seconds. Add the butter pieces and mix until the dough pulls away cleanly from the side of the bowl and forms a smooth dough, about 1 minute 15 seconds. The dough looks smooth but will have some flecks of butter showing. Form the dough into a smooth ball. Flatten the ball into a 2-inch-thick disk, cover with plastic wrap, and refrigerate for 30 minutes or as long as overnight.

2. Position an oven rack in the upper third of the oven. Preheat the oven to 350°F. Cut parchment or wax paper to fit the bottom of eight 3-inch-wide ramekins (small soufflé cups) with a 5- or 6-ounce capacity and line the bottom of each ramekin with the paper. Put the ramekins on a baking sheet.

3. On a lightly floured surface, roll the dough to an even ¾-inch thickness. This will be about a 7½-inch circle. Cut 4 rounds with a 2¾-inch metal cutter. Roll the dough scraps ¾ inch thick and cut 4 more circles. The last galette may be a little skimpy but will spread as it bakes. Slide a small knife under the galettes to loosen them from the rolling surface. Brush the rounds with the beaten egg yolk. Use a small knife or fork to lightly score the top of the rounds with crisscrossing lines in a diamond pattern. Put each galette, scored side up, in a ramekin. Bake until the tops are golden brown, about 35 minutes. Reverse the baking sheet, front to back, after 20 minutes to ensure even browning. Immediately turn the galettes out onto a rack to cool. They will drop out of the ramekins. Be careful lifting the hot ramekins; they are slippery. Remove the paper and turn the galettes right side up. Cool thoroughly.

# Autumn Apple Cupcakes with Cream Cheese Frosting

**Makes twelve 2½-inch cupcakes**

Somewhere along the way since my cupcake-in-every-kitchen childhood, cupcakes went out of fashion. Cupcakes are a down-home American dessert; they suit family reunions, picnics, lunch boxes, and afternoon snacks, and they are too easy and too good to forget about. When you read the directions for this recipe, the easy part will be clear. When you taste these cupcakes, filled with grated apples and spices and topped with a smooth cream cheese frosting, you'll be left with no doubt about the good part.

### Apple Cupcakes

**1 cup peeled and grated Granny Smith apple (1 large apple)**
**1 tablespoon cognac or brandy**
**1¼ cups unbleached all-purpose flour**
**¾ cup sugar**
**1 teaspoon baking soda**
**½ teaspoon salt**
**1 teaspoon ground cinnamon**
**⅛ teaspoon ground nutmeg**
**¼ teaspoon ground cloves**
**2 large eggs**
**½ cup canola or corn oil**
**1 teaspoon vanilla extract**

### Cream Cheese Frosting

**4 tablespoons (½ stick) soft unsalted butter**
**3 ounces cream cheese, softened**
**1 teaspoon vanilla extract**
**1½ cups powdered sugar**

1. Position a rack in the middle of the oven. Preheat the oven to 350°F. Line 12 medium (½-cup) muffin tins with paper cupcake liners.

## Prepare the cupcakes

2. Put the grated apple in a small bowl and stir in the brandy. Put the flour, sugar, baking soda, salt, cinnamon, nutmeg, and cloves in the large bowl of an electric mixer. Mix on low speed just to combine the ingredients. Mix in the eggs, oil, vanilla, and apple mixture. Divide the batter among the 12 muffin tins, about 3 tablespoons batter each. Bake until a toothpick inserted in the center of a cupcake comes out clean, about 23 to 25 minutes. Reverse the baking sheets after 12 minutes, front to back, to ensure the cupcakes bake evenly. Cool the cupcakes for 5 minutes in the pan. Transfer the cupcakes in their paper liners to a wire cooling rack to cool completely.

### Good Advice

Use paper liners for easier clean-up.

### Doubling the Recipe

Use ¾ teaspoon salt and double the remaining ingredients for the cupcakes and frosting.

### To Freeze Plain Cupcakes

Wrap each cooled cupcake tightly with plastic wrap. Place the cupcakes in a single layer in a metal or plastic freezer container. Cover tightly and label with date and contents. Freeze up to 2 months.

### To Freeze Frosted Cupcakes

Freeze the cupcakes uncovered, for 30 minutes, until the frosting is firm. Wrap each cupcake in plastic wrap. Place the cupcakes in a single layer in a metal or plastic freezer container and cover tightly. Label with date and contents. Freeze up to 1 month.

### To Serve

Defrost the wrapped cupcakes for 5 hours or overnight in the refrigerator. Unwrap and let sit at room temperature for 1 hour before serving. Cover leftover cupcakes with plastic wrap and store up to 3 days in the refrigerator, but serve them at room temperature.

## Frost the cupcakes

3. Put the butter, cream cheese, and vanilla in the large bowl of an electric mixer and beat on medium-low speed for about 1 minute until the mixture is smooth and the butter and cream cheese are thoroughly combined. Decrease the speed to low and add the powdered sugar in 2 additions. Beat until the powdered sugar is incorporated and the frosting is smooth. Spread the cream cheese frosting over the top of each cupcake. If plain cupcakes have been frozen, they can be frosted while still frozen.

# Fresh Berry Shortcakes

**Serves 4**

One of the most luxurious summer desserts I know is a buttery shortcake covered with lots of juicy berries and generous dollops of whipped cream. If you have shortcakes in the freezer, this dessert can be prepared in a matter of minutes. For a summer party dessert, serve a platter of shortcakes with big bowls of berries and whipped cream and let your guests create their own shortcake extravaganza, or two, or three . . .

In Maine, we have a berry for each summer month: strawberries in late June, raspberries in July, and blackberries in August. Blueberries also arrive in August, but I prefer to use them in combination with one of the other juicier berries. Good shortcakes should have plenty of berry juice soaking into them.

**3 cups raspberries or blackberries, or a combination of berries, or 4 cups sliced strawberries**
**1 to 3 tablespoons sugar**
**1 cup cold heavy whipping cream**
**1 teaspoon vanilla extract**
**1 tablespoon powdered sugar**
**4 Shortcakes, baked and cooled or defrosted (page 41)**

1. One to 6 hours before serving, toss the berries with 1 tablespoon of sugar. Crush raspberries or blackberries slightly to release the juices. Taste the berries and decide if they need more sugar and add up to 2 more tablespoons. Usually, blackberries and raspberries will need more sugar and strawberries will not. Cover the berries and refrigerate for 1 to 6 hours, until you are ready to serve the shortcakes.

2. Chill a large mixing bowl and the beaters from an electric mixer in the freezer for 30 minutes. Put the cream, vanilla, and powdered sugar in the chilled bowl. Beat the cream with an electric mixer at medium speed for about 4 to 5 minutes, until soft peaks form. To check for soft peaks, lift up a spoonful of cream in the bowl and see if a point forms, then falls over. Also at that point, the beaters will form smooth curving lines as they move in the cream. Serve immediately or cover and refrigerate up to 2 hours.

### Good Advice

- Refrigerate the sugared berries at least one hour to draw juice from the berries and melt the sugar. Do not let the sugared berries sit overnight as they will soften too much.
- Strawberries have a milder flavor than other berries, so I use more of them for each shortcake.
- I whip cream with a standing electric mixer on medium rather than high speed. Whipping cream with a less powerful hand-held mixer takes high speed. Cream whipped this way holds its shape longer and can be whipped up to two hours in advance of serving. It is also easier to observe the whipping stages and to stop whipping at just the right point. One cup of whipping cream will make about 2½ cups of softly whipped cream.

### Doubling the Recipe

Multiply the amount of fruit and whipped cream to cover as many shortcakes as desired.

### To Serve

Either serve the shortcakes the day they are baked or warm defrosted shortcakes in a 225°F. oven for 10 minutes. Pull the shortcakes apart. They will split in half easily. Place the shortcakes cut side up on individual serving plates. Cover each shortcake with berries and their juice. Top with whipped cream. Dig in!

# Caramel-Cashew Bars

**Makes 24 bars, about 2 inches square**

I'll go on record here: Cashew nuts are one of my favorite foods, and I always look for good excuses to eat more of them. These bars are one of my best excuses.

Cashew Crust

**2 cups unbleached all-purpose flour**
**1 cup (packed) light brown sugar**
**4 ounces (1 stick) cold unsalted butter, cut into 8 pieces**
**1½ cups roasted unsalted cashew halves or pieces**

Caramel Layer

**¼ pound plus 3 tablespoons (1 stick plus 3 tablespoons) unsalted butter**
**½ cup (packed) light brown sugar**
**½ cup (about 3 ounces) chopped white chocolate, Callebaut preferred**

1. Position a rack in the center of the oven. Preheat the oven to 350°F. Butter a 13 × 9 × 2-inch pan.

## Prepare the crust

2. Put the flour, brown sugar, and butter in the large bowl of an electric mixer. Mix on low speed until pea-size crumbs form. Press the crust firmly into the prepared pan. Sprinkle the cashew nuts evenly over the crust.

## Prepare the caramel layer

3. Put the butter and brown sugar in a medium saucepan. Cook over low-medium heat until the butter and brown sugar melt, stirring constantly. Increase the heat to medium and bring to a boil for 1 minute, stirring constantly. Pour the hot mixture evenly over the cashew nuts in the baking pan.

4. Bake until the mixture bubbles, about 25 minutes. Remove from the oven and let sit for 5 minutes at room temperature. Sprinkle the chopped white chocolate evenly over the bars. Let sit for another 5 minutes; the chocolate will melt. With the back of a spoon, swirl the chocolate over the bars. Cool thoroughly until the topping is firm. Refrigerate the bars for 15 minutes to speed the cooling process. To cut 24 bars, cut 6 rows across and 4 rows the long way. The bars will be about 2 inches square.

### Good Advice

If the bars are refrigerated, cut the bars as soon as the white chocolate topping is firm. If the bars chill firm, they will be difficult to cut.

### Doubling the Recipe

Double the ingredients and bake the bars in two pans.

### To Freeze

Place the bottoms of 2 bars together and wrap them in plastic wrap. Put the wrapped bars in a metal or plastic freezer container and cover tightly. Label with date and contents. Freeze up to 3 months.

### To Serve

Remove as many bars from the freezer as needed and defrost the wrapped bars at room temperature for about 3 hours. Serve within 3 days.

# Caramel Butterscotch Squares

**Makes thirty-five 2 inch squares**

When you want a big batch of quick-to-prepare yet classy dessert bars, these are the ones. There isn't even a bowl to clean since the bars are mixed right in the saucepan used to melt the butter and brown sugar. Chopped walnuts add an attractive finish, while at the same time protecting the soft frosting and making the bars easier to store, transport, or mail.

Butterscotch Squares

**1½ cups unbleached all-purpose flour**
**2 teaspoons baking powder**
**¼ teaspoon salt**
**¼ pound (1 stick) unsalted butter**
**2 cups (packed) light brown sugar**
**2 large eggs**
**2 teaspoons vanilla extract**
**¾ cup coarsely chopped walnuts**

Caramel Frosting

**½ cup whipping cream**
**½ cup granulated sugar**
**¼ pound (1 stick) soft unsalted butter**
**1 cup powdered sugar**
**2 teaspoons vanilla extract**

**¾ cup finely chopped walnuts**

1. Position a rack in the middle of the oven. Preheat the oven to 325°F. Butter a jelly-roll pan, 15½ × 10½ × 1 inch.

## Make the squares

2. Sift the flour, baking powder, and salt together and set aside. Put the butter and brown sugar in a medium saucepan and stir together over medium heat until they melt and become smooth. Set aside to cool at room temperature for 10 minutes. Add the eggs and vanilla to the cooled butter mixture and stir vigorously with a wooden spoon until smooth. Add the flour mixture and mix just until the flour is incorporated. Stir in the coarsely chopped walnuts.

3. Pour the batter into the prepared pan. Use a thin metal spatula to spread the batter evenly in the pan. Bake just until a toothpick inserted in the center of the bars no longer has liquid clinging to it, about 13 to 14 minutes. After 6 minutes, reverse the pan, front to back, to ensure even baking. Watch the bars carefully as they bake. Cool the bars in the pan. They will firm as they cool.

### Good Advice

• Watch the bars carefully during baking. They are thin and the edges can quickly become too crisp.

• Before adding the caramel sauce to the frosting, check to see that it is soft and pourable but not hot to the touch. If the sauce is too hot, it can melt the butter in the frosting, if it is too cool, it can harden and form pieces in the frosting. The temperature should be about 85°F. on a food thermometer. The caramel sauce can be gently warmed and cooled repeatedly to obtain the right temperature.

### Doubling the Recipe

Use 1 tablespoon baking powder for the bars and double the ingredients. Bake the bars in two pans. Double the frosting ingredients.

### To Freeze

Wrap 2 frosted squares, placed side by side, in plastic wrap. Put them in a metal or plastic freezer container and cover tightly. Do not crowd or crush the squares. Label with date and contents. Freeze up to 3 months.

### To Serve

**Remove as many squares from the freezer as needed. Defrost the wrapped squares at room temperature. Store leftover squares, wrapped in plastic wrap, up to 3 days at room temperature.**

## Prepare the frosting

4. Heat the cream in a small saucepan and keep it hot, about 150°F. if measured with a food thermometer, without boiling it. Put the sugar in a heavy-bottomed medium saucepan and cook over low heat until the sugar begins to melt. Increase the heat to medium-high and cook until the sugar melts, caramelizes, and turns a dark golden color, about 4 minutes. Watch the sugar carefully and stir it with a wooden spoon occasionally to ensure that it cooks evenly. Remove the caramel from the heat. Slowly add the warm cream to the hot sugar. The mixture will bubble up, so be careful. Return the saucepan to medium heat and cook the mixture, stirring with the wooden spoon, until the caramel is completely dissolved and the sauce is smooth. Set the sauce aside to cool for about 20 minutes. When it is beaten into the frosting, the caramel should be soft and pourable and cool to the touch, about 85°F. if measured with a food thermometer. Put the butter in a large mixing bowl and mix with an electric mixer on low speed just to smooth it. Add the powdered sugar and beat the mixture until it is smooth, about 1 minute. Add the cooled caramel sauce and vanilla and beat until the frosting is smooth and creamy, about 30 seconds.

## Frost the squares

5. Use a thin metal spatula to spread the frosting evenly over the cooled squares in the baking pan. Sprinkle evenly with the finely chopped walnuts. Freeze the squares, uncovered, to firm the frosting, about 30 minutes. To cut 35 squares about 2 inches square, cut 7 rows across and 5 rows the long way.

## Variation

Rather than frosting the squares, serve them plain as butterscotch brownies.

# Pat's Toffee Bars

**Makes 36 bars**

My husband, Jeff, loves sweets, and he often cajoles friends and colleagues into bringing him cookies and candy. One night he arrived home with a tin of these toffee bars which he coaxed out of his friend Pat Stover. After tasting six or eight of them (I admit we lost all control), we knew why Pat was renowned for these crunchy butter toffee bars. Generous Pat shared the recipe, which turned out to be one of the easiest cookies I have ever baked. Saltine crackers provide the base for the bars, and Heath Bits 'O Brickle are combined with butter and brown sugar for the toffee layer. The saltines are absorbed by the toffee. In a million years no one would guess they are part of this recipe.

**24 saltine crackers**
**½ pound (2 sticks) unsalted butter**
**1 cup (packed) light brown sugar**
**1 cup Heath Bits 'O Brickle, one 6-ounce package**
**2 cups (about 12 ounces) white chocolate, chopped, Callebaut preferred**
**1 cup pecans, finely chopped**

1. Position a rack in the center of the oven. Preheat the oven to 375°F. Line a 13 × 9 × 2-inch pan with heavy foil, letting the foil extend over the ends of the pan.

2. Line the bottom of the pan with the saltine crackers. There will be 4 rows of 6 crackers each. Put the butter in a medium saucepan and melt it over medium heat. Add the brown sugar and, stirring constantly, boil the mixture for 2 minutes. Pour the hot mixture over the crackers. Sprinkle the Heath Bits 'O Brickle evenly over the butter mixture.

3. Bake 5 minutes. The mixture will be bubbling. Remove from the oven and immediately sprinkle the white chocolate pieces over the hot toffee. Let sit at room temperature for 5 minutes or until the white chocolate melts. Use the back of a spoon to spread the white chocolate evenly over the toffee. Sprinkle the pecans evenly over the white chocolate. Refrigerate just until the white chocolate and toffee are firm. Use the overhanging ends of aluminum foil to lift the toffee out of the pan. Remove the aluminum foil. Place the toffee on a cutting surface and use a large sharp knife to cut the bars. To cut 36 bars, cut 4 rows lengthwise and 9 rows across. The bars will measure about 2 inches by a scant 1½ inches.

### Good Advice

For easy cutting, chill the bars just until the white chocolate firms but before the toffee hardens completely. If the bars are cold and hard, they will break and crumble as they are cut; not a disaster, but the bars will have irregular shapes.

### Doubling the Recipe

Double the ingredients. Use two pans.

### To Freeze

Place the bottoms of 2 bars together and wrap them in plastic wrap. Put the wrapped bars in a metal or plastic freezer container and cover tightly. Label with date and contents. Freeze up to 3 months.

### To Serve

Remove as many bars from the freezer as needed and defrost the wrapped bars for about 3 hours at room temperature. Serve within 3 days.

## Good Advice

It is easy to cut through the toffee topping if you mark the brownies while the toffee is warm.

## Doubling the Recipe

Double the ingredients, but bake the brownies in two pans.

## To Freeze

Wrap individual brownies tightly in plastic wrap. Place in a plastic freezer container and cover tightly. Label with date and contents. Freeze up to 3 months.

## To Serve

Remove as many brownies as needed from the freezer and defrost the wrapped brownies at room temperature for about 3 hours. Store leftover brownies up to 3 days at room temperature.

# Toffee Fudge Brownies

**Makes 12 brownies**

These dark chocolate brownies have a crunchy toffee topping. They are excellent in their own right but are spectacular topped with ice cream and warm caramel sauce (page 124).

**8 ounces semisweet chocolate, cut into ¾-inch pieces**
**2 ounces unsweetened chocolate, cut into ¾-inch pieces**
**½ pound (2 sticks) unsalted butter, cut into ½-inch pieces**
**¾ cup unbleached all-purpose flour**
**1 teaspoon baking powder**
**¼ teaspoon salt**
**3 large eggs**
**1 cup sugar**
**2 teaspoons vanilla extract**
**1 cup (about 5½ ounces) coarsely crushed toffee crunch candy, such as Heath Bars**

1. Position a rack in the middle of the oven. Preheat the oven to 350°F. Butter a 13 × 9 × 2-inch baking pan.

2. Put the semisweet chocolate, unsweetened chocolate, and butter in a heatproof container and place it over, but not touching, a saucepan of barely simmering water. Stir the mixture over the hot water until the chocolates and butter are melted and smooth. Remove the container from over the water and cool 5 minutes.

3. Stir the flour, baking powder, and salt together in a small bowl and set aside. Put the eggs in the large bowl of an electric mixer and mix at medium speed for 10 seconds. Add the sugar and vanilla and beat for 1 minute until the mixture thickens and the color lightens slightly. Decrease the speed to low and mix in the melted chocolate mixture until it is combined thoroughly with the egg mixture. Add the flour mixture and mix just until the flour is incorporated.

4. Spread the batter evenly in the prepared pan. Bake 15 minutes. Sprinkle the crushed toffee evenly over the top and return the pan to the oven. Bake until a toothpick inserted in center of the brownies comes out with a few moist crumbs clinging to it, about 10 more minutes. Cool the brownies in the pan. Mark the top of the brownie with a sharp knife while the toffee is still warm and can be easily cut. Use a large sharp knife to cut the cooled brownies into 12 pieces.

### Good Advice

Let the fudge bars chill firm before cutting them, but serve them at room temperature for the best chocolate flavor.

### Doubling the Recipe

Double the ingredients for either recipe and use two pans. A double recipe of the larger pan of brownies needs to be mixed in a five-quart bowl.

### To Freeze

Wrap individual pieces in plastic wrap. Place in a metal or plastic freezer container and cover tightly. To freeze the Fudge Bars in one piece, wrap the entire bar tightly in plastic wrap, then heavy aluminum foil. Label with date and contents. Freeze up to 3 months.

### To Serve

Remove only as many bars from the freezer as you need. Defrost the wrapped bars at room temperature or in the refrigerator for 3 to 5 hours. Store the bars in the refrigerator up to 5 days. Serve at room temperature.

# Fudge Bars

**Makes 8 to 16 bars**

These are the ultimate brownie, my kind of brownie, dark and moist through and through. I can't think of a time in the past few years when these bars haven't been in my freezer, ready to top with ice cream and fudge sauce, form into Chocolate Thunder cake, crumble into an ice cream pie, or mail to a lucky person. These easy bars will make you the toast of Brownie Town.

For an 8 × 8 × 2-inch pan, 8 to 9 bars

**1⅓ cups semisweet chocolate chips or chopped semisweet chocolate**
**½ ounce unsweetened chocolate, chopped**
**¼ pound (1 stick) unsalted butter, cut into 8 pieces**
**1 teaspoon instant decaffeinated coffee, dissolved in 1 tablespoon hot water**
**2 large eggs**
**¾ cup sugar**
**⅛ teaspoon salt**
**1 teaspoon vanilla extract**
**¼ cup unbleached all-purpose flour**

For a 13 × 9 × 2-inch pan, 12 to 16 bars

**2½ cups (15 ounces) semisweet chocolate chips or chopped semisweet chocolate**
**1 ounce unsweetened chocolate, chopped**
**½ pound (2 sticks) unsalted butter, cut into 16 pieces**
**2 teaspoons instant decaffeinated coffee, dissolved in 2 tablespoons hot water**
**4 large eggs**
**1½ cups sugar**
**¼ teaspoon salt**
**2 teaspoons vanilla extract**
**½ cup unbleached all-purpose flour**

1. Position a rack in the middle of the oven. Preheat the oven to 375°F. Line the pan of your choice with heavy aluminum foil, letting the foil extend over the ends of the pan. Butter the aluminum foil.

2. Put the semisweet chocolate, unsweetened chocolate, butter, and dissolved coffee in a heatproof container and place it over, but not touching, a saucepan of barely simmering water. Stir the mixture over the hot water until the chocolates and butter are melted and smooth. Remove from over the water and cool 5 minutes.

3. Meanwhile, put the eggs in the large bowl of an electric mixer and mix the eggs at medium speed for 10 seconds. Add the sugar, salt, and vanilla and beat for 2 minutes, until the egg mixture thickens and is a light yellow color. Decrease the speed to low and mix in the melted chocolate mixture. Add the flour and mix just until no white streaks of flour remain.

4. Spread the batter evenly in the prepared pan. Bake 28 minutes. The brownies will look soft. Cool 1 hour at room temperature, then cover and refrigerate at least 5 hours or overnight. Use the overhanging ends of aluminum foil to lift the brownies out of the pan. Remove the aluminum foil. If using them for Chocolate Thunder cake, wrap and freeze the larger pan of brownies without cutting them. If freezing them in individual pieces, cut the smaller pan of brownies into 8 or 9 squares and the larger pan into 12 to 16 pieces.

## White Chocolate Chip Brownies

**Makes 12 to 16 brownies**

You can never get too much of a good thing, or brownies, but sometimes I find white chocolate brownies have little flavor. I took no chances with these and used one pound of white chocolate to give them a pure white chocolate taste.

**½ pound (2 sticks) unsalted butter**
**16 ounces white chocolate, chopped, Callebaut preferred**
**¼ cup warm water**
**4 large eggs**
**1 cup sugar**
**¾ teaspoon salt**
**1 teaspoon vanilla extract**
**1 cup unbleached all-purpose flour**
**1½ cups (9 ounces) miniature semisweet chocolate chips**

1. Position an oven rack in the middle of the oven. Preheat the oven to 375°F. Line a 15 × 10 × 2-inch baking pan with a piece of heavy aluminum foil long enough to overhang the ends of the pan. Butter the foil.

2. Put the butter, white chocolate, and water in a heatproof container and place it over, but not touching, a saucepan of barely simmering water. Stir the mixture until the chocolate and butter melt and the mixture is smooth. Remove the mixture from over the hot water and set aside.

3. Put the eggs in a large bowl and beat with an electric mixer just to blend. Add the sugar, salt, and vanilla. Beat at medium speed until thick and fluffy, about 2 minutes. Mix in the melted white chocolate mixture. Add the flour and stir just to incorporate it into the batter. Mix in the chocolate chips.

4. Pour the batter into the foil-lined pan. Bake for 30 minutes. Cool the brownies in the pan. Cover the pan and chill the brownies until they are firm, about 6 hours or overnight. Use the overhanging ends of aluminum foil to lift the brownies out of the pan. Remove the aluminum foil. If using them for White Lightning cake (page 128), wrap and freeze the brownies without cutting them. If freezing in individual pieces, cut into 12 to 16 pieces.

### Good Advice

- The brownies will still be soft when removed from the oven, chilling firms them.

### Doubling the Recipe

Double all ingredients. Use two pans.

### To Freeze

Wrap individual pieces in plastic wrap. Place in a metal or plastic freezer container and cover tightly. To freeze the brownie in one piece, wrap the brownie tightly in plastic wrap, then heavy aluminum foil. Label with date and contents. Freeze up to 3 months.

### To Serve

Remove only as many brownies from the freezer as you need. Defrost the wrapped brownies at room temperature or in the refrigerator for 3 to 5 hours. Store the brownies in the refrigerator up to 3 days. Serve at room temperature.

## Good Advice

The brownies should still feel soft when removed from the oven.

## Doubling the Recipe

Use 1½ teaspoons baking powder and 1 teaspoon salt and double the remaining ingredients. Bake in two pans.

## To Freeze

Wrap each brownie tightly in plastic wrap. Place in a metal or plastic freezer container and cover tightly. Label with date and contents. Freeze up to 3 months.

## To Serve

Defrost the wrapped bars at room temperature for about 3 hours. Store leftover brownies, wrapped tightly in plastic wrap, up to 3 days at room temperature.

# Espresso Brownies

**Makes 12 brownies**

A twist on the classic brownie, these not-too-sweet, golden-colored brownies get their flavor from coffee.

**1½ cups unbleached all-purpose flour**
**1 teaspoon baking powder**
**¾ teaspoon salt**
**6 ounces (1½ sticks) soft unsalted butter**
**¾ cup granulated sugar**
**1 cup (packed) light brown sugar**
**2 large eggs**
**2 tablespoons instant espresso granules, decaffeinated preferred, or instant decaffeinated coffee, dissolved in 2 tablespoons hot water**
**2 teaspoons vanilla extract**
**1 cup (6 ounces) semisweet chocolate chips**

1. Position a rack in the middle of the oven. Preheat the oven to 325°F. Butter a 13 × 9 × 2-inch baking pan.

2. Put the flour, baking powder, and salt in a small bowl and stir them together.

3. Put the butter in the large bowl of an electric mixer and mix on medium speed for 15 seconds. Add the granulated sugar and brown sugar and beat until the butter and sugars are creamed thoroughly, about 1 minute. Decrease the speed to low and mix in the eggs, dissolved espresso, and vanilla, mixing just until the eggs are incorporated. The mixture will look curdled. Stop the mixer and scrape the sides of the bowl once during this mixing. Slowly add the flour mixture and mix just until the flour is incorporated and the mixture is smooth.
Mix in the chocolate chips.

4. Spread the batter evenly in the prepared pan. Bake until a toothpick inserted in the center no longer has liquid clinging to it, but the brownies still feel soft, 28 to 30 minutes. Leave the brownies in the pan to cool thoroughly. Cut the brownies into 12 pieces.

# Chocolate Chip Desserts

Whenever I buy a new cookbook, I immediately turn to the index to find any chocolate chip desserts. Show me a cake, cookie, or pie with nuggets of chocolate chips, and I'm sold—so you can see why I give chocolate chip desserts their own chapter.

I prefer Nestlé or Guittard brands, because they taste more like chocolate and less like sugar to me. I contacted the major chocolate chip companies in the United States and asked them for the percentage of chocolate in their chips. None of the companies would give out this information, so I conducted my own survey by tasting all the brands in my supermarket. Several hundred chocolate chips later, I confirmed that Nestlé and Guittard brands, the ones I had been using for years, should remain my favorites. When I bake with miniature chocolate chips, I use these same brands.

Chocolate chip cookies fall into two categories—chewy or crisp. Each type has its champions, and here there are Big Chocolate Chip Cookies and Little Crisp Chocolate Chip Cookies for both persuasions. The small chocolate chip cookies also work for bite-size ice cream sandwiches.

Chocolate chips usually signal a homestyle dessert, but the Toasted Hazelnut–Chocolate Chip Meringue Cake, in which hazelnut and chocolate chip meringues are filled with chocolate buttercream, is as sophisticated a dessert as you'll find anywhere.

My Mom's Extraordinary Chocolate Chip Cake has been our family's traditional snack cake for three generations, including all aunts, uncles, and cousins. I once told a friend that a cookbook was worth its price to me if I found three great recipes in it. Cookbooks are better now, and prices are certainly higher than when I made that statement. Today a cookbook must give a lot more than three great recipes to be worth its price. But just supposing I still believed in that premise, My Mom's Extraordinary Chocolate Chip Cake would be worth the price of this book.

For many years, I had an idea in the back of my mind to bake a coffee-flavored coffee cake that had chocolate chips everywhere, even in the crumb topping. I decided to develop one for this book, and the Coffee Chocolate Chip Coffee Cake is it.

Several recipes in other chapters contain chocolate chips, but this chapter highlights them. Since many of these desserts are established family favorites, I guess I'm not alone in my chocolate chip cravings.

# Big Chocolate Chip Cookies

**Makes about fifteen 3-inch cookies**

Under normal circumstances, I display some self-control around desserts. I eat one piece of cake, one dish of ice cream, or one cookie. Except when I bake chocolate chip cookies. Well, no one is perfect, and I do have a passion for big, thick chocolate chip cookies that are soft inside and crisp outside—just like these.

**1¼ cups unbleached all-purpose flour**
**1 teaspoon baking soda**
**½ teaspoon salt**
**¼ pound (1 stick) unsalted butter, softened slightly for about 30 minutes**
**½ cup (packed) light brown sugar**
**6 tablespoons granulated sugar**
**1 large cold egg**
**1 teaspoon vanilla extract**
**2 cups (12 ounces) semisweet chocolate chips**

1. Position 2 oven racks in the middle and upper third of the oven. Preheat the oven to 350°F. Line 2 baking sheets with heavy aluminum foil.

2. Sift the flour, baking soda, and salt together and set aside. Put the butter, brown sugar, and granulated sugar in the large bowl of an electric mixer and beat on medium speed for about 1 minute, until the mixture is smooth. Add the egg and vanilla and mix on low speed for about 15 seconds, until they are blended thoroughly. Stop the mixer and scrape the bowl during this mixing. Decrease the speed to low and add the flour mixture, mixing just until the flour is incorporated. Mix in the chocolate chips.

3. Using 2 tablespoons of dough for each cookie, roll the dough between the palms of your hands into a ball about 1¾ inches in diameter. Place the cookie balls about 2½ inches apart on the prepared baking sheets. Bake the cookies 13 to 15 minutes, until the centers are golden and the edges are light brown. Reverse the baking sheets after 7 minutes, front to back and top to bottom, to ensure even browning. Watch the cookies carefully as they near the end of their baking time. Remove the cookies from the oven as soon as the center is golden and the edges are light brown. Cool the cookies thoroughly on the cookie sheet. The top of the cookies will look wrinkled and slightly crackled. Wrinkled tops indicate an excellent chocolate chip cookie.

## Variation

If you like nuts in chocolate chip cookies, stir ¾ cup chopped pecans or walnuts into the dough along with the chocolate chips.

## Good Advice

- The butter should be softened slightly so that it is firm but not hard, and the egg should be cold. Cool butter and a cold egg make a fairly stiff dough, which in turn makes nice ½-inch-thick cookies.
- After overbaking more chocolate chip cookies than I care to admit, I found that lining the baking sheet with heavy aluminum foil prevents blackened cookie bottoms. As the cookies reach the end of their baking time, check often; opening the oven to have a look will not harm them.

## Doubling the Recipe

Use 1½ teaspoons baking soda and ¾ teaspoon salt and double the remaining ingredients.

## To Freeze

Place the bottoms of 2 cookies together and wrap them in plastic wrap. Put the wrapped cookies in a metal or plastic freezer container and cover tightly. Label with date and contents. Freeze up to 3 months.

## To Serve

Remove as many cookies from the freezer as needed and defrost the wrapped cookies at room temperature. Serve within 3 days. For cookies with soft chocolate chips, spread the defrosted cookies in a single layer on a baking sheet and warm them in a preheated 200°F. oven for 5 minutes.

# Little Crisp Chocolate Chip Cookies

**Makes about ninety 1½-inch cookies**

These mini cookies are rich with miniature chocolate chips and chopped walnuts. Margarine rather than butter is used for the shortening for a crisper cookie.

**1 cup unbleached all-purpose flour**
**¾ teaspoon baking soda**
**⅛ teaspoon salt**
**⅛ teaspoon cinnamon**
**6 tablespoons cold margarine**
**¼ cup granulated sugar**
**½ cup (packed) light brown sugar**
**1 cold large egg**
**1 teaspoon vanilla extract**
**¾ cup (4½ ounces) miniature chocolate chips**
**½ cup walnuts, coarsely chopped**

1. Position 2 oven racks in the middle and upper third of the oven. Preheat the oven to 350°F. Line 3 baking sheets with heavy aluminum foil.

2. Sift the flour, baking soda, salt, and cinnamon together and set aside. Put the margarine, granulated sugar, and brown sugar in the large bowl of an electric mixer. Beat on medium speed for about 15 seconds, until the mixture is smooth. Add the egg and vanilla extract and mix on low speed for about 15 seconds, until blended thoroughly. Stop the mixer and scrape the bowl during this beating. Add the flour mixture and mix just until the flour is incorporated. Mix in the chocolate chips and walnuts.

3. Pinch off 1 level teaspoon of dough for each cookie. Measure the dough for the first cookie and note the amount. Place the cookies 1½ inches apart on the prepared baking sheets. Bake 2 sheets of cookies 8 to 9 minutes until the cookies are an even light brown. Repeat with the third baking sheet. Cool the cookies thoroughly on the baking sheet.

### Good Advice

These cookies are so small that I just line the freezing container with plastic wrap and fill it with cookies. The plastic wrap clings to the cookies and eliminates the air spaces.

### Doubling the Recipe

Double the ingredients.

### To Freeze

Line a metal or plastic freezer container with plastic wrap. A 2-quart container will hold all of the cookies. Fill the container with the cooled cookies, press plastic wrap onto the cookies, and cover tightly. Label with date and contents. Freeze up to 3 months.

### To Serve

Remove as many cookies from the freezer as needed, cover the cookies with plastic wrap, and defrost at room temperature. Serve within 3 days.

# Little Chocolate Chip Cookie Ice Cream Sandwiches

**Makes 18 ice cream sandwiches**

A little dessert that is always a big hit, bite-size chocolate chip cookie ice cream sandwiches bring out the kid in everyone.

**3 ounces (about ½ cup) chopped semisweet chocolate or semisweet chocolate chips**
**2 teaspoons vegetable oil**
**36 Little Crisp Chocolate Chip Cookies, frozen (page 82)**
**1 pint good-quality (not premium) vanilla ice cream**

1. Put the chocolate and vegetable oil in a heatproof container and place it over, but not touching, a saucepan of barely simmering water. Stir the mixture over the hot water until the chocolate is melted and the mixture is smooth. Remove the heatproof container from over the water.

2. Put a baking sheet in the freezer.

3. Spread ½ teaspoon of chocolate coating on the bottom of each cookie. If the coating is not firm, chill the chocolate-coated cookies for 5 minutes. Spread 1 tablespoon ice cream on the bottom of a cookie. Place another cookie, chocolate-coated side facing the ice cream, on the ice cream. Gently press the cookies together just to flatten the ice cream a little. As soon as 3 ice cream sandwiches are prepared, place them on the baking sheet in the freezer. Continue filling and freezing the remaining cookies. You will not use all the ice cream. Let the ice cream sandwiches freeze firm in the freezer, about 1 hour.

## Variations

- Fill the ice cream sandwiches with different flavor and colors of ice cream. Vanilla, chocolate, peppermint, coffee, and strawberry are good choices.
- Serve a bowl of warm chocolate coating for dipping the ice cream sandwiches.

### Good Advice

- The ice cream should be softened just enough to be spreadable but still firm. It shouldn't drip on the cookies. The softening time will depend on how cold your freezer is. One pint of ice cream will fill about thirty ice cream sandwiches.
- These ice cream sandwiches are a great dessert for a summer barbecue. Plan on three ice cream sandwiches per person, but have some more in the freezer—just in case.

### Doubling the Recipe

Double the ingredients or prepare as many ice cream sandwiches as you need.

### To Freeze

Wrap each ice cream sandwich in plastic wrap. Place in a metal or plastic freezer container and cover tightly. Label with date and contents. The cookies will remain crisp for about 10 days. After 10 days the cookies will soften slightly, but the ice cream sandwiches will still taste fine for up to 2 weeks.

### To Serve

Unwrap the ice cream sandwiches, pile them in a bowl or stack them on a platter, and serve immediately.

# Jeff's Chocolate Chip Crumb Cookie Cake

Serves 8 to 10

I can never decide whether to call this a cookie or a cake. On the day the cake is baked, the chocolate chips stay soft, and the cake can be eaten with a fork. The day after the cake is baked or after it's been frozen, the chocolate chips become firm, so it's best to pick the cake up and eat it like a cookie. As for taste, it's delicious either way.

**3 cups unbleached all-purpose flour**
**1 teaspoon baking powder**
**7 ounces (1¾ sticks) cold margarine, cut into 7 pieces**
**1 cup sugar**
**1 large egg**
**1 teaspoon grated lemon zest**
**1 teaspoon vanilla extract**
**1⅓ cups (6 ounces) semisweet chocolate chips**
**Powdered sugar, for dusting**

1. Position a rack in the center of the oven. Preheat the oven to 375°F. Butter a 9-inch springform pan at least 2¾ inches high.

2. Sift the flour and baking powder together and set aside. Put the margarine and sugar in the large bowl of an electric mixer and beat on low speed until the mixture is creamed thoroughly, about 1 minute. Mix in the egg, lemon zest, and vanilla. Add the flour mixture and beat just until the mixture forms crumbs and all of the flour is incorporated.

3. Press half of the crumbs into the bottom and ½ inch up the sides of the pan. Cover the crumbs evenly with the chocolate chips. Sprinkle the remaining crumbs evenly over the chocolate chips. Bake 35 to 40 minutes, until the top of the cake is light brown. Cool the cake in the pan on a wire cooling rack for about 2 hours. Use a small sharp knife to loosen the cake from the sides of the pan. Remove the sides of the springform pan. Sift powdered sugar over the cooled cake.

### Good Advice

The chocolate chip filling can be softened after freezing by warming the cake in a preheated 250°F. oven for ten minutes.

### Doubling the Recipe

Use two pans and double the ingredients

### To Freeze

Use a wide metal spatula to slide the cake onto a piece of plastic wrap. Wrap tightly with plastic wrap, then heavy aluminum foil. Label with date and contents. Freeze up to 3 months.

### To Serve

Remove the cake from the freezer and defrost the wrapped cake at room temperature, at least 5 hours or overnight. To warm the defrosted cake and soften the chocolate chip filling, preheat the oven to 250°F. Unwrap the cake and place it on a baking sheet. Bake, uncovered, 10 to 12 minutes. Serve the cake at room temperature. Store leftover cake, wrapped in plastic wrap, up to 3 days at room temperature.

# My Mom's Extraordinary Chocolate Chip Cake

**Makes 20 pieces, about 2 × 1¾ inches**

You are going to love this cake. Many families have a special cake recipe they treasure, and this is ours. It takes about ten minutes to prepare, it keeps well, freezes beautifully, mails easily, and tastes wonderful. I have carried this cake to potluck suppers, shipped it to my children at college, offered it for Christmas presents, flown it to Japan, and baked it for my own birthday cake. This cake has never let me down. It's a gift from my family to yours.

**2 cups unbleached all-purpose flour**
**2 cups (packed) light brown sugar**
**½ teaspoon ground cinnamon**
**¼ pound (1 stick) cold unsalted butter, cut into 6 pieces**
**1 large egg**
**1 teaspoon baking soda**
**1 cup sour cream**
**2 tablespoons milk (optional)**
**1½ cups (9 ounces) semisweet chocolate chips**

1. Position the oven rack in the middle of the oven and preheat to 325°F. Butter a 11 × 7 × 1¾-inch baking pan or ovenproof glass baking dish.

2. Put the flour, brown sugar, and cinnamon in the large bowl of an electric mixer and mix on low speed for 15 seconds. Add the butter and mix until the butter pieces are the size of peas, about 1 minute. You will still see loose flour. Mix in the egg. The mixture will still look dry. Rub any lumps out of the baking soda and gently mix the baking soda into the sour cream. Stir the sour cream mixture and the milk, if used (see Good Advice), into the batter. Stir just until the batter is evenly moistened. Stir in the chocolate chips. The batter will be thick.

3. Spread the batter in the prepared baking pan. Bake about 40 minutes. To test for doneness, gently press your fingers on the top of the cake. The middle should feel slightly soft and the edges firm. Insert a toothpick in the center of the cake. When the toothpick comes out with a few crumbs clinging to it, the cake is done. Cool the cake thoroughly in the baking pan on a wire cooling rack. The center of the cake will sink slightly.

## Variation

The cake can be dusted with powdered sugar before serving and/or served with vanilla ice cream.

## Good Advice

- Some brands of sour cream are drier and thicker than others. If the sour cream is thick and has no liquid on top of it when opened, add the milk. If in doubt, add the milk.
- On occasion, I have substituted margarine for the butter, and the results were fine.
- I use an electric mixer to prepare the batter, but the cake can also be mixed by hand with a pastry blender and mixing spoon.

## Doubling the Recipe

Double the ingredients. Bake in two pans.

## To Freeze

Either cut the cake into 2 or 3 large pieces or 20 individual pieces. Remove from the baking pan. Wrap large cake pieces in plastic wrap then heavy aluminum foil. Label with date and contents and freeze. After they are frozen, the large cake pieces can be stacked in the freezer. Wrap small pieces of cake in plastic wrap, place in a metal or plastic freezer container, and cover tightly. Label with date and contents. Freeze up to 3 months.

## To Serve

Remove as much cake from the freezer as needed and defrost the wrapped cake at room temperature. Serve within 3 days.

# Toasted Hazelnut–Chocolate Chip Meringue Cake

Serves 8 to 9

This idea behind this cake is to alternate layers of crisp and creamy chocolate. I flavor chocolate meringues with chocolate chips and toasted hazelnuts and fill them with a smooth chocolate buttercream. The buttercream is prepared with Italian meringue; it's a light buttercream that suits the light, crisp meringues. A mixture of ground chocolate and hazelnuts makes a quick, attractive topping for the cake. This was a good idea that turned out great.

**Toasted Hazelnut Meringues**

1 tablespoon cornstarch
2 tablespoons unsweetened Dutch Process cocoa powder
¾ cup plus 2 tablespoons toasted hazelnuts (page 6)
2 tablespoons powdered sugar
5 large egg whites
½ teaspoon cream of tartar
1 cup granulated sugar
1 teaspoon vanilla extract
1 cup (6 ounces) miniature semisweet chocolate chips

**Chocolate Rum Buttercream**

5 ounces semisweet chocolate, cut into ¾- to 1-inch pieces
1 ounce unsweetened chocolate
½ cup plus 1 tablespoon granulated sugar
3 tablespoons hot water
2 teaspoons light corn syrup
5 large egg whites
¼ teaspoon cream of tartar
5 ounces (1¼ sticks) unsalted butter, softened to about the same temperature as the cooled meringue (72°F. to 78°F.)
1 teaspoon vanilla extract
1 tablespoon dark rum

4 teaspoons semisweet chocolate, finely grated on the smallest holes of a grater
Powdered sugar, for dusting
1 cup Cold Chocolate Sauce, for serving (page 46)

## Prepare the meringues

1. Position 2 oven racks in the middle and upper third of the oven. Preheat the oven to 275°F. Line 2 large baking sheets with aluminum foil. Butter the aluminum foil and lightly coat it with powdered sugar. Mark two 8-inch circles on 1 baking sheet and one 8-inch circle on the other baking sheet with a dull knife.

### Good Advice

- When beating sugar into the egg whites for the meringues, add it slowly. If the meringues need trimming, it's easier to cut them while they are still warm and soft. If a meringue breaks, simply piece it together as you layer the cake and buttercream. The buttercream will hold it together.
- Preparing these meringues with granulated sugar, and no powdered sugar, makes them especially crisp.
- The base for this buttercream is an Italian meringue, which is prepared by beating a hot sugar syrup into egg whites that have been whipped to soft peaks. The resulting buttercream is a stable mixture with a light, silky texture, which is easy to work with and worth some effort. Italian meringue requires careful attention while the sugar syrup boils and when the hot syrup is beaten into the egg whites. Cook the sugar syrup carefully so that the sugar does not crystallize; adding some corn syrup also inhibits crystallization. Any bowls, pots, and utensils used for the meringue should be clean and grease-free.
- Beat the egg whites just to soft peaks. If the syrup reaches 240°F. before the egg whites are ready, remove the syrup from the heat for a few seconds

and finish beating the egg whites.

• When butter is beaten into the Italian meringue, the butter must be very soft and feel the same temperature as the meringue. If checked with an instant-read food thermometer, both the beaten meringue and the softened butter should be about 72°F. to 78°F. If the butter is too cold, it will form small lumps in the buttercream. If this should happen, whisk the bowl of buttercream over a pan of hot water until the butter lumps disappear and the buttercream becomes smooth, then continue with the recipe.

### Doubling the Recipe

Double the ingredients for the meringue, buttercream, and topping. Use a five-quart bowl to mix the baked meringue and buttercream mixtures. Use three baking sheets to bake the meringues. Double the amount of Cold Chocolate Sauce.

### To Freeze the Meringues

Stack the meringues on a cardboard cake circle or plate, placing plastic wrap between each layer. Carefully wrap the stack of meringues with plastic wrap, then heavy aluminum foil. Meringues may be frozen for up to 1 month. Do not defrost the meringues before using them.

2. Sift the cornstarch and cocoa together and set aside. Put the hazelnuts and powdered sugar in a food processor fitted with a metal blade and process the nuts until they are finely ground. Remove 2 tablespoons of the ground nuts and set them aside for the cake topping. Put the egg whites and cream of tartar in the large bowl of an electric mixer and beat on low speed until the egg whites are frothy. Increase the speed to medium-high and beat until soft peaks form. Reduce the speed to medium and slowly beat in the granulated sugar, 1 tablespoon every 30 seconds. Mix in the vanilla. Remove the bowl from the mixer and use a rubber spatula to fold the cocoa mixture into the egg whites. Fold in the rest of the ground hazelnuts, then the chocolate chips.

3. With a thin metal spatula spread the meringue mixture over the 3 marked circles. Smooth the edges with the metal spatula. Or, fit a clean greasefree pastry bag with a ½-inch plain tip, fill the pastry bag with the meringue, and pipe it evenly onto the 3 marked circles. If a chocolate chip obstructs the pastry tip, poke it with a toothpick to free it. The meringues will be about ½ inch thick. Bake 70 to 75 minutes until the meringues are crisp and dry. Turn off the oven and leave the meringues in the oven 1 hour. Remove from the oven. With a small sharp knife, trim any rough edges from the meringues. Cool the meringues on the baking sheets.

## Prepare the buttercream

4. Preheat the oven to 175°F. Put the semisweet chocolate and unsweetened chocolate in a small baking pan. Melt the chocolate in the oven, about 8 to 10 minutes. Remove the chocolate from the oven as soon as it is melted and stir it smooth. Put ½ cup of the sugar, the water, and corn syrup in a small saucepan. Cover the saucepan and cook over low heat until all of the sugar is dissolved, stirring occasionally to help it dissolve. Do not let the syrup boil until the sugar dissolves. Increase the heat to high and boil, without stirring, until the syrup reaches 240°F. measured on a candy thermometer. Brush the sides of the pan with a pastry brush dipped in hot water to dissolve any sugar crystals that form on the side of the pan.

5. When the syrup begins to boil, start beating the egg whites. Put the egg whites and cream of tartar in the large bowl of an electric mixer and beat on low speed for 30 seconds to dissolve the cream of tartar. Raise the speed to medium-high and beat the egg whites to soft peaks. Beat in the remaining 1 tablespoon of sugar. As soon as the syrup reaches 240°F., and with the mixer on low speed, slowly pour the hot syrup in a thin stream onto the softly beaten egg whites. Try to pour the syrup in the space between the beaters and the sides of the bowl to prevent as much sugar syrup as possible from splashing onto the sides of the bowl and the beater. Beat the meringue on medium speed about 5 minutes; the outside of the bowl will be lukewarm and the meringue will be stiff and have a temperature of about 72°F t.o 78°F., if measured with a food thermometer. Beat in the softened butter, 2 tablespoons at a time. The meringue will deflate slightly. Stop the

*continued*

mixer and scrape the bowl once, but do not scrape in any sugar syrup that may have splashed onto the side of the bowl and hardened. On low speed, gradually beat in the slightly cooled melted chocolate, the vanilla, and rum. If the buttercream is too soft to spread easily, refrigerate it 15 minutes. The buttercream can be covered and refrigerated up to 1 week. Soften chilled buttercream at room temperature until it is spreadable and whisk it for 30 seconds to smooth it.

## Assemble the cake

6. Spread 1 tablespoon of buttercream in the center of a plate or cardboard cake circle to prevent the cake from sliding around on the plate. Place a meringue layer on the plate. Spread 1 cup of buttercream evenly over the meringue. Top with another meringue layer and repeat with 1 cup of buttercream. Top the cake with the remaining meringue layer. Spread a thin layer of buttercream, about ¼ cup, over the top of the cake and spread the remaining buttercream evenly over the sides of the cake. Mix the grated chocolate and reserved 2 tablespoons ground hazelnuts from Step 2 together and sprinkle evenly over the top of the cake. Sift powdered sugar over the top of the cake.

### To Freeze

Chill the cake in the freezer until the buttercream is firm, about 30 minutes. Wrap with plastic wrap. Gently press heavy aluminum foil around the cake. Label with date and contents. Freeze up to 1 month.

### To Serve

Defrost the wrapped cake at least 5 hours or overnight in the refrigerator. Unwrap the cake and let it sit at room temperature 15 minutes before serving. Slice the cake with a large sharp knife. Pour about 2 tablespoons of Cold Chocolate Sauce on 1 side of each slice of meringue cake. Leftover meringue cake can be covered with plastic wrap and stored in the refrigerator; it will remain crisp up to 5 days.

# Coffee Chocolate Chip Coffee Cake

**Makes 9 servings**

Don't worry, you're not seeing double. The word *coffee* appears twice in the title, and chocolate chips show up everywhere in the cake.

**1¾ cups plus 2 tablespoons unbleached all-purpose flour**
**¾ cup (packed) light brown sugar**
**½ cup plus 1 tablespoon granulated sugar**
**1½ teaspoons ground cinnamon**
**½ cup plus 1 tablespoon canola or corn oil**
**4 teaspoons instant decaffeinated coffee granules, dissolved in 4 teaspoons hot water**
**1½ cups (9 ounces) miniature semisweet chocolate chips**
**1 cup sour cream**
**1 large egg**
**1 teaspoon baking powder**
**¾ teaspoon baking soda**
**Whipped cream or coffee ice cream, for serving with the cake (optional)**

1. Position an oven rack in the middle of the oven. Preheat the oven to 300°F. Oil an 8 × 8 × 2-inch baking pan.

2. Put the flour, brown sugar, granulated sugar, and cinnamon in a large mixing bowl. Stir the ingredients together. There will be small lumps of brown sugar in the mixture. Add the oil and dissolved coffee and stir until the flour is evenly moistened. The mixture will be crumbly. Put ½ cup of the mixture in a small bowl and mix in ½ cup of the chocolate chips. Set aside. Put the sour cream and egg in a small bowl and stir them together until the egg is incorporated. Gently stir in the baking powder and baking soda. Add the sour cream mixture to the flour mixture and stir until the batter is evenly moistened. Stir in the remaining 1 cup of chocolate chips.

3. Spread the batter evenly in the prepared pan. Sprinkle the reserved crumb mixture evenly over the cake. Bake about 55 minutes, until a toothpick inserted into the center of the cake comes out clean. If the toothpick penetrates chocolate chips, test another spot in the cake. Let the cake cool in the pan on a wire cooling rack until the chocolate chips are firm, about 5 hours. To speed the cooling of the chocolate chips in the topping, refrigerate the cake for 30 minutes.

## Good Advice

- The cake requires only mixing, rather than beating, and can easily be mixed by hand.
- Let the cake cool completely, or it will be hard to handle because the chocolate chip topping will still be soft. This is not a serious problem, just a little messy. When the cake sits overnight the coffee flavor intensifies.
- The cake is baked in an eight-inch square pan, but a nine-inch round layer pan may be substituted. Either pan must have two-inch high sides.

## Doubling the Recipe

Use 1½ teaspoons baking powder, double the ingredients, and bake the cake in two pans.

## To Freeze

Cut the cooled cake into 9 pieces and wrap each piece in plastic wrap. Put the cake pieces in a metal or plastic freezer container and cover tightly. Label with date and contents. Freeze up to 3 months.

## To Serve

Remove as many pieces of cake as you need from the freezer and defrost the wrapped cake at room temperature. Leftover cake can be covered with plastic wrap and stored at room temperature up to 3 days. Serve with whipped cream or coffee ice cream, if desired.

# Double Chocolate Chip Pie

**Serves 8**

I tried many combinations of ingredients before I came up with this pie, which meets all my requirements for a great chocolate chip pie. The pie had to be easy and fast to prepare, be moist throughout, have plenty of chocolate chips in every bite, and store well. With a pie crust from your freezer, this pie can be ready to bake in about five minutes, and it keeps so well it can even be mailed successfully. Double Chocolate Chip Pie was the pie I baked and mailed to our son, Peter, for his twenty-first birthday—need I say more?

**¼ pound (1 stick) soft unsalted butter**
**1½ cups (packed) light brown sugar**
**3 large eggs**
**½ cup half-and-half**
**1 teaspoon vanilla extract**
**2 cups (12 ounces) semisweet chocolate chips**
**1 10-inch Easy as Pie Crust, unbaked and frozen in pie pan (page 32)**
**Whipped cream or ice cream, for serving with pie (optional)**

1. Position a rack in the middle of the oven. Preheat the oven to 400°F.

2. Put the butter in the large bowl of an electric mixer. Mix on low speed 15 seconds. Add the brown sugar and beat on medium speed 1 minute, until the mixture is smooth. Beat in the eggs, one at a time. Stop the mixer and scrape the sides of bowl after adding each egg. Add the half-and-half and vanilla and mix on low speed just to combine the ingredients. The mixture will look curdled. Stir in the chocolate chips.

3. Pour the filling into the pie crust. Bake 15 minutes. Reduce the oven temperature to 350°F. Bake until the pie is set in the center, about 40 minutes. Check to see that the pie is set by giving it a gentle shake; the center should remain firm. Cool thoroughly at room temperature.

### Good Advice

For mailing the pie in disposable pie pans, divide 1½ recipes of filling between two 8¾-inch aluminum foil pie pans lined with frozen pie crust.

### Doubling the Recipe

Use two pie crusts and double the remaining ingredients.

### To Freeze

Wrap the cooled pie with plastic wrap, then heavy aluminum foil. Label with date and contents. Freeze up to 2 months.

### To Serve

Bring the wrapped pie to room temperature. Or refrigerate the pie and serve it cold. Refrigerate leftover pie, covered with plastic wrap, up to 5 days.

### To Mail the Pie

Leave the cooled or frozen pie in its baking pan, wrapped with the plastic wrap and heavy aluminum foil. Place cardboard circles that extend 1 inch beyond the edges of the pie on top of the pie and under the pie pan. Tape the cardboard circles together. Fill a carton with several inches of crumpled newspaper or tissue paper. Place the pie on the crushed paper and cover with several more inches of crushed paper. Stuff paper around the sides of the pie. Seal the carton and mail. Send the pie by a method that will guarantee delivery within 2 or 3 days.

# Cakes Without Frosting

These are the everyday cakes that sit on my kitchen counter ready for family or friends who drop by to help themselves. None of these cakes need refrigeration. Many are the eat-anytime-of-day cakes that will add excitement to breakfast, perk up a lunch box, revive you in the afternoon, or top off a family dinner.

Although these cakes have no frosting, they could never be called plain. Several cakes like the Banana Crunch Cake, Kuign Aman, and the Butter Crumb Cake have crunchy toppings that bake with the cake. Others like the Gingerbread, Raspberry Buckle, or Sharrow Bay's Sticky Toffee Pudding are served with a sauce or ice cream.

Pithiviers is a village cake from France that I freeze before or after baking. Its layers of puff pastry and almond filling may look complicated, but the pastry is made with Fast Puff Pastry and the creamy almond filling is made in the food processor.

After these cakes bake and cool, they are ready to serve or freeze.

# Sticky Toffee Pudding with Warm Toffee Sauce and Cream

**Serves 8**

Sharrow Bay Country House Hotel in the English lake district serves Sticky Toffee Pudding every day with their extraordinary multicourse lunches. The owners, Brian Sack and Francis Coulson, want guests to feel as if they're visiting them in their luxurious country home. Fortunately, this philosophy includes sharing treasured recipes, like Sticky Toffee Pudding.

This dessert is not, however, a pudding as we would think of one, but a moist golden date cake, British-English words not having quite the same meaning as American-English words. A toffee sauce is poured over slices of the cake, and it is served with a pitcher of cold cream. It's a true comfort dessert. So whenever you're feeling peckish, cosset yourself a little and indulge in Sticky Toffee Pudding.

**Toffee Sauce**

**3 cups whipping cream**
**2 teaspoons molasses**
**2¼ cups (packed) light or dark brown sugar**

**Sticky Toffee Pudding**

**1 cup (6 ounces) date pieces, coated with oat flour preferred**
**1 cup water**
**1 cup plus 2 tablespoons unbleached all-purpose flour**
**1 teaspoon baking powder**
**½ teaspoon salt**
**4 tablespoons (½ stick) soft unsalted butter**
**¾ cup granulated sugar**
**2 large eggs**
**1 teaspoon vanilla extract**
**1 teaspoon baking soda**

**1½ cups cold heavy whipping cream, for serving**

## Cook the toffee sauce

1. Stir the cream, molasses, and brown sugar together in a large saucepan. Heat over medium heat, stirring, until the brown sugar dissolves. Simmer gently, uncovered, for 30 minutes. The sauce will reduce slightly.

## Prepare the pudding

2. Position an oven rack in the middle of the oven. Preheat the oven to 350°F. Butter the loaf pan of your choice. Line the bottom of the pan with parchment or wax paper and butter the paper.

### Good Advice

- I prefer using a long narrow loaf pan, the type used for terrines, for this cake. An ordinary loaf pan can also be used. Any loaf pan with a capacity of six to eight cups works fine.
- Date pieces coated with oat flour give the best results. They are found in health food stores.

### Doubling the Recipe

Double the ingredients. Bake the cake in 2 pans.

### To Freeze the Sauce

Pour the toffee sauce into a plastic container, leaving 1 inch of space at the top. Refrigerate the sauce until it is cold. Press plastic wrap onto the top of the sauce. Cover the container tightly and freeze up to 2 months.

### To Freeze the Pudding

Use a small sharp knife to loosen the sides of the cooled cake from the pan. Unmold the cake onto a piece of plastic wrap. Remove the paper from the bottom of the cake and discard it. Wrap the cake tightly in the plastic wrap and turn top side up. Wrap the cake with heavy aluminum foil. Freeze up to 2 months.

### To Serve

Defrost the wrapped cake at room temperature. Defrost the covered toffee sauce in the refrigerator overnight. Pour the toffee sauce into a medium saucepan and warm over medium heat, stirring constantly. Slice the cake and place in 8 individual serving bowls. If the cake was baked in a long narrow loaf pan, cut 16 slices and serve 2 slices per serving. If the cake was baked in an ordinary loaf pan, cut 8 slices, cut each slice in half, and serve 2 half slices per serving. Pour warm toffee sauce over each serving and pass cold heavy whipping cream in a pitcher. Cover leftover cake and sauce with plastic wrap and store up to 5 days in the refrigerator.

3. Put the dates and water in a medium saucepan and bring to a boil. Remove from the heat and set aside to cool while you prepare the pudding.

4. Sift the flour, baking powder, and salt together and set aside. Put the butter in the large bowl of an electric mixer. Add the granulated sugar and beat on medium speed until the mixture lightens in color and looks fluffy, about 1 minute. Add the eggs and vanilla and beat until smooth, about 30 seconds. Decrease the speed to low and mix in the flour mixture just until the flour is incorporated. Press any lumps out of the baking soda and gently stir it into the date mixture. Mix the dates and any liquid into the cake batter.

5. Pour the batter into the prepared loaf pan and bake 35 minutes. Gently touch the cake, it should feel firm. If the cake is not firm, bake another 5 minutes. Reduce the oven heat to 250°F. Pour ¾ cup of the warm toffee sauce over the top of the cake and bake another 25 minutes. The sauce will look like a wet glaze on top of the cake. The cake will sink slightly in the middle. Remove the cake from the oven and let the cake cool in the pan.

## Good Advice

Butter the center tube of the pan well. After baking, carefully loosen the baked cake from the center tube.

## Doubling the Recipe

Use 1 tablespoon baking powder and ¾ teaspoon salt and double the remaining ingredients. A double recipe of cake has to be mixed in a five-quart bowl.

## To Freeze

Invert the cooled cake onto plastic wrap. Carefully remove and discard the paper liner. Wrap the cake tightly with plastic wrap then heavy aluminum foil. Label with date and contents. Freeze up to 3 months. The cooled cake can be cut in half before freezing and wrapped and frozen in 2 pieces.

## To Serve

Defrost the wrapped cake at room temperature 5 hours or overnight. Unwrap the cake and place it on a serving plate. Cut into slices and serve with fresh berries and whipped cream, if desired. Leftover cake can be covered with plastic wrap and stored up to 4 days at room temperature.

# Mazie MacKay's Hot Milk Cake

**Makes 12 servings**

My dessert memories last a long time. When I used to play with Mazie MacKay's daughter after school, I would hope there was a Hot Milk Cake in the house for our snack. One day about forty years later, I had a sudden craving for Hot Milk Cake and wrote the MacKays for the recipe. Luckily, families hold on to their recipes, and I soon received the directions. It was the same delicious yellow cake that I remembered, and it turned out to be extremely quick and easy to prepare. It's baked in a tube pan and has a flavor similar to pound cake but with a much lighter texture. I serve the cake plain or with fresh berries and whipped cream.

**2 cups unbleached all-purpose flour**
**2 teaspoons baking powder**
**½ teaspoon salt**
**1 cup whole milk**
**¼ pound (1 stick) unsalted butter, cut into 8 pieces**
**4 large eggs**
**2 cups sugar**
**1 teaspoon vanilla extract**

1. Position a rack in the middle of the oven. Preheat the oven to 350°F. Butter the bottom, sides, and center tube of a 9- or 9¼-inch tube pan. Line the bottom of the tube pan with parchment or wax paper and butter the paper.

2. Sift the flour, baking powder, and salt together and set aside. Put the milk and butter in a medium saucepan and heat over medium heat until the butter melts and the mixture is hot, about 140°F. if measured on a food thermometer. Put the eggs in the large bowl of an electric mixer and mix on medium speed just to combine the yolks and whites. Add the sugar and beat for about 1 minute until the mixture is fluffy, thick, and lightened in color. Mix in the vanilla. Decrease the speed to low and mix in the flour mixture just until it is incorporated. Slowly add the hot milk mixture and mix for about 30 seconds until smooth. Stop the mixer and scrape the sides of the bowl once during this mixing. The batter will be thin.

3. Pour the batter into the prepared pan. Bake about 45 minutes. To check for doneness, gently press your fingers on the top of the cake. It should feel firm. If it does, insert a toothpick in the center of the cake. When the toothpick come out clean the cake is done. Cool the cake in the pan on a wire cooking rack. Use a small, sharp knife to loosen the sides of the cake from the sides and the center tube of the pan.

# Peach Upside-Down Cake with Red Raspberry Ice Cream

**Serves 9**

Upside-down cake can take on a different personality each season by baking it with different seasonal fruits. Peaches are one of my favorite summer choices. In the fall, fresh cranberries are a good alternative. My grandmother's butter cake recipe is just right for upside-down cake. It is dense enough to stand up to the fruit topping, yet it is still light textured. Serving the cake with homemade raspberry ice cream may be gilding the lily, but you've got to gild lilies once in a while.

Brown Sugar Glaze

**4 tablespoons (½ stick) unsalted butter**
**1 tablespoon light corn syrup**
**¾ cup (packed) light brown sugar**

**4 to 5 large ripe peaches**
**One 9-inch Yellow Butter Cake Layer (page 36), batter only**
**Red Raspberry Ice Cream (page 240) or storebought ice cream for serving with the cake**

1. Position an oven rack in the middle of the oven. Preheat the oven to 350°F. Butter an 8 × 8 × 2-inch baking pan. Line the bottom of the pan with parchment paper.

## Prepare the glaze

2. Put the butter, corn syrup, and brown sugar in a small saucepan. Stirring constantly, cook over low-medium heat until the butter and sugar melt and the mixture is smooth. Pour the glaze into the prepared pan and spread the glaze evenly in the pan.

## Peel the peaches

3. Fill a large bowl with ice cubes and water. Have ready a saucepan of boiling water large enough to cover the peaches. Use a slotted spoon to gently place the peaches in the boiling water. Boil for 30 seconds. Use the slotted spoon to transfer the peaches to the ice water. Leave the peaches in the ice water just until they are cool enough to handle, about 5 minutes. Peel the peaches and pat them with a paper towel to remove excess water. Cut the peaches into wedges about ¾ inch thick. You should have 30 peach slices (about 2½ cups). Place 3 rows of peaches, overlapping them slightly, on top of the glaze in the pan. Each row of peaches will have about 10 slices. Holding your hand over the peaches (they will stick to the glaze), pour off any juices that have accumulated in the pan. If any peaches slide around, put them back in place.

*continued*

### Good Advice

- A tablespoon of corn syrup added to the glaze makes it smooth; it doesn't separate or become grainy as it bakes.
- In order for the baking pan to hold all of the fruit and batter it must be two inches deep. Line the baking pan with parchment paper and neither the fruit nor glaze will stick to the pan when you remove the cake.
- Cooling the cake in the pan for five minutes, before removing the cake from the pan, prevents the glaze from dripping off the cake when you turn it over.

### Doubling the Recipe

Prepare batter for two 9-inch Yellow Butter Cake Layers. Double the remaining ingredients. Bake the cake in two pans.

### To Freeze

Cover the cooled cake with plastic wrap then heavy aluminum foil. Label the cake with date and contents. Place the cake in the freezer, fruit side up, and freeze up to 1 month.

4. Prepare the cake batter and pour it over the peaches in the pan. Smooth the top of the batter.

5. Bake for about 55 minutes, reversing the pan after 30 minutes to ensure even baking. To test for doneness gently press your fingers on the top of the middle of the cake. It should feel firm. If so, insert a toothpick in the center of the cake. Be sure to insert the toothpick in the cake, not in the peaches. When the toothpick comes out clean, the cake is done. Cool the cake in the pan for 5 minutes only. Loosen the sides of the cake from the pan with a thin knife blade. Place a wire cooling rack on top of the cake and invert the cake onto the rack. The parchment will probably remain in the pan; if not, carefully remove it from the bottom of the cake. Replace any peaches that stick to the paper. Cool the cake at room temperature, about 2 hours.

### To Serve

**Remove the cake from the freezer and defrost the wrapped cake at room temperature, about 5 hours. Preheat the oven to 250°F. Unwrap the cake and place it on a baking sheet. Bake, uncovered, 10 to 12 minutes. This warming will return the just-baked taste to the cake. Cut the cake into 9 squares. Serve the cake warm or at room temperature with raspberry ice cream. Store left-over cake, wrapped in plastic wrap, at room temperature up to 3 days.**

# Butter Crumb Cake

Serves 12

When I buy crumb-topped cakes, they never seem to have enough crumb topping. Sometimes there are even bare spots with no crumbs at all—a big disappointment for a crumb lover like me. This cake has plenty of crumbs, almost four cups. For my fellow crumb lovers, I promise plenty of crumbs and no bare spots.

**Butter Crumb Topping**

**1¼ cups unbleached all-purpose flour**
**½ cup granulated sugar**
**½ cup (packed) light brown sugar**
**6 ounces (1½ sticks) cold unsalted butter, cut into 12 pieces**

**Pound Cake batter, prepared with 2 large eggs (page 40), unbaked**
**Powdered sugar, for dusting**

## Mix the crumb topping

1. Put the flour, sugar, and brown sugar in a large bowl and stir to break up the pieces of brown sugar. Add the butter pieces. Using an electric mixer on low speed, a pastry blender, or your fingertips, mix the ingredients together until coarse crumbs form and no streaks of flour remain. Mixing the crumbs with an electric mixer will take about 1 minute. The crumbs will be different sizes, with the largest crumbs the size of peas. Set the mixture aside.

2. Position an oven rack in the middle of the oven. Preheat the oven to 325°F. Butter the bottom and sides of a 10-inch layer pan 1¾ to 2 inches deep. Line the bottom of the pan with parchment or wax paper and butter the paper.

## Prepare the cake

3. Pour the Pound Cake batter into the pan and smooth the top. Reserve 1 cup of the crumbs and gently sprinkle the remaining crumbs evenly over the cake. Bake 20 minutes. Gently sprinkle the reserved crumbs evenly over the cake. Bake the cake another 35 to 40 minutes, until a toothpick inserted in the center of the cake comes out clean. Thoroughly cool the cake in the pan on a wire cooling rack, about 2 hours. Use a small sharp knife to loosen the sides of the cake from the pan. Place a flat plate on top of the cake and invert the cake onto the plate. Carefully remove the paper liner from the bottom of the cake. Place a flat plate or cardboard cake circle on the cake and invert the cake. The cake is now right side up. Sift powdered sugar over the top.

### Good Advice

Part of the crumb topping is added to the cake after it is partially baked so the crumbs don't sink.

### Doubling the Recipe

For the cake batter, use ¾ teaspoon salt and 2 teaspoons baking powder and double the remaining ingredients. Double the ingredients for the crumb topping. Bake the cake in two pans.

### To Freeze

Wrap the cooled cake tightly with plastic wrap then with heavy aluminum foil. Label with date and contents. Freeze up to 3 months.

### To Serve

Remove the cake from the freezer and defrost the wrapped cake at room temperature, at least 5 hours or overnight. To prevent the crisp topping from cracking, use a serrated knife and a sawing motion to cut the cake into wedges. Serve the cake at room temperature. Store leftover cake, wrapped in plastic wrap, up to 2 days at room temperature.

Kuign Aman

# Breton Butter Cake

**Makes 8 servings**

Several years ago, a Frenchwoman from Brittany spent the winter in Camden to improve her English. We became good friends, helping each other with French and English and spending many snowy days cooking together. The first cake we baked was this little-known specialty from her native Brittany. It is a rustic, family-style cake with a crisp, puffy topping; it looks just like my idea of a French country cake. A simple flour and water yeast dough is quickly folded and rolled with butter and sugar to form a multilayered pastry. The technique is like preparing puff pastry but with no waiting or chilling time involved. After the dough is patted into a pan, it is glazed with egg and sugar, which gives it the crisp topping. As the cake bakes, some of the butter and sugar melt and spread under the cake, forming a candy-like base. After one taste of this buttery yeast cake, I knew exactly why Kuign Aman is a Breton family tradition.

**¼ pound plus 1 tablespoon (1⅛ sticks) soft unsalted butter**
**¾ cup warm water (95° to 105°F.)**
**2 teaspoons granulated active dry yeast**
**Pinch sugar**
**2¼ cups unbleached all-purpose flour**
**⅛ teaspoon salt**
**½ cup plus 3 tablespoons sugar**
**1 large egg yolk, lightly beaten**

1. Position a rack in the middle of the oven. Have ready a 9-inch layer pan 1¾ to 2 inches deep. When you put the dough in the baking pan for its final rising, preheat the oven to 400°F.

2. Remove the butter from the refrigerator. Softening the butter will take about 1½ hours if the kitchen is between 65° and 75°F.

3. Put ¼ cup of the warm water in a large bowl. Sprinkle the yeast and pinch of sugar over the water and stir until the yeast dissolves. Let the mixture sit for 10 minutes. If the yeast is alive and active, it will begin to foam on top. Add ¼ cup of the flour and stir to incorporate the flour. The dough will look like a thick liquid. Cover the bowl with plastic wrap and let the mixture rest 15 minutes.

4. Stir the remaining ½ cup warm water into the yeast mixture. Mix the remaining flour and salt and stir the flour mixture into the yeast mixture. The dough will look floury and ragged. Scrape the dough onto a work surface. Knead the dough until smooth, about 3 minutes. Knead the dough by pushing down on it, folding it over on itself, and turning the dough as you knead it. Place the dough in a clean, buttered bowl and turn the dough over in the

## Good Advice

- Just remember two things about yeast when preparing this cake and you'll have no trouble. Use warm water, between 95° and 105°F. if measured with a food thermometer, to dissolve the yeast. My test is that the water should feel comfortably warm to my hand; if the water burns my hand, it will burn the yeast. Also check to see that the yeast is fresh and alive by mixing it with warm water and a little sugar. After about ten minutes, the mixture will look creamy and spongy. If you watch the mixture, you will see movement. If nothing happens, the yeast is not fresh, and you must buy fresh yeast. Yeast packages are dated and should be fine if used by the date on the package. I use dried granular yeast which dissolves easily. One ¼-ounce package contains a scant tablespoon of yeast. You will not use the whole envelope.
- The dough rises for a total of one hour and forty-five minutes. This means you have to be available when the dough needs rolling or baking; between risings it is not necessary pay attention to it. Dough rises well if the room temperature is between 65° and 70°F., but this is not always possible. This is not a finicky cake, however; it has been rising for generations in heated and unheated French farmhouses, so don't be too

concerned about exact room temperatures. If the room is cool, let the dough rise a little longer; if warm, let the dough rise for a shorter time.

• The butter is at the correct temperature to roll with the dough when it yields to about the same pressure when pressed with a finger as the dough does. If the butter is too hard it can break through the dough; if too soft, it can blend into the dough and the layering effect is lost.

## Doubling the Recipe

Double the ingredients. Before adding the butter and sugar, divide the dough into two parts and fill and roll each piece of dough separately.

## To Freeze

Cover the cooled cake tightly with plastic wrap then heavy aluminum foil. Label with date and contents. Freeze up to 3 months.

## To Serve

Remove the cake from the freezer and defrost the wrapped cake at room temperature, about 5 hours. Preheat the oven to 250°F. Unwrap the cake and place it on a baking sheet. Bake, uncovered, 10 to 12 minutes, just to warm the cake slightly. Cut in squares and serve warm. Cover with plastic wrap and store leftover cake at room temperature up to 2 days.

bowl to coat it with butter. Cover with plastic wrap and let the dough rise for 1 hour.

5. Punch the air out of the dough and place the dough on a lightly floured surface. Roll the dough into a rectangle about 14 × 10 inches. Leaving a 1½-inch border of plain dough, sprinkle ¼ cup of the sugar over the dough. Break off teaspoon-size pieces of butter and place them evenly over the dough. Sprinkle another ¼ cup of sugar evenly over the butter. It will look like a lot of sugar. The shorter end of the rectangle should be facing you. Fold the top quarter of the dough to the center, then fold the bottom quarter of the dough to the center so the edges meet in the center. Fold the dough package in half. There will be 4 layers in a long narrow rectangle, about 10 × 3½ inches. Turn the dough so an open end faces you. Pinch both open ends to seal them. Pat the dough gently to level it. Roll it into a rectangle, about 14 × 6 inches. Fold the top third of the dough to the center, then fold the bottom third of the dough over the top. There will be 3 layers. Turn the dough so that an open end faces you. Immediately repeat this rolling and folding. The final dough package will measure about 6 × 5 inches.

6. Carefully roll the dough into a square, about 8 inches. If any butter breaks through the dough, rub a small amount of flour over the butter. Place the dough in the layer pan and gently press it to fill the pan. The dough is elastic from the rolling and may pull away a little from the edges of the pan. Cover with plastic wrap and let rise 30 minutes. The top of the cake will puff slightly. Remove the plastic wrap, use a pastry brush to lightly brush the dough with the egg yolk, and sprinkle with the remaining 3 tablespoons of sugar.

7. Bake until the top of the cake is a dark golden brown, 30 to 35 minutes. Some of the butter and sugar will melt and bubble up under the cake as it bakes; this forms the bottom glaze. Watch the cake carefully during the last few minutes of baking as the topping can burn quickly. Cool the cake in the pan 5 minutes. Spread a piece of wax paper under a wire cooling rack to catch any drips. Use a small sharp knife to loosen the sides of the cake from the pan. Place the wire cooling rack on top of the cake, invert the cake onto the rack, and place the rack on the wax paper. If any sugar-butter mixture sticks to the bottom of the pan, spread it on the bottom of the cake. Turn the cake right side up to cool.

Pithiviers

# Butter Almond Cake

**Serves 12**

Although Pithiviers originated in a village of the same name south of Paris, the French know a good cake when they taste it, and Pithiviers is now popular all over France. This low round cake has an almond filling sealed between two layers of flaky puff pastry. Shallow cuts made on the top of the cake before it bakes give it an attractive spiral pattern. The finished cake looks so impressive that every time I remove it from my oven, I feel as if it just came out of the window of a fancy French pâtisserie.

Everything about traditional Pithiviers is easy, except the puff pastry. Few cooks will deny that making classic puff pastry is time consuming and, as far as I'm concerned, a nuisance. My version of Pithiviers replaces the classic pastry with a clever, Fast Puff Pastry. The pastry dough, with almost equal parts of butter to flour, is mixed like a pie crust dough (no bulky butter packages to roll into the dough), then quickly folded and rolled (no long waiting times between rollings). Whenever I bake Fast Puff Pastry, I'm impressed with its simplicity and the results. It does not rise quite as high as traditional puff pastry, but otherwise it has all of the tender, buttery, flaky, multilayered qualities required for Pithiviers. Fast Puff Pastry is no poor cousin to traditional puff pastry, and I use it not only for Pithiviers but anytime I need puff pastry for a dessert.

### Fast Puff Pastry

2 cups unbleached all-purpose flour
½ cup cake flour
¾ teaspoon salt
½ pound plus 6 tablespoons (2¾ sticks) cold unsalted butter, cut into 22 pieces
1 tablespoon sour cream
½ cup ice water
Sifted cake flour, for rolling the pastry

### Almond Filling

1¼ cups blanched almonds
2 tablespoons sugar
¼ pound (1 stick) soft unsalted butter
¾ cup powdered sugar
1 large egg
1 large egg yolk
1 tablespoon whipping cream
1 tablespoon fresh lemon juice
2 teaspoons dark rum
1 teaspoon vanilla extract
½ teaspoon almond extract
1 teaspoon cornstarch

## Good Advice

• When the butter is added to the flour, it must be so cold that pieces of butter remain visible in the dough after rolling. After mixing the butter and flour, the butter pieces should be rather large—½ to ¾ inch. It is these butter pieces that help lift and separate the layers of pastry during baking.

• Using a combination of all-purpose and cake flour for the pastry reduces the stretchy gluten content, and makes the dough more tender and somewhat easier to roll.

## Doubling the Recipe

Mix the dough in separate batches. Double the ingredients for the filling.

## To Freeze

Wrap the Pithiviers on the pan tightly with plastic wrap, then with heavy foil, gently pressing the foil against dough. Label with date and contents. Once frozen the Pithiviers can be removed from the baking pan and rewrapped. Freeze up to 3 weeks.

## To Bake and Serve

Position a rack in the middle of the oven. Preheat the oven to 425°F. Unwrap the frozen Pithiviers. Using a pastry brush, lightly brush the Pithiviers evenly with the egg wash. Wipe up any egg that splashes on the baking pan. Cut a ¼-inch hole in the center of the cake to let steam escape. Use a small sharp knife to cut evenly spaced curving lines from the center to the edge of the cake. The lines will form a spiral pattern. The bottom of each line should end at a cut along the scalloped edge. This will space the lines at 1-inch intervals along the edge of the cake. Make the cuts shallow so they do not penetrate to the filling.

Bake for 20 minutes. Reduce the oven heat to 350°F. and bake another 25 minutes. Remove the cake from the oven and increase the oven temperature to 425°F. Sift 2 tablespoons of powdered sugar evenly over the cake. Bake about 7 minutes, just until the powdered sugar melts and forms a golden glaze over the top of the cake. Reverse the pan, front to back, after 4 minutes of baking to ensure the glaze bakes evenly. Watch carefully as the sugar can burn easily. Remove the cake from the oven and slide it onto a wire cooling rack to cool completely. Cut into wedges to serve. Pithiviers stores well; leftover cake can be covered with plastic wrap and stored up to 5 days at room temperature.

**1 large egg, mixed with 1 tablespoon whipping cream, for egg wash**
**2 tablespoons powdered sugar, for glaze**

1. Have ready a 12- to 14-inch round baking pan. A pizza pan works well.

## Prepare the fast puff pastry

2. Put the all-purpose flour, cake flour, and salt in the large bowl of an electric mixer and mix on low speed just to blend. With the mixer running, add the butter and mix just until the butter forms ½- to ¾-inch pieces, about 30 seconds. You will still see loose flour. Add the sour cream, then slowly pour in the water. Stop mixing as soon as the mixture holds together and pulls away from the sides of the bowl, about 20 seconds. Add up to 1 additional tablespoon of water, if needed. Turn the dough onto a rolling surface and with the heel of your hand push the dough down and forward against the rolling surface. Fold the dough in half and repeat 4 or 5 times until the dough looks smooth. Form the dough into a smooth 6-inch square about 1½ inches thick. You will see butter pieces in the dough. Cover with plastic wrap and refrigerate 15 minutes to rest the dough.

3. Place the dough on a rolling surface lightly dusted with sifted cake flour and roll into a rectangle about 14 × 10 inches. Don't flip the dough over while rolling it, but lift and turn the dough several times to prevent it from sticking to the surface. Dust the rolling surface and rolling pin with a little more flour as necessary. Brush any loose flour off the dough. The shorter end of the rectangle should be facing you. Fold the top quarter of the dough to the center then fold the bottom quarter of the dough to the center. The edges of the dough will meet in the center. Fold the dough package in half. There will be 4 layers shaped in a long narrow rectangle, about 10 × 3½ inches. Turn the dough so an open end faces you. Pat the dough gently to level it. Roll into another rectangle, about 14 × 8 inches. The dough becomes more resistant with each rolling and will need firmer rolling each time. Repeat the folding to form 4 layers. Turn the dough so that an open end faces you and immediately repeat the rolling and folding. The final dough package will measure about 8 × 3½ inches. The dough has now been rolled and folded 3 times. Cover with plastic wrap and refrigerate 30 minutes.

## Mix the almond filling

4. Put the almonds and sugar in a food processor fitted with a metal blade. Process until the almonds are finely ground, about 20 seconds. Put the butter in the large bowl of an electric mixer and mix on low speed 15 seconds. Add the powdered sugar and beat for 30 seconds until the mixture is smooth. Mix in the almond mixture. Add the egg, egg yolk, cream, lemon juice, rum, vanilla, and almond extract. Mix for 30 seconds until blended completely. Stir in the cornstarch.

*continued*

### To Freeze Baked Pithiviers

Cool the baked Pithiviers completely. Wrap the cooled Pithiviers with plastic wrap then heavy aluminum foil, gently pressing the foil against the cake. Label with date and contents. Freeze up to 2 months.

### To Serve Previously Frozen Baked Pithiviers

Remove the cake from the freezer and defrost the wrapped cake at room temperature, about 5 hours. Preheat the oven to 250°F. Remove the wrapping from the defrosted cake and place it on a baking sheet. Bake, uncovered, 12 to 15 minutes. This warming will return the just-baked taste to the cake. Cut into wedges to serve. Store leftover cake, wrapped in plastic wrap, up to 5 days at room temperature.

### Good Advice

Use frozen unsweetened raspberries that are still frozen for the buckle. The batter is thick and frozen raspberries will not be crushed when they are stirred into the batter.

## Fill the Pithiviers

5. Remove the dough from the refrigerator and cut it into 2 equal pieces. Roll 1 piece of dough into an 11-inch circle. Roll the dough from the center out to the edges. Place the dough on the baking pan. Leaving a 1½-inch plain border, spread the center of the dough with almond filling, mounding the filling slightly toward the center. Lightly brush the plain border with cold water. Roll the remaining dough to another 11-inch circle. Cover the filling with this dough circle. Press the edges of the dough together tightly to seal. The edges of the dough will probably not fit together exactly. Place a 10-inch cake layer pan or bowl over the cake as a guide and trim the cake to a neat 10-inch round. If any edges do not look sealed, press them together. Use a small knife to cut ½-inch slits at 1-inch intervals around the edge of the dough. When making the cuts pull the knife toward the inside of the circle and a scallop pattern will form. Check to see that the slits go all the way through the dough.

# Raspberry Buckle

**Serves 12**

If Raspberry Buckle sales are a measure, our customers at Peter Ott's would like this cake to be on the menu every day. It is a moist, homey cake filled with lots of raspberries and topped with cinnamon-flavored crumbs. I bake the cake in a rectangular pan and serve large squares of the warm buckle topped with vanilla ice cream. The cake was inspired by a recipe of Maida Heatter's for buckle with blueberries and peaches.

**Cinnamon Crumb Topping**

**6 ounces (1½ sticks) cold unsalted butter, cut into 12 pieces**
**2 teaspoons ground cinnamon**
**1 cup (packed) light brown sugar**
**1 cup unbleached all-purpose flour**

### Doubling the Recipe

Double the ingredients for the crumb topping. Prepare one recipe of cake batter at a time and bake the buckle in two pans.

### To Freeze

The cake can be frozen whole in the pan or cut into 12 squares before freezing. To freeze the cake in the pan wrap tightly with plastic wrap then heavy aluminum foil. Or wrap cake pieces individually in plastic wrap. Put the wrapped cake pieces in a metal or plastic freezer container and cover tightly. Label with date and contents. Freeze up to 3 months.

### To Serve

Remove the cake or as many pieces as you need from the freezer and defrost the wrapped cake at room temperature about 2 hours. Preheat the oven to 250°F. Unwrap the whole defrosted cake and bake it, uncovered, about 15 minutes, until it is warm. Unwrap individual pieces of cake, place them on a baking sheet, and cover tightly with standard weight aluminum foil. Bake about 10 minutes until warm. Serve the cake warm, with vanilla ice cream. Leftover cake can be wrapped with plastic wrap and stored at room temperature up to 3 days.

Buckle Cake

**4 cups unbleached all-purpose flour**
**1 tablespoon baking powder**
**¾ teaspoon salt**
**6 ounces (1½ sticks) soft unsalted butter**
**1⅓ cups sugar**
**2 large eggs**
**2 teaspoons vanilla extract**
**1 teaspoon almond extract**
**1 cup milk**
**3 cups frozen unsweetened raspberries, not defrosted**

**Vanilla ice cream, for serving with the cake**

## Mix the cinnamon crumb topping

1. Put the cold butter, cinnamon, brown sugar, and flour in the large bowl of an electric mixer. Mix on low speed for about 1 minute until crumbs about the size of small lima beans form. Or use a pastry blender or your fingertips to mix the ingredients together until the crumbs form. The crumbs will vary in size from small grains to lima bean. Pour the crumbs into a bowl and set aside.

2. Position an oven rack in the middle of the oven. Preheat the oven to 325°F. Butter a 15 × 10 × 2-inch baking pan.

## Prepare the buckle cake

3. Sift the flour, baking powder, and salt for the cake together and set aside. Put the butter in the large bowl of an electric mixer and mix on low speed 15 seconds, just until smooth. Add the sugar and beat on medium speed about 1 minute, until the mixture lightens in color and the mixture is smooth. Add the eggs, one at a time, then beat for 1 minute. Stop the mixer and scrape the sides of the bowl once during the beating. Add the vanilla and almond extract to the milk. Decrease the speed to low and add the flour mixture and the milk alternately, beginning and ending with the flour mixture (3 flour, 2 milk). Scrape the sides of the bowl again after the last addition of flour. The batter is ready when the final addition of flour is mixed completely into the batter. If any flour is clinging to the sides of the bowl, stir it into the batter. The batter will be thick. Use a large mixing spoon to gently stir the frozen raspberries into the batter. The cold raspberries will thicken the batter further.

4. Spread the batter evenly in the pan. Sprinkle the crumbs evenly over the batter. Bake 50 to 55 minutes, reversing the pan from front to back after 40 minutes to ensure even browning. To test for doneness, insert a toothpick in the center of the cake. When the toothpick comes out clean, the cake is done. If the toothpick penetrates raspberries, test another spot in the cake. Cool the cake thoroughly in the pan on a wire cooling rack, about 3 hours.

# Chocolate-Cherry Buckle

Serves 12

This triple chocolate combination includes chocolate chips in a light chocolate cake topped with chocolate crumbs. Bing cherries marinated in kirsch add a chewy texture and good flavor.

### Cocoa Crumb Topping

¼ pound (1 stick) cold unsalted butter, cut into 8 pieces
⅓ cup unbleached all-purpose flour
⅔ cup (packed) light brown sugar
⅓ cup unsweetened Dutch process cocoa powder
1 teaspoon ground cinnamon

### Chocolate-Cherry Cake

3 cups fresh, frozen, or canned and drained pitted Bing cherries
3 tablespoons kirsch
3½ cups unbleached all-purpose flour
¼ cup unsweetened Dutch process cocoa powder
1 tablespoon baking powder
¾ teaspoon salt
1 teaspoon ground cinnamon
¼ pound (1 stick) soft unsalted butter
1⅓ cups sugar
2 large eggs
2 teaspoons vanilla extract
¾ teaspoon almond extract
1 cup milk
2 cups (12 ounces) semisweet chocolate chips
Powdered sugar, for dusting
Cherry or vanilla ice cream, for serving with the buckle

## Prepare the cocoa crumb topping

1. Put the butter, flour, brown sugar, cocoa powder, and cinnamon in the large bowl of an electric mixer. Mix on low speed until crumbs about the size of small lima beans form. Alternatively rub the ingredients together between your fingertips until crumbs form. Set the crumbs aside.

2. Cut the Bing cherries in half and put them in a small bowl. Add the kirsch and marinate for 30 minutes. Drain the cherries.

3. Position an oven rack in the middle of the oven. Preheat the oven to 325°F. Butter a 15 × 10 × 2-inch baking pan.

## Prepare the chocolate-cherry cake

4. Sift the flour, cocoa powder, baking powder, salt, and cinnamon together and set aside. Put the butter in the large bowl of an electric mixer and mix on low speed for 15 seconds. Increase the speed to medium, add the sugar, and beat for 1 minute, until the color lightens slightly and the mixture is smooth. Add the eggs, one at a time. Beat for 1 minute. Stop the mixer

### Good Advice

Contrary to many crumb cakes, this one should be served at room temperature rather than warm.

### Doubling the Recipe

Double the ingredients for the crumb topping. Prepare one recipe of cake batter at a time and bake the cake in two pans.

### To Freeze

The cake can be frozen whole in the pan or cut into 12 squares and frozen in pieces. Wrap the cake in the pan tightly with plastic wrap then heavy aluminum foil. Or, wrap cake pieces tightly in plastic wrap. Put the wrapped cake pieces in a metal or plastic freezer container and cover tightly. Label with date and contents. Freeze up to 3 months.

### To Serve

Remove the cake or as many pieces as you need from the freezer and defrost the wrapped cake at room temperature. Serve the cake topped with a scoop of ice cream. Leftover cake can be wrapped with plastic wrap and stored at room temperature up to 3 days.

and scrape the sides of the bowl once during the beating. Add the vanilla and almond extract to the milk. Decrease the speed to low and add the flour mixture and the milk mixture alternately, beginning and ending with the flour mixture (3 flour, 2 milk). Scrape the sides of the bowl again after the last addition of flour. The batter is ready when the final addition of flour is mixed completely into the batter. If any flour is clinging to the sides of the bowl, stir it into the batter. Gently stir the cherries and chocolate chips into the batter.

5. Spread the batter evenly in the pan. Sprinkle the crumbs evenly over the batter. Bake 50 to 55 minutes, reversing the pan front to back to ensure even browning. To test for doneness, insert a toothpick in the center of the cake. When the toothpick comes out clean the cake is done. The top of the cake will look dark brown. Cool the cake in the pan on a wire cooling rack, about 2 hours. Sift powdered sugar over the top of the cooled cake.

# Banana Crunch Cake

**Serves 8 to 10**

For this moist banana cake I wanted a crunchy topping that repeated the banana flavor of the cake. I finally thought of using crushed banana chips. Usually I serve this informal cake as a daytime snack or family dessert, but for a fancier occasion I dress it up with a scoop of Banana Sorbet or banana ice cream.

### Banana Crunch Topping

**1 cup (about 4 ounces) dried banana chips unsalted but sweetened**
**4 tablespoons (½ stick) unsalted butter**
**½ cup packed light brown sugar**
**¾ cup pecans, coarsely chopped**

### Banana Cake

**1½ cups unbleached all-purpose flour**
**¾ teaspoon baking powder**
**½ teaspoon salt**
**1 teaspoon ground cinnamon**
**6 tablespoons (¾ stick) soft unsalted butter**
**1 cup sugar**
**2 large eggs**
**1 teaspoon vanilla extract**
**2 teaspoons dark rum**
**¾ teaspoon baking soda**
**½ cup sour cream**
**1½ cups (about 3) mashed bananas**

**Banana Sorbet (page 244) or banana ice cream, for serving with the cake (optional)**

## Mix the banana crunch topping

1. Put the banana chips between 2 pieces of wax paper and crush them with a rolling pin or the flat side of a meat pounder into approximately ½-inch pieces. You should have about ¾ cup banana chip pieces. Melt the butter and brown sugar in a small saucepan over medium heat. Bring the mixture to a boil and cook for 30 seconds, stirring constantly. Remove the pan from the heat and stir in the banana chips and chopped pecans until they are well coated with the brown sugar mixture. Set aside.

2. Position an oven rack in the middle of the oven. Preheat the oven to 325°F. Butter the bottom and sides of a 9-inch layer pan 2 inches deep. Line the bottom of the pan with parchment or wax paper and butter the paper.

### Good Advice

- Natural food stores and most supermarkets sell dried banana chips. Unsweetened banana chips have little flavor, so buy the lightly sweetened kind.
- The cake is thick; it must be baked in a layer pan that is two inches deep.
- Use a plate or a foil-wrapped or moisture-resistant cardboard circle to store the cake since the moist cake will stick to a cardboard circle.

### Doubling the Recipe

Double the ingredients and bake in two pans.

### To Freeze

Wrap the cooled cake tightly with plastic wrap then heavy aluminum foil. Label with date and contents. Freeze up to 3 months.

### To Serve

Remove the cake from the freezer and defrost the wrapped cake at room temperature, at least 5 hours or overnight. Serve the cake warm or at room temperature. To warm the cake, heat the defrosted cake in a preheated 250°F. oven, uncovered, for about 15 minutes. Use a serrated knife and a sawing motion to cut through the crisp topping. Store leftover cake, wrapped in plastic wrap, up to 3 days at room temperature. Serve with Banana Sorbet or ice cream, if desired.

### Prepare the banana cake

3. Sift the flour, baking powder, salt, and cinnamon together. Set aside. Put the butter in the large bowl of an electric mixer and beat on medium speed 15 seconds. Slowly add the sugar and beat 2 minutes. The mixture will be thick. Add the eggs and beat for 1 minute. Stop the mixer and scrape the bowl once during this beating. Add the vanilla and rum. Gently stir the baking soda into the sour cream. Stir the sour cream mixture into the mashed bananas. The banana mixture will be lumpy. Decrease the speed to low and add the flour mixture and the banana mixture alternately, beginning and ending with the flour mixture (3 flour, 2 banana). Stop mixing as soon as the last addition of flour is incorporated.

4. Spread half the batter in the prepared pan. Sprinkle ½ cup of the topping evenly over the batter. Spread the remaining batter evenly over the crunch. Sprinkle the remaining banana crunch evenly over the batter. Bake until a toothpick inserted into the center of the cake comes out clean, about 1 hour. Cool the cake in the pan on a wire cooling rack for about 2 hours. Use a small sharp knife to loosen the sides of the cake from the pan. Place a flat plate on top of the cake and invert the cake onto the plate. Carefully remove and discard the paper liner. Place another flat plate or a moisture-resistant cardboard cake circle on the bottom of the cake and invert the cake. The cake is now right side up. Replace any of the crunch that may have fallen off the cake.

# Pumpkin–Pine Nut Cake

**Serves 9**

Pumpkin gives an appealing dark golden color to this lightly spiced cake. Pine nuts add a subtle buttery nut flavor without overpowering the pumpkin. After a fall afternoon of bulb planting and leaf raking, I serve generous squares of this cake as a reward for all that hard work.

**1 cup pine nuts (4 ounces)**
**2¼ cups unbleached all-purpose flour**
**2 teaspoons baking powder**
**½ teaspoon salt**
**1 teaspoon ground cinnamon**
**½ teaspoon ground nutmeg**
**¼ teaspoon ground cloves**
**¼ pound (1 stick) soft unsalted butter**
**1¾ cups (packed) light brown sugar**
**3 large eggs**
**1 teaspoon vanilla extract**
**1¼ cups canned pumpkin**

1. Position an oven rack in the middle of the oven. Preheat the oven to 300°F. Butter an 8 × 8 × 2-inch baking pan.

2. Spread ½ cup of the pine nuts in an even layer in a small baking pan and toast 8 to 10 minutes, until the nuts are golden, stirring once. Set aside to cool. Increase the oven temperature to 350°F.

3. Sift the flour, baking powder, salt, cinnamon, nutmeg, and cloves together and set aside. Put the butter and brown sugar in the large bowl of an electric mixer and beat on medium speed 30 seconds, until the butter and sugar are smooth. Add the eggs and vanilla and beat 30 seconds. Decrease the speed to low and mix in the pumpkin just until it is incorporated. Add the flour mixture and mix just until the flour is incorporated. Stir in the ½ cup of toasted pine nuts.

4. Spread the batter evenly in the prepared pan. Sprinkle the remaining ½ cup of pine nuts evenly over the top of the cake and gently press the nuts into the cake. Bake about 55 minutes. A toothpick inserted in the center of the cake will come out clean but slightly moist. Cool the cake in the pan on a wire cooling rack, about 2 hours.

### Good Advice

Check to see that the label on the can of pumpkin says pumpkin rather than pumpkin pie filling.

### Doubling the Recipe

Use 1 tablespoon baking powder and double the remaining ingredients. Bake in two pans.

### To Freeze

Cut the cooled cake into 9 pieces and wrap each piece in plastic wrap. Put the cake pieces in a metal or plastic freezer container and cover tightly. Label with date and contents. Freeze up to 3 months.

### To Serve

Remove as many pieces of cake as you need from the freezer and defrost the wrapped cake at room temperature. Leftover cake can be wrapped with plastic wrap and stored at room temperature up to 3 days.

# Mom's Walnut and Wine Passover Cake

**Serves 12**

Passover cakes, since they must be baked without wheat flour and leavening, are notorious for their dry, unappealing texture. Not our family's traditional Passover cake. It's a light spongy cake, enriched with ground walnuts and flavored with sweet red wine and lemon. Every Passover my mother asks, "The cake isn't dry, is it?" "Moist, definitely moist this year," we always reply.

**9 large eggs, separated**
**1½ cups sugar**
**1 teaspoon grated lemon zest**
**3 tablespoons fresh lemon juice**
**2 tablespoons canola or corn oil**
**2 tablespoons Concord grape wine**
**¼ teaspoon salt**
**½ cup matzo cake meal**
**1 tablespoon potato starch**
**2½ cups (8 ounces) ground walnuts**
**Powdered sugar, for dusting (optional)**

1. Position an oven rack in the middle of the oven. Preheat the oven to 325°F. Oil a 10-inch springform or cake pan with 3-inch-high sides. Line the bottom of the pan with parchment or wax paper and oil the paper.

2. Put the egg yolks in the large bowl of an electric mixer and mix on medium speed for 15 seconds, just to break up the yolks. Add ¾ cup of the sugar and beat about 90 seconds until the mixture thickens and the color lightens to pale yellow. Add the lemon zest, lemon juice, oil, wine, and salt and mix on low speed until the ingredients are blended. Add the cake meal and potato starch and mix until evenly moistened. Mix in the walnuts. Set aside. Put the egg whites in another clean large bowl and with clean dry beaters beat the egg whites on medium speed to soft peaks. Slowly beat in the remaining ¾ cup sugar, 2 tablespoons at a time. Use a rubber spatula to fold half of the whites into the yolk mixture. Fold in the remaining whites.

3. Pour the batter into the prepared pan and smooth the top. Bake 60 to 70 minutes, until a toothpick inserted in the center of the cake comes out clean. Cool the cake in the pan on a wire cooling rack for 20 minutes. Loosen the sides of the cake from the pan with a thin knife blade. Place a wire cooling rack on top of the cake and invert it onto the rack. If using a springform pan, remove the springform sides and bottom. Carefully remove the paper liner from the bottom of the cake and discard it. Place another wire cooling rack on the cake and invert the cake onto the rack to cool right side up. Cool the cake thoroughly.

### Good Advice

- This large cake must be baked in a ten-inch diameter springform or cake pan with three-inch-high sides.
- Cake meal and potato starch can be found in the kosher foods sections of supermarkets.
- Store leftover boxes of cake meal and potato starch, wrapped tightly in plastic freezer bags, up to two years in the freezer.

### Doubling the Recipe

Prepare separate batches of batter.

### To Freeze

Wrap the cooled cake tightly with plastic wrap then heavy aluminum foil. Label with date and contents. Freeze up to 1 month.

### To Serve

Defrost the wrapped cake at room temperature for 5 hours or overnight. Unwrap the cake and place it on a serving plate. Sprinkle the cake with powdered sugar, if desired. Leftover cake can be wrapped with plastic wrap and stored at room temperature up to 3 days.

# Gingerbread with Ice Cream and Warm Butterscotch Sauce

Serves 12

Serving traditional gingerbread with vanilla ice cream and butterscotch sauce makes a new classic out of an old one.

**Gingerbread**

**2½ cups unbleached all-purpose flour**
**2 teaspoons baking powder**
**½ teaspoon salt**
**1½ teaspoons ground cinnamon**
**2 teaspoons ground ginger**
**¼ teaspoon ground cloves**
**¼ pound (1 stick) unsalted butter, melted**
**1¼ cups (packed) light brown sugar**
**2 large eggs**
**¾ cup molasses**
**1 teaspoon instant decaffeinated coffee granules**
**1½ cups warm water**
**½ teaspoon baking soda**

**Butterscotch Sauce**

**⅔ cup whipping cream**
**6 tablespoons (¾ stick) unsalted butter**
**1 cup (packed) dark brown sugar**
**⅓ cup light corn syrup**
**1 teaspoon vanilla extract**

**Vanilla ice cream, for serving with the gingerbread**

1. Position an oven rack in the middle of the oven. Preheat the oven to 350°F. Butter a 13 × 9 × 2-inch pan.

## Prepare the gingerbread

2. Sift the flour, baking powder, salt, cinnamon, ginger, and cloves together and set aside. Put the melted butter, light brown sugar, eggs, and molasses in a large bowl. Mix on low speed until combined thoroughly. Dissolve the instant coffee in the warm water. Gently stir the baking soda into the coffee. Add the flour mixture and the coffee alternately, beginning and ending with the flour mixture (3 flour, 2 coffee). Stop the mixer and scrape the bowl after the last addition of flour and stir to incorporate all the flour. The batter will be thin.

3. Pour the batter into the prepared baking pan. Bake 30 minutes. To test for doneness gently press your fingers on the middle of the cake. It

### Good Advice

Since the butterscotch sauce can be stored in the refrigerator up to two weeks, you may not want to freeze it. If the sauce separates during storage, whisk it as it warms to restore the smooth texture.

### Doubling the Recipe

Double the ingredients. Mix a double recipe of gingerbread in a bowl with a five-quart capacity. Bake the cake in two pans.

### To Freeze the Gingerbread

Cut the cooled gingerbread into 12 pieces. Wrap each piece tightly in plastic wrap and place in a plastic freezer container. Cover tightly and label with date and contents. Freeze up to 3 months. Remove as many pieces of cake as you need and defrost the wrapped cake at room temperature. Store at room temperature up to 3 days.

### To Freeze the Sauce

Place cold butterscotch sauce in a plastic container, leaving a 1-inch space in the top of the container. Press plastic wrap onto the sauce. Cover the container tightly. Label with date and contents. Freeze up to 2 months.

### To Serve

When you are ready to use the butterscotch sauce, defrost it in the refrigerator 6 hours or overnight. Warm the sauce in a medium saucepan over low heat, stirring occasionally. Place a piece of gingerbread in a shallow bowl, top with a scoop of vanilla ice cream, and cover with the warm butterscotch sauce.

should feel firm. If so, insert a toothpick in the center of the cake. When the toothpick comes out clean, the cake is done. Cool the cake in the baking pan on a wire cooling rack.

## Prepare the butterscotch sauce

4. Put the cream, butter, dark brown sugar, and corn syrup in a medium saucepan. Cook over low heat until the butter and sugar are melted, stirring occasionally. Increase the heat to medium-high and bring the sauce to a boil. Stirring constantly, boil the sauce for 1 minute. Remove the sauce from the heat and whisk in the vanilla. Pour the sauce into a small bowl, cover, and refrigerate up to 2 weeks, or freeze the sauce.

# Cakes *with* Frosting

Every weekend I bake at least one frosted layer cake for the restaurant where I work. The possibilities are endless, and it's fun for me to mix and match fillings, frostings, and cakes. With some Chocolate Truffle Sauce and melted white chocolate, I turn a pan of Fudge Bars into Chocolate Thunder cake. Layers like Chocolate Butter Cake are so versatile that they take to almost any type of filling or frosting. I often bake two recipes of Chocolate Butter Cake Layers, and turn one into a Fallen Leaves Chocolate Cake and the other into a Deep Dark Chocolate Cake.

All of the cakes in this chapter can be baked and frozen before they are frosted; this divides the preparation time into separate steps. When I freeze cake layers prior to frosting, I store them only two months, rather than the usual three, since they will be frozen again with the frosting for up to one month more. I frost frozen cake layers and return the cake to the freezer. If the layers require splitting, I defrost them to the point where they can be split, add the filling and frosting, and return the finished cake to the freezer. The slight defrosting does not harm the cake. If I am preparing the entire cake in one day, I make the frosting and filling, if any, while the cakes cool.

Cakes bake evenly in good quality heavyweight pans. I prefer heavy aluminum cake pans, which do not rust. Using cake pans with two-inch-high sides prevents cakes from rising over the rim of the pan and burning. Invest in two or four nine- and ten-inch cake pans to bake beautiful cakes for years—more than thirty years so far for me.

After years of buttering and flouring pans and still having cakes stick to the bottom of the pan, I learned to take the time to line the bottom with wax or parchment paper. Now my cakes never stick.

To bake cakes evenly—no overbaked bottoms or tops—the middle of the oven is the best position. If you need to use two racks for four layers, place the racks in the lower middle and upper middle of the oven. Space the pans on the rack so they are not placed directly over each other and rotate them front to back and top to bottom after the batter is set, usually after twenty minutes of baking.

An underbaked cake will collapse in the center and an overbaked cake will be dry, so keep a careful watch on a cake toward the end of its baking time. To test a dense or fairly firm cake for doneness, first touch the center to check to see if it feels firm, then insert a wooden toothpick into the center of the cake. If the toothpick comes out clean, the cake is done. When checking a delicate sponge cake or a cake with a firm crunch topping, use only the toothpick. I test cakes with a wooden toothpick rather than a metal cake tester. It is easier to see the batter on a toothpick than on a metal tester and to judge more accurately what's happening inside the cake. Sometimes crumbs will adhere to a toothpick when a thin metal tester inserted in the same cake comes out perfectly clean.

When I began baking at Peter Ott's and had to cool many cake layers at a time, I discovered that most cakes cool perfectly in the pan. I place the cakes, in their pans, on a wire cooling rack for good air circulation. Some cakes, though, like the moist Date Cake with Cream Cheese Frosting (page 150) must be removed from the pan before it sticks to the pan and should be cooled on a rack. For these, I use a cooling rack with crosswoven wires, which do not leave deep indentations in the cake as the ones with parallel wires can.

When splitting cake layers into thinner layers, I use the removable bottom of a tart pan to separate the cake layers. The pan bottom slides in easily and supports the whole layer so there is no chance of its breaking apart when you move it to the side.

I usually brush butter cake and sponge cake layers lightly with a sugar syrup, with the flavor of the syrup suited to the flavor of the cake. Rum and coffee go well with chocolate cakes, framboise (raspberry) syrups with raspberry cakes. Syrup also adds moistness to cakes and helps the frosting adhere.

When I'm filling cakes, I can almost hear the great pastry chef and teacher Albert Kumin saying, "Remember the last bite." So I spread that buttercream to the edge, brush that syrup to the edge. The last bite is the most important bite—the one that will be remembered.

Neatness also counts. This means smooth frostings and glazes evenly applied, attractive serving platters without frosting streaks, and cleanly cut slices made with a sharp knife. Slide wax paper strips under the bottom of the cake before frosting it to keep the platter clean. After frosting the cake, pull out and discard the strips. Smooth frosting with a clean thin metal spatula wiped clean each time you use it. Let glazes cool until they thicken slightly so they do not run off the cake; they should be thick enough to cling to the sides of the cake. Pour the glaze over the top of a cake and gently tilt it to spread the glaze evenly. If the glaze needs to be spread, use a thin metal spatula dipped in hot water and dried. A warm spatula spreads sticky glazes smooth. Use the same spatula, without warming it, to spread the glaze over the sides of the cake.

I'm not a big fan of cakes that are overly decorated and garnished. As far as I'm concerned, a shiny glaze, an ivory buttercream, or a swirl of frosting is enough most of the time. When looking for an extra touch, I use big petal-like chocolate curls or glazed nuts, which I keep on hand in the freezer, fresh raspberries, or shiny strips of glazed citrus rind. And I try to match the garnish to the cake's flavor. Raspberries scattered on a Chocolate Hazelnut Truffle Cake might look nice, but hazelnuts will taste better.

# Fallen Leaves Chocolate Cake

**Serves 12**

About fifteen years ago while planning a trip to Italy, I read in a travel guide about a restaurant in Nice, France, that served "the best chocolate cake in the world." It was a chocolate cake covered with chocolate curls, which looked like fallen leaves. Now I'll go anywhere for a great chocolate cake, so my husband and I figured out that if we drove for twelve hours in one day on our way to Milan from western France, we could stop at the restaurant for lunch. I didn't take any chances. I wrote the restaurant to check that they would be open and requested that their Fallen Leaves Chocolate Cake be available for lunch. We started our drive before dawn and managed to arrive at the restaurant in time for lunch. As we walked into the empty restaurant, I assured myself that "March on the Riviera is always quiet." After introductions were made and assurances were given that they had the cake waiting for us, we quickly polished off a good lunch. Then came the cake. It was one of the worst cakes I've ever eaten. Not one to give up, I returned home, reread the description of the cake in the travel guide, and created my own version. This cake is definitely worth a detour.

**Rum Syrup**

4 tablespoons hot water
2 tablespoons sugar
1 tablespoon dark rum

**Chocolate Whipped Cream**

3 ounces semisweet chocolate, chopped
1½ cups cold heavy whipping cream
⅓ cup powdered sugar
3 tablespoons unsweetened Dutch process cocoa powder
½ teaspoon instant decaffeinated coffee granules
1 teaspoon vanilla extract

Two 9-inch Chocolate Butter Cake Layers (page 38), cooled or defrosted just until soft enough to split

**Chocolate Buttercream**

8 ounces semisweet chocolate, chopped
1 ounce unsweetened chocolate, chopped
¾ cup plus 2 tablespoons sugar
¼ cup hot water
1 tablespoon light corn syrup
5 large egg whites
½ teaspoon cream of tartar

## Good Advice

- Since the chocolate for the whipped cream and buttercream are melted without other ingredients, I melt them in a 175°F. oven.
- When preparing the chocolate whipped cream, whisk a cup of the whipped cream mixture thoroughly into the melted chocolate. This is a simple but important mixing technique that will prevent the warm chocolate from hardening when it is combined with the cold whipped cream and thus keep the chocolate whipped cream smooth.
- The base for the buttercream is an Italian meringue. For details on making the meringue and beating in the butter, see page 86.
- Placing the cake on a turntable makes it easy to turn the cake as you pipe the border on top of the cake.

## Doubling the Recipe

Use four cake layers. Double the ingredients for the whipped cream filling. Double the ingredients for the buttercream if using a heavy-duty mixer with a five-quart bowl and plan to beat the Italian meringue for about ten minutes rather than five minutes; otherwise prepare two batches of buttercream. Double the amount of chocolate curls.

### To Freeze

Chill the frosted cake, uncovered, in the freezer until the buttercream is firm, about 1 hour. Wrap tightly with plastic wrap. Gently press heavy aluminum foil around the cake. Label with date and contents. Freeze up to 1 month.

### To Serve

Defrost the wrapped cake overnight in the refrigerator. Unwrap the cake and allow to sit at room temperature about 1 hour before serving, until the buttercream softens. Leftover cake can be covered with plastic wrap and stored in the refrigerator up to 4 days.

**½ pound (2 sticks) unsalted butter, softened to about the same temperature as the cooled meringue, 72° to 78°F. if tested with a food thermometer**
**1 teaspoon vanilla extract**

**2 cups (2 to 3 ounces) semisweet or bittersweet Chocolate Curls and Curves (page 47)**

### Prepare the rum syrup

1. Put the water and sugar in a small saucepan and mix over low heat just until the sugar dissolves. Remove from the heat, stir in the rum, and cool the syrup. The syrup may be covered and stored in the refrigerator up to 1 week.

### Prepare the chocolate whipped cream

2. Preheat the oven to 175°F. Put the 3 ounces of semisweet chocolate in a small ovenproof container and melt in the oven, about 8 to 10 minutes. Remove the chocolate from the oven as soon as it is melted and stir until smooth. Put the cream, powdered sugar, cocoa powder, coffee, and vanilla in the large bowl of an electric mixer. Beat at medium speed to soft peaks. Scrape the melted chocolate into a clean large bowl. Whisk about 1 cup of the whipped cream mixture into the chocolate until smooth. Use a rubber spatula to fold the remaining whipped cream into the chocolate mixture.

### Fill the cake

3. Place 1 cake layer on a serving plate or cardboard cake circle. With a serrated knife, split the cake into 2 horizontal layers. Slide the removable bottom of a tart pan under the top layer and move it to the side. Slide strips of wax paper under the bottom layer to keep the cake plate clean. Use a pastry brush to lightly brush the bottom cake layer with rum syrup. Use a thin metal spatula to spread about 1 cup of the chocolate whipped cream over the bottom layer. Slide the bottom of the tart pan under the top layer and carefully place it on the cake. Brush with rum syrup and spread with 1 cup of chocolate whipped cream. Split the remaining chocolate layer and separate the layers using the bottom of the tart pan. Slide the bottom of the tart pan under the bottom layer and carefully place it on the cake. Brush with rum syrup and spread with the remaining chocolate whipped cream. Top with the remaining layer and brush the cake with the remaining syrup. Smooth the sides of the cake with the spatula. There will be 3 cream-filled layers topped with a cake layer brushed with rum syrup. Refrigerate the cake and prepare the chocolate buttercream.

### Prepare the chocolate buttercream

4. Preheat the oven to 175°F. Put the 8 ounces of semisweet chocolate and the unsweetened chocolate in an ovenproof container. Melt the chocolate in the oven, about 8 to 10 minutes. Remove the chocolate from the

*continued*

oven as soon as it is melted and stir it smooth. Put ¾ cup of sugar, the water, and corn syrup in a small saucepan. Cover and cook the syrup over low heat until all of the sugar is dissolved, stirring occasionally to help the sugar dissolve. Do not let the syrup boil until the sugar dissolves. Increase the heat to high and boil, without stirring, until the syrup reaches 240°F. measured with a candy thermometer. Wipe down the sides of the pan with a pastry brush dipped in hot water to dissolve any sugar crystals that form on the side of the pan.

5. Begin beating the egg whites when the sugar syrup starts to boil. Put the egg whites and cream of tartar in the clean large bowl of an electric mixer. With clean dry beaters, beat on low speed for 30 seconds, until the egg whites are foamy and the cream of tartar is dissolved. Increase the speed to medium-high and beat the egg whites to soft peaks. Add the remaining 2 tablespoons of sugar, 1 tablespoon at a time. As soon as the syrup reaches 240°F., with the mixer on low speed, slowly pour the hot syrup in a thin stream onto the softly beaten egg whites. If the syrup reaches 240°F. before the egg whites are ready, remove the syrup from the heat for a few seconds and finish beating the egg whites. Try to pour the syrup in the space between the beaters and the sides of the bowl to prevent as much sugar syrup as possible from splashing onto the sides of the bowl and the beater. Continue beating the meringue at medium-low speed for 5 minutes. The outside of the bowl will be lukewarm and the meringue will be stiff and have a temperature of 72°F. to 78°F. if measured with a food thermometer.

6. Beat in the softened butter, 2 tablespoons at a time. Stop the mixer and scrape the bowl once, but do not scrape any sugar syrup that may have splashed onto the side of the bowl and hardened. The meringue will deflate slightly when the butter is added. Add the slightly cooled melted chocolate and the vanilla and mix on low speed until incorporated. If the buttercream seems too soft to spread, refrigerate for about 20 minutes to firm slightly then whisk for a few seconds until smooth. The buttercream can be covered and refrigerated up to 1 week in a tightly covered plastic container. If the buttercream has been chilled, bring it back to room temperature and whisk until smooth and spreadable.

## Frost the cake

7. Place the cake on a turntable. Spoon 1 cup of the buttercream into a large pastry bag fitted with a large open star tip and set aside. Cover the top and sides of the chilled cake with the remaining buttercream (about 3 cups). Pipe a border of buttercream swirls around the top of the cake, turning the turntable as necessary.

8. To pipe swirls, hold the pastry tip a ½ inch above and at a 45° angle to the cake. Pipe the frosting in a tight zigzag motion around the edge of the cake. Spoon the chocolate curls on the top of the cake inside the buttercream border. Try not to touch the curls since the heat of your hand can melt them. Remove the wax paper strips.

# Deep Dark Chocolate Cake

**Serves 12**

This cake reminds me of the cakes served with ice cream at birthday parties in my childhood. With chocolate cake layers from the freezer and an easy no-cook frosting, the cake is fast to put together.

### Good Advice

- For a creamy frosting, use soft butter. Press your finger against the butter; it should feel like room-temperature peanut butter.
- Turn the cake on a turntable as you pipe the border of shells.

### Doubling the Recipe

Use four cake layers. Mix the frosting in two batches, since a smaller quantity is easier to beat to a creamy consistency.

### To Freeze

Chill the cake in the freezer for 1 hour until the frosting is firm. Wrap tightly with plastic wrap. Gently press heavy aluminum foil around the cake. Label with date and contents. Freeze up to 1 month.

### To Serve

Defrost the wrapped cake overnight in the refrigerator. Unwrap the cake and let it sit at room temperature 30 minutes before serving so the frosting can soften. Serve with ice cream. Leftover cake can be covered with plastic wrap and stored in the refrigerator up to 4 days.

Chocolate Frosting

**4 ounces unsweetened chocolate, in 1-ounce pieces**
**½ pound (2 sticks) soft unsalted butter**
**3 cups powdered sugar, sifted**
**2 teaspoons fresh lemon juice**
**2 teaspoons vanilla extract**
**¼ cup whipping cream, at room temperature**

**Two 9-inch Chocolate Butter Cake Layers (page 38), cooled or defrosted just until soft enough to split**

**Vanilla ice cream, for serving with the cake**

## Prepare the chocolate frosting

1. Preheat the oven to 175°F. Put the chocolate in a small heatproof container. Melt the chocolate in the oven, about 8 to 10 minutes. Remove the chocolate from the oven as soon as it is melted and stir it smooth. Set the chocolate aside to cool slightly. Put the butter in a large mixing bowl and mix with an electric mixer on low speed just to smooth it. Add the powdered sugar and beat until the mixture is smooth, about 1 minute. Mix in the chocolate, lemon juice, and vanilla. Stop the mixer and scrape the sides of the bowl. Add the whipping cream and beat on medium-low speed until the frosting becomes fluffy and smooth, and lightens in color, about 2 minutes.

## Frost the cake

2. Place 1 cake layer on a cardboard circle or cake plate. Place the cake on a turntable. Place wax paper strips under the bottom of the cake. Spoon 1 cup of the frosting into a large pastry bag fitted with a large open or closed star tip and set aside. (I use a 2-inch-long Ateco # 5 closed star tip.) Spread about 1¼ cups frosting over the top of the cake layer. Top with the second layer. Spread a thin layer of frosting over the top and sides of the cake so that any crumbs will adhere. Spread the remaining frosting over the top and sides of the cake. Use the reserved frosting to pipe a border of shells around the top edge of the cake, turning the turntable as necessary. To form the shells, hold the pastry tip a ½ inch above and at a 60° angle to the cake. Pipe a mound of frosting about ½ inch in diameter, pull the tip forward ¼ inch while reducing the pressure on and lowering the angle of the pastry bag slightly to form a tail on the shell. Stop the pressure, lift the bag, and pipe a second mound of frosting over the edge of the tail to form another shell and tail. Repeat until you have formed a shell border around the top of the cake. Carefully slide out the wax paper strips.

# Brooklyn's Famous Chocolate Blackout Cake

Serves 12

When I was a girl, our family spent every summer visiting my grandfather in Brooklyn. People used to laugh at the idea of spending summer vacation in Brooklyn, but we had a great time. It was a lot cooler than where we lived in Florida, and we enjoyed the big city treats—museums, department stores, Broadway shows, subway rides (they were a treat then), restaurants, delicatessens, and our daily trip to Ebinger's bakery. Parker House rolls, Macaroon Tarts (page 64), crumb cakes, blueberry crumb pies, lemon meringue tarts—there was something different for each day of the week—but for extra-special dinners we always bought Blackout Cake. Blackout Cake was all chocolate: crumbly and moist chocolate cake; creamy chocolate filling; thick chocolate glaze; and the entire cake covered with chocolate cake crumbs.

After my grandfather died, we began spending summers on Long Island where there was no Ebinger's, and several summers later the unheard-of happened—Ebinger's bakery chain had financial problems and closed. I assumed I had eaten my last blackout cake. Then several years ago the *New York Times* ran a nostalgic article about Ebinger's and at the end of the article they included a recipe for Blackout Cake. It took me about five minutes to start baking the cake, and I wasn't disappointed. It was the same moist, crumbly chocolate cake, the same soft chocolate pudding–type filling, and the same dark fudge frosting. I revised several of the recipe instructions and made slight changes in the ingredients and directions printed in the *New York Times* article.

### Good Advice

- The chocolate filling is like a light chocolate pudding made with water instead of milk. It must be chilled well, or it will run right off the cake. The easiest way to be sure the filling is thick enough is to prepare it a day ahead and chill it overnight.
- The chocolate frosting combines lukewarm water with melted chocolate. It is important for the chocolate mixture and the water to be at a similar temperature. Cold water would harden the chocolate and hot water could overheat it and cause it to become grainy. Touch the chocolate with a finger, then the water with another finger, and adjust the water temperature until it feels the same as the chocolate temperature. It is not necessary to use a thermometer, but if you do, the water and chocolate temperatures should read 88°F. to 90°F.

### Doubling the Recipe

Prepare only two cake layers at a time. Double the filling and frosting ingredients.

#### Chocolate Cake

**2 cups cake flour**
**1 teaspoon baking powder**
**1 teaspoon baking soda**
**1 teaspoon salt**
**½ cup unsweetened Dutch process cocoa powder**
**2 tablespoons water**
**2 ounces unsweetened chocolate, chopped**
**¾ cup whole milk**
**½ pound (2 sticks) soft unsalted butter**
**2 cups sugar**
**4 large eggs, separated**
**2 teaspoons vanilla extract**

### To Freeze and Defrost the Cake Layers

Invert the cooled cake layers onto plastic wrap and remove the paper liner. Wrap the layers tightly with the plastic wrap then heavy aluminum foil. Label with date and contents. Freeze up to 2 months. After the cake layers are frozen, they may be stacked in the freezer. Defrost the wrapped cake at room temperature. Fill and frost the layers as soon as they are thawed enough to cut. Cold layers are easier to handle.

### To Freeze

Freeze the cake, uncovered, for about 1 hour, until the frosting is firm. Wrap tightly with plastic wrap and heavy aluminum foil. Label with date and contents. Freeze up to 1 month.

### To Serve

Refrigerate the wrapped cake 8 hours or overnight. Unwrap the cake and bring to room temperature before serving, about 45 minutes. Cut into wedges and serve. Leftover cake can be covered with plastic wrap and stored in the refrigerator up to 3 days.

Chocolate Filling

**1 tablespoon plus 2 teaspoons unsweetened Dutch process cocoa powder**
**1½ cups hot water**
**¾ cup sugar**
**1 ounce semisweet chocolate, chopped**
**2 tablespoons plus 1 teaspoon cornstarch**
**2 tablespoons cold water**
**½ teaspoon salt**
**2 tablespoons unsalted butter, cut into 2 pieces**
**1 teaspoon vanilla extract**

Chocolate Fudge Frosting

**12 ounces semisweet chocolate, chopped**
**6 ounces (1½ sticks) unsalted butter, softened, cut in 12 pieces**
**½ cup lukewarm water, at the same temperature as melted chocolate mixture, 88°F. to 90°F. if tested with a food thermometer**
**1 tablespoon light corn syrup**
**1 tablespoon vanilla extract**

1. Position an oven rack in the center of the oven. Preheat the oven to 350°F. Butter the bottom and sides of two 9-inch diameter baking pans 1¾ to 2 inches deep. Line the bottom of each pan with parchment or wax paper and butter the paper.

## Prepare the cake

2. Sift the flour, baking powder, baking soda, and salt together and set aside. Put the cocoa powder, water, unsweetened chocolate, and milk in a medium saucepan and cook over low heat, stirring constantly, until the chocolate melts. Remove the saucepan from the heat to cool.

3. Put the butter in the large bowl of an electric mixer and mix on low speed until smooth, about 15 seconds. Add the sugar and beat on medium speed for 2 minutes. Stop the mixer and scrape the sides of the bowl during the beating. Add the egg yolks, two at a time, beating well after each addition. Stop the mixer and scrape the sides of the bowl again during this beating. Add the vanilla and beat for 2 more minutes at medium speed. With the mixer on low speed, add the cooled chocolate mixture, mixing just until the chocolate is combined thoroughly. Slowly add the flour mixture, mixing just until the flour is incorporated and the mixture looks smooth. Stop the mixer and scrape the bowl again during this beating. Set the mixture aside. Put the egg whites in a large clean bowl of an electric mixer and with clean dry beaters beat the egg whites to soft peaks. Use a rubber spatula to fold about ¼ of the beaten egg whites into the chocolate batter. Fold the remaining egg whites into the chocolate batter.

4. Pour the batter into the prepared baking pans. Smooth the top of the batter. Bake 30 to 35 minutes. To test for doneness, gently press your fingers on the middle of the cake. It should feel firm. If the cake feels firm, insert a toothpick in the center of the cake. When the toothpick comes out clean, the

*continued*

cake is done. Cool the cake layers in the baking pans on a wire cooling rack. Use a small, sharp knife to loosen the sides of the cakes from the pan.

## Cook the chocolate filling

5. Put the cocoa, hot water, sugar, and chocolate in a medium saucepan and cook over low heat, stirring often, until the chocolate dissolves. Dissolve the cornstarch in the cold water, stirring to make a smooth paste. Add the cornstarch mixture and the salt to the saucepan. Bring to a boil over medium-high heat and boil gently for 1 minute, stirring constantly. Stir the mixture often where the sides and the bottom of the pan meet. Remove the pan from the heat and add the butter and vanilla, stirring until the butter melts. Pour the mixture into a bowl and press plastic wrap onto the surface of the chocolate filling to prevent a skin from forming. Chill at least 5 hours or overnight. The filling will thicken to the consistency of pastry cream or soft pudding.

## Mix the frosting

6. Put the semisweet chocolate in a heatproof container and place it over, but not touching, a saucepan of barely simmering water. Stir the chocolate until it is melted and smooth. Remove the chocolate from over the water, add the butter pieces, and stir until the butter is melted. If necessary, replace the container over hot water to melt the butter completely. Measure out the lukewarm water. Check with your fingertips that the water temperature feels similar to the chocolate temperature. Add the lukewarm water to the chocolate mixture all at once and gently whisk the mixture until the frosting is smooth. Stir in the corn syrup and vanilla. Cool the frosting at room temperature for about 30 minutes, until it thickens slightly.

## Fill and frost the cake

7. Defrost the cake layers if they have been frozen. Use a serrated knife to split each layer into 2 layers. You will have 4 layers. To separate the layers slide the removable bottom of a tart pan under each layer and move it to the side. Place a cake layer on a cardboard cake circle or serving plate. Slide wax paper strips under the layer to protect the plate. Cover the layer with half of the cold chocolate filling, leaving a ¼-inch plain edge as the filling may run slightly. Slide the bottom of the tart pan under another layer and carefully place it on the bottom layer. Cover the layer with the remaining filling. Slide the bottom of the tart pan under a layer, using a layer from the top half of the cake, and carefully place it on the cake. There will be 2 filled layers topped with a plain layer and 1 remaining layer set aside. If any filling has run over onto the sides of the cake, spread it out onto the sides of the cake with a thin metal spatula. Cover the top and sides of the cake with a thin layer of the chocolate fudge frosting and refrigerate the cake for 15 minutes to firm the cake and filling. Spread the remaining frosting over the top and sides of the cake. Use your fingers to crumble the remaining cake layer into small crumbs. Sprinkle the cake crumbs over the top and press them onto the sides of the cake. Use all of the crumbs to make a thick crumb coating. Remove the wax paper strips.

# Chocolate-Caramel Fudge Cake

**Serves 12**

One afternoon as I was eating a chocolate-covered caramel, I thought, "What a good combination this would be for a cake—a rather sinful cake with lots of dark chocolate and gooey caramel." Using a long narrow loaf pan, I baked a chocolate cake with a dense, fine-grained texture that would keep its cake identity when combined with several layers of chocolate and caramel. I split the cake into three layers, filled each layer with caramel sauce and whipped chocolate ganache, and covered the whole cake with a smooth chocolate ganache glaze. The finished cake looks like a giant chocolate-covered caramel bar, but it is much better than any candy bar I ever tasted.

### Cake

1 cup unbleached all-purpose flour
1 teaspoon baking powder
9 ounces semisweet chocolate, chopped
6 ounces (1½ sticks) unsalted butter
5 large eggs separated
½ cup (packed) light brown sugar
1 teaspoon vanilla extract
¼ teaspoon cream of tartar
½ cup granulated sugar

### Caramel Sauce

1 cup whipping cream
1½ cups granulated sugar

### Ganache Filling and Glaze

3 ounces (¾ stick) unsalted butter
1¼ cups whipping cream
12 ounces bittersweet chocolate, chopped, Callebaut, Lindt, or Guittard preferred
1 teaspoon vanilla extract

1. Position a rack in the center of the oven. Preheat the oven to 350°F. Butter the bottom and sides of a long, narrow loaf pan, about 12¾ × 4¼ × 2½-inches (8-cup capacity). Line the bottom of the pan with parchment or wax paper and butter the paper.

## Prepare the cake

2. Sift the flour and baking powder together and set aside. Melt the chocolate and butter in a large heatproof container set over, but not touching, a saucepan of simmering water, stirring until the chocolate and butter melt

*continued*

## Good Advice

• Caramelizing sugar is easy. Just watch it carefully so that it doesn't burn, and use a wooden spoon for any stirring since a metal spoon could become hot and a plastic one could melt. Be careful also that the hot caramel doesn't splash on you.
• The caramel sauce must be chilled until it is firm, so that it doesn't drip off the cake.
• Ganache is prepared from cream, butter, and chocolate. Here some of the ganache is whisked for a creamy filling, and the remaining ganache is spread over the cake for a fudge glaze. Use a bittersweet chocolate such as Callebaut, Lindt, or Guittard. Chill the ganache for the filling only until it thickens, is cold to the touch throughout, and the edges are just beginning to firm. Whip the cold ganache by hand with a whisk.

## Doubling the Recipe

Double the ingredients. Bake the cake in two pans.

### To Freeze and Defrost the Cake

Invert the cooled cake onto plastic wrap. Wrap the cake tightly with plastic wrap then heavy aluminum foil. Label with date and contents. Freeze up to 2 months. Defrost the wrapped cake at room temperature. Fill and glaze the cake as soon as it is thawed enough to cut. The cold cake is easier to handle.

### To Freeze

Freeze the cake, uncovered, for about 1 hour, until the glaze is firm. Wrap tightly with plastic wrap then heavy aluminum foil. Label with date and contents. Freeze up to 1 month.

### To Serve

Refrigerate the wrapped cake 8 hours or overnight. Unwrap the cake and bring it to room temperature before serving, about 45 minutes. Cut into approximately 1-inch slices and serve. Leftover cake can be covered with plastic wrap and stored in the refrigerator up to 5 days.

and the mixture is smooth. Remove the mixture from over the water and set aside.

3. Put the egg yolks in the large bowl of an electric mixer and beat on medium speed for 15 seconds. Add the brown sugar and beat for 1 minute, until the mixture is smooth and thick. Add the melted chocolate mixture and vanilla and mix on low speed just until the chocolate is incorporated. Add the flour mixture and mix just until the flour is incorporated into the batter. Put the egg whites and cream of tartar in the clean large bowl of an electric mixer and with clean dry beaters, beat on low speed until the egg whites are foamy and the cream of tartar is dissolved. Increase the speed to medium-high and beat the egg whites until soft peaks form. Slowly add the granulated sugar, 1 tablespoon every 30 seconds. Use a rubber spatula to fold a third of the egg white mixture into the chocolate mixture. Fold in the remaining egg white mixture.

4. Pour the batter into the prepared pan. Smooth the top of the batter. The batter will come to within ½ inch of the top of the pan. Bake just until a toothpick inserted in the center comes out clean, about 45 minutes. Cool the cake in the pan on a wire cooling rack. Use a small sharp knife to loosen the sides of the cake from the pan. Turn the cake out onto a long platter. Peel the paper liner from the bottom of the cake and discard it. Leave the cake bottom side up. The cake can be frozen before it is filled and frosted.

## Prepare the caramel sauce

5. Heat the cream in a small saucepan and keep it hot while you cook the sugar, about 150°F. if measured with an instant-read food thermometer. Do not boil the cream. Put the sugar in a medium saucepan with a heavy bottom and cook over low heat until the sugar begins to melt. Increase the heat to medium-high and cook until the sugar melts, caramelizes, and turns a dark golden color. Watch the sugar carefully and stir it with a wooden spoon occasionally to ensure the sugar cooks evenly. Remove the caramel from the heat. Slowly and carefully add the hot cream to the hot sugar. The mixture will bubble up, so be careful. Return the saucepan to medium heat and cook the mixture, stirring with the wooden spoon, until the caramel is completely dissolved and the sauce is smooth. Cover and refrigerate the caramel sauce for about 2 hours, until it is cool and firm. The caramel sauce should be soft enough to spread but thick enough to form a firm layer on the cake. If the sauce becomes too cold to spread, warm it gently in a heatproof bowl placed over hot water just until the sauce becomes spreadable.

## Prepare the ganache

6. Heat the butter and cream in a medium saucepan until the butter melts and the mixture is hot, about 150°F. on a food thermometer. Remove the saucepan from the heat and add the chopped chocolate. Let the chocolate melt in the cream for 1 minute. Add the vanilla and stir until the sauce is smooth and all of the chocolate is melted. Remove 1¼ cups of the ganache for the glaze and set it aside at room temperature. Pour the remaining

ganache into a large mixing bowl and press plastic wrap onto the surface. Refrigerate just until the chocolate is cold to the touch and is beginning to harden around the edges, about 1 hour. Stir the mixture occasionally to ensure it chills throughout.

## Assemble the cake

7. Place wax paper strips under the cake to protect the serving platter. Split the loaf cake into 3 layers, about 1 inch thick. Use a long wide spatula to separate the layers and slide each of the 2 top layers onto the removable bottom of a tart pan. Spread ½ cup of the caramel sauce over each of the 3 layers. Put the cold ganache in a large bowl and whisk until the color lightens somewhat to a medium chocolate color and the ganache thickens slightly, about 30 seconds. Immediately spread half of the whipped ganache over the bottom layer of caramel-covered cake. Use the long wide spatula to slide a second cake layer on the cake and spread the remaining whipped ganache over the layer. Use the spatula to slide the remaining cake layer on top of the cake. Smooth the sides of the cake with a metal spatula. Use a serrated knife to trim any uneven edges from the cake. Freeze the uncovered cake for 30 minutes to firm the filling. Spread the reserved ganache glaze over the top and sides of the cake. Remove and discard the wax paper strips.

# Chocolate Hazelnut Truffle Cake

**Serves 12**

One of my fondest childhood memories is of buying small squares of striped chocolate truffles at the local Barton's candy store. It wasn't until years later that I discovered the flavor was a combination of chocolate and hazelnuts. Those striped chocolate truffles inspired this cake. A chocolate layer is split in three, filled with a whipped chocolate and hazelnut ganache cream, and covered with a shiny, dark chocolate glaze. Since the layers are thin, the cake has equal proportions of filling and cake and a creamy truffle-like consistency. A border of hazelnuts, half-dipped in the chocolate glaze, makes an easy but sophisticated garnish.

### Dark Rum Syrup

4 tablespoons water
2 tablespoons sugar
2 tablespoons dark rum

### Chocolate Glaze

4 tablespoons (½ stick) unsalted butter
½ cup whipping cream
1 tablespoon light corn syrup
8 ounces semisweet chocolate, chopped

12 whole toasted peeled hazelnuts for garnish (page 6)

### Chocolate Hazelnut Ganache

6 tablespoons (¾ stick) unsalted butter, room temperature
1¼ cups whipping cream
12 ounces semisweet chocolate, chopped
1 teaspoon vanilla extract
½ cup ground toasted hazelnuts (page 6)
One 10-inch Chocolate Butter Cake Layer (page 38), cooled or defrosted just until soft enough to split

## Prepare the syrup

1. Put the water and sugar in a small saucepan and mix over low heat just until the sugar dissolves. Remove from the heat, stir in the rum, and cool the syrup. The syrup may be covered and stored in the refrigerator up to 1 week.

## Prepare the chocolate glaze

2. Heat the butter, cream, and corn syrup in a medium saucepan until the mixture is hot, about 150°F. on a food thermometer. Remove from the heat, add the chocolate, and gently stir until the chocolate melts. Dip half of each whole toasted hazelnut in the warm glaze. Put the nuts on a piece of wax paper, glazed side up, to let the chocolate firm. Set the remaining glaze

## Good Advice

• Preparing ganache is simple, but note a few important points: The chilled ganache is ready to be whipped when it is cold and thickened but not hard. Chill it only until the edges begin to harden and the mixture feels cold to the touch. Beating time for ganache is short, just until the color lightens from dark brown to medium brown and it thickens slightly. There is also a flavor change from fudge-like to cream-like. It is this change that gives ganache its wonderful taste. If the ganache is whipped too long, it will be grainy. This seldom happen, but if it does, melt the ganache over low heat, chill it, and whip it again. Use the ganache immediately after whipping, as it firms up quickly.
• The glaze can be prepared up to a week ahead and refrigerated. Warm the glaze over low heat just to a spreading consistency.

## Doubling the Recipe

Use two ten-inch cake layers and double the syrup, ganache, and glaze ingredients.

## To Freeze

Freeze the cake, uncovered, to firm the chocolate glaze and filling, about 1 hour. Wrap tightly with plastic wrap. Gently press heavy aluminum foil around the cake. Label with date and contents. Freeze up to 1 month.

### To Serve

Defrost the wrapped cake overnight in the refrigerator. Unwrap and let the cake sit at room temperature about 1 hour before serving. It is important that the cake be served at room temperature; at that point the full flavor of the chocolate comes out and the glaze and filling become soft and creamy. Leftover cake can be covered with plastic wrap and refrigerated up to 4 days.

aside to cool and thicken for about 20 minutes. The glaze should be pourable but thick enough to spread on the sides of the cake without dripping off.

### Prepare the ganache

3. Heat the butter and cream in a medium saucepan just until the mixture is hot, about 150°F. on a food thermometer. Remove the saucepan from the heat and stir in the chocolate and vanilla. Stir the mixture until it is smooth and the chocolate is melted. Put the ganache in a medium bowl and press plastic wrap onto the surface. Refrigerate until the ganache is cold to the touch, thick, and just begins to harden around the edges, about 45 minutes. Stir once to ensure the mixture chills throughout. The mixture should not be hard. Whisk the chilled mixture for about 30 seconds until the chocolate lightens slightly in color from dark to medium brown. Mix in the ground hazelnuts. Use immediately.

### Assemble the cake

4. With a serrated knife, cut the cake layer into 3 horizontal layers. To remove the 2 top layers, slide the removable bottom of a tart pan under each layer and move it to the side. Place the bottom of the cake layer on a serving plate or cardboard cake circle. Slide wax paper strips under the cake to protect the plate. Use a pastry brush to lightly brush the cake layer with syrup. Spread half of the ganache on the layer. Slide the bottom of the tart pan under the middle layer and carefully place it on the cake. Brush with syrup, and spread with the remaining ganache. If the ganache becomes too firm to spread easily, dip a metal spatula in hot water, dry it, and spread the ganache on the cake with the warm spatula. Cover with the third cake layer and brush with the remaining syrup. Pour about three quarters of the cooled glaze over the top of the cake and tilt the cake to spread the glaze evenly. Use a metal spatula to smooth any glaze that has dripped onto the sides of the cake, then use the spatula to spread the remaining glaze on the sides of the cake. Carefully remove and discard the wax paper strips. Let the cake sit about 20 minutes for the glaze to firm, then place a border of the chocolate-dipped hazelnuts around the top of the cake.

# Mocha Buttercrunch Cookie/Cake

Serves 10

This crisp and creamy cookie/cake is like a triple-decker sandwich of butter pecan pastry with a mocha cream filling. It's covered with coffee whipped cream, and then coated with crushed pieces of the pastry. Yes, this cake tastes as good as it sounds. I cut the pastry layers into three different size circles for an attractive dome shape. This recipe may look long, but the techniques are all simple and the dessert assembles quickly.

### Good Advice

- The butter pecan pastry is mixed like a pie crust. I use an electric mixer to combine the ingredients—a portable mixer works fine.
- Because of the large amount of butter and the chopped nuts, this dough would be difficult to roll so it is simply pressed onto the cookie sheet. Use a flat cookie sheet or baking sheet as opposed to one with sides so that the pastry circles will be easy to remove. Or use a cookie sheet or jelly-roll pan turned upside-down. For the circles used as guides for cutting the pastry, I use the bottoms of three springform pans; you could also cut out parchment paper or cardboard circles.
- The butter for the mocha filling must be very soft. I soften the butter in a sunny window for about an hour.
- The coffee whipped cream topping has a large amount of powdered sugar, which contains cornstarch; this helps stabilize the whipped cream during freezing.

### Doubling the Recipe

Double all the ingredients. Use two cookie sheets for the pastry.

**Butter Pecan Layers**

**1½ cups unbleached all-purpose flour**
**½ cup cake flour**
**¼ teaspoon salt**
**½ cup (packed) light brown sugar**
**½ pound (2 sticks) cold unsalted butter, cut into 16 pieces**
**1 cup finely chopped pecans**
**1 teaspoon vanilla extract**
**2 teaspoons cold water**

**Mocha Cream Filling**

**3 ounces unsweetened chocolate, chopped**
**½ cup heavy whipping cream**
**6 ounces (1½ sticks) unsalted butter, very soft**
**1 cup (packed) light brown sugar**
**1 teaspoon instant decaffeinated coffee granules**
**1 teaspoon vanilla extract**

**Coffee Whipped Cream Topping**

**1 cup cold heavy whipping cream**
**1 tablespoon instant decaffeinated coffee granules**
**¼ cup powdered sugar**
**1 teaspoon vanilla extract**

1. Position a rack in the middle of the oven. Preheat the oven to 375°F. Butter an open-ended 17 × 14-inch cookie sheet. Have ready 3 circles to use as guides, with diameters of 8 inches, 7 inches, and 6 inches.

## Prepare the butter pecan layers

2. Place the all-purpose flour, cake flour, salt, and brown sugar in the large bowl of an electric mixer and mix them together on low speed. Add the cold butter pieces and mix until the butter pieces are the size of peas. You will still see loose flour. Mix in the pecans. Add the vanilla and cold water and mix just until the dough holds together. The pastry will look like a cookie dough.

3. Press the pastry in an even layer onto the prepared cookie sheet, leaving a ½-inch uncovered border around the cookie sheet. The pastry will

### To Freeze

Freeze the cake, uncovered, until firm, about 2 hours. Wrap tightly in plastic wrap then heavy aluminum foil. Label with date and contents. Freeze up to 2 months.

### To Serve

Place the wrapped frozen cake in the refrigerator 2 to 2½ hours before serving. The cake should be soft frozen, not hard frozen, when served. Use a large sharp knife to cut into slices and serve. Leftover cake can be wrapped again in plastic wrap and heavy aluminum foil and returned to the freezer, but it is best to serve the cake within 2 months of the initial freezing.

be about ¼ inch thick. Bake for 15 minutes, reversing the baking sheet front to back to ensure the pastry browns evenly. The baked pastry should look golden brown. Remove the pastry from the oven, and immediately place the 3 prepared circles on the warm pastry. Use a small sharp knife to cut 3 pastry circles. Leave the pastry on the cookie sheet to cool.

### Prepare the mocha cream filling

4. Put the unsweetened chocolate and cream in a heatproof container and place it over, but not touching, barely simmering water. Stir the chocolate and cream together until the chocolate is melted. Remove from over the water. Let cool to room temperature, 65° to 75°F. Put the butter in the large bowl of an electric mixer and beat at medium speed until smooth. Mix in the brown sugar, coffee, and vanilla and beat until the mixture is smooth and fluffy, about 2 minutes. Add the cooled chocolate mixture and beat another minute. Stop the mixer and scrape the sides of the bowl to incorporate all of the chocolate. If the chocolate cream is too soft to spread easily, refrigerate it 10 to 15 minutes.

### Fill the pastry

5. Cut away the scraps of butter pecan pastry, leaving the 3 circles on the pastry sheet. Put the pastry scraps between 2 sheets of wax paper and use a rolling pin to crush the pastry into crumbs. Set the crumbs aside. Slide the removable bottom of a tart pan under the 8-inch pastry layer and move it to a serving plate or foil-covered cardboard cake circle. Spread the pastry with half of the mocha cream. Top with the 7-inch pastry layer. Reserve about a quarter of the remaining mocha cream and spread the rest of the cream over the pastry. Top with the 6-inch pastry circle. Spread the reserved cream around the sides of the cake. Freeze the cake 30 minutes to firm the chocolate filling.

### Prepare the coffee whipped cream topping

6. Place the cream, coffee, powdered sugar, and vanilla in the large bowl of an electric mixer. Beat at medium speed to firm peaks. Spread the topping over the chilled cake. Spread a thicker layer of cream over the top of the cake and a thinner layer over the sides to form a dome shape. Freeze the cake about 30 minutes to firm the topping. Cover the cake with the reserved pastry crumbs.

## Good Advice

The Fudge Bar brownie should be cold, so that it is easy to handle. Freeze a pan of Fudge Bars without cutting them into pieces.

## Doubling the Recipe

For each Chocolate Thunder, use two large pans of Fudge Bars, two cups Chocolate Truffle Sauce, and two ounces white chocolate.

## To Freeze

Wrap the chilled cake tightly in plastic wrap. Gently press heavy aluminum foil around the cake. Label with date and contents. Freeze up to 3 months.

## To Serve

Defrost the covered cake in the refrigerator 6 hours or overnight. Let the cake sit at room temperature 15 minutes before serving. Use a large sharp knife to cut the cake into wedges. For easier cutting, dip the knife in hot water and wipe it clean after cutting each slice. Leftover cake can be covered with plastic wrap and stored in the refrigerator up to 4 days.

# Chocolate Thunder

Serves 8 to 10

This cake is like a clap of chocolate thunder. The mountain-shaped cake consists of Fudge Bar pieces layered with a thick chocolate sauce. Melted white chocolate is drizzled over the cake for a professional finish. Everyone is always impressed by the look of this cake, but it is actually fast and easy to assemble.

**1 ounce white chocolate, chopped, Callebaut preferred**
**One 13 × 9 × 2-inch Fudge Bar (page 76), defrosted but still cold, in 1 piece**
**1 cup Chocolate Truffle Sauce (page 45), warmed to spreading consistency**

1. Preheat the oven to 175°F. Place the white chocolate in a small nonreactive ovenproof container and place it in the oven to melt, 2 to 3 minutes. Remove the white chocolate from the oven as soon as it is melted and stir until smooth.

2. Place the entire Fudge Bar on a cutting surface. Cut out an 8-inch circle from the Fudge Bar and transfer the circle to a serving plate or cardboard cake circle. Cut a 3-inch circle and a 1½-inch circle from the remaining piece of Fudge Bar and set aside. Spread ¼ cup of the truffle sauce over the top of the 8-inch circle. Leaving about a ¾-inch edge, fill in a circle with the leftover Fudge Bar pieces. The edges of the circle will not be even. Spread 2 tablespoons truffle sauce over the top of the circle. Leaving about a 1-inch edge and using more leftover Fudge Bar pieces, top with another circle of Fudge Bar pieces. Spread with about 2 tablespoons of the truffle sauce. Place the 3-inch Fudge Bar circle on top and spread with 2 tablespoons of the truffle sauce. Place the 1½-inch Fudge Bar circle on top. There will be 4 brownie layers on top of the big brownie circle. Spoon or spread the remaining truffle sauce over the entire cake. Turn the cake to check the shape and press thin pieces of Fudge Bars on the cake wherever it looks lopsided. The cake should look lumpy. Chill the cake, uncovered, just until the truffle sauce is firm, about 15 minutes.

3. Dip a fork into the melted white chocolate and wave it over the cake to form thin lines of white chocolate. Working quickly, wave the fork in a random pattern, crisscrossing back and forth over the cake. Keep dipping the fork and sprinkling the white chocolate until all of the white chocolate is used. Try to sprinkle the chocolate quickly to create thin lines. Chill the cake, uncovered, just until the white chocolate is firm, about 30 minutes.

# White Lightning

Serves 10

When does lightning follow thunder? Only here. As soon as I tasted Chocolate Thunder, I knew I had to have White Lightning, a white chocolate variation. White Chocolate Chip Brownies and a white chocolate truffle glaze form a seven-inch-high mountain of a cake, which is drizzled with melted dark chocolate for a quick, fancy finish.

White Chocolate Truffle Glaze

**¾ cup heavy cream**
**2 tablespoons unsalted butter, softened**
**1 tablespoon light corn syrup**
**12 ounces white chocolate, cut into ½-inch pieces, Callebaut preferred**
**1 teaspoon vanilla extract**

**1 ounce semisweet chocolate**
**One 15 × 10 × 2-inch White Chocolate Chip Brownie (page 77), defrosted but still cold, in 1 piece**

## Prepare the white chocolate truffle glaze

1. Put the cream, butter, and corn syrup in a small saucepan and heat until the cream is hot and the butter is melted. The hot cream mixture will form tiny bubbles and measure about 175°F. on a food thermometer. Do not let the mixture boil. Remove from the heat and add the white chocolate. Gently stir the mixture until the white chocolate is melted and the glaze is smooth. Return the mixture to low heat if necessary to melt the chocolate completely. Stir in the vanilla. Chill the glaze until it is firm enough to spread, stirring occasionally, about 45 minutes. Or, chill the glaze overnight and warm it over hot water just until it is soft enough to spread.

## Melt the semisweet chocolate

2. Preheat the oven to 175°F. Place the semisweet chocolate in a small ovenproof container. Melt the chocolate in the oven, about 5 minutes. Remove the chocolate from the oven as soon as it is melted and stir it smooth.

## Assemble the Cake

3. Place the entire White Chocolate Chip Brownie on a cutting surface. Cut out an 8-inch circle and transfer it to a serving plate or cardboard cake circle. Cut a 3-inch circle and a 1½-inch circle from the remaining piece of brownie and set aside. Spread ¾ cup of white chocolate glaze over the top and sides of the 8-inch circle. Leaving approximately a 1-inch edge, fill in the remainder of the circle with a layer of brownie pieces. The edge of the circle will not be even. Spread with 3 tablespoons of glaze. Leaving about a 1-inch edge add a smaller circle of brownie pieces. Spread with 2 table-

*continued*

### Good Advice

- White Chocolate Chip Brownies are thicker than Fudge Bars, so the finished White Lightning will be higher than Chocolate Thunder.
- Gently press the brownie layers together to eliminate any air spaces.
- You will have leftover brownies to sample.
- Before the melted dark chocolate is sprinkled over the cake, it looks rather plain. The dark chocolate garnish changes the cake from plain to stunning.

### Doubling the Recipe

Double all ingredients.

### To Freeze

Wrap the chilled cake tightly in plastic wrap. Gently press heavy aluminum foil around the cake. Label with date and contents. Freeze up to 3 months.

### To Serve

Defrost the wrapped cake in the refrigerator 6 hours or overnight. Let the cake sit at room temperature 15 minutes before serving. Use a large sharp knife to cut the cake into wedges. For easier cutting, dip the knife in hot water and wipe it clean after cutting each slice. Leftover cake can be covered with plastic wrap and stored in the refrigerator up to 4 days.

spoons of glaze. Add the 3-inch brownie circle and spread with 2 tablespoons of glaze. Add the 1½-inch brownie circle. There will be 4 brownie layers on top of the brownie circle. Spoon or spread the remaining glaze over the entire cake. It will look lumpy, and the glaze will not cover the cake completely. Turn the cake to check the shape and press thin pieces of white chocolate brownie on the cake wherever it looks lopsided. Chill the cake, uncovered, just until the glaze is firm.

4. Dip a fork in the melted chocolate and sprinkle thin lines of dark chocolate over the cake. Sprinkle the chocolate in a random pattern, crossing back and forth over all sides of the cake. Keep dipping the fork in the chocolate and sprinkling until all of the chocolate is used. Sprinkle the chocolate quickly to create thin lines. Stop and take a look at the cake. It will look beautiful. Chill the cake, uncovered, until the dark chocolate is firm.

## Good Advice

- The cake and chocolate bark can be prepared ahead and frozen.
- The buttercream can be prepared up to one week ahead and refrigerated. Since the finished cake will be frozen, I do not recommend freezing the buttercream, then defrosting and refreezing it.
- Line the baking sheet with parchment paper, which will not stick to the cake when it is unrolled as wax paper might.
- The chocolate bark is prepared by spreading melted chocolate on wax paper strips. Don't worry about rough edges or if some bark breaks as you work with it; irregular pieces look fine, like real bark. The white chocolate adds a nice pattern to the bark.

## Doubling the Recipe

Double the ingredients. Bake the cake in two pans. Mix the cake and buttercream in a five-quart bowl.

## To Freeze

- Chill the cake, uncovered, in the freezer for 1 hour. Wrap with plastic wrap, gently pressing the plastic wrap on the cake. Gently press heavy aluminum foil around the cake. Label with date and contents. Freeze up to 1 month.

Bûche de Noël

# Yule Log

**Serves 12**

Bûche de Noël is a French Christmas cake shaped and decorated to represent a traditional holiday yule log. At Christmastime throughout France, pâtisserie windows are filled with Bûches de Noël, ranging in size from miniature to gargantuan and trimmed with everything from whimsical marzipan figures to elaborate spun sugar decorations.

Every year I prepare several Christmas logs for our holiday dinner and for special gifts. My logs have a sophisticated appearance that looks difficult but is actually simple and fun to prepare. This Bûche de Noël is an all-chocolate (of course) version: chocolate sponge cake roll, filled and frosted with chocolate buttercream and covered with slabs of chocolate "bark." I swirl white chocolate with some of the dark chocolate bark to create a marbled look. During the holiday frenzies, it is especially nice to have this festive cake ready and waiting in your freezer.

Chocolate Sponge Cake

**½ cup cake flour**
**2 tablespoons cornstarch**
**¼ cup unsweetened Dutch process cocoa powder**
**6 large eggs, separated**
**1 large egg yolk**
**¾ cup sugar**
**1 teaspoon vanilla**
**⅛ teaspoon almond extract**
**½ teaspoon cream of tartar**

**Chocolate Buttercream (page 116)**

Thick Rum Syrup

**2 tablespoons hot water**
**2 tablespoons sugar**
**1 tablespoon dark rum**

Chocolate Bark

**10 ounces semisweet chocolate, chopped**
**1 ounce white chocolate, chopped**

1. Position a rack in the middle of the oven. Preheat the oven to 350°F. Butter a 15½ × 10½ × 1-inch baking sheet (jelly-roll pan). Line the bottom of the baking sheet with parchment paper and butter the paper.

## Prepare the cake

2. Sift the flour, cornstarch, and cocoa together and set aside. Put the 7 egg yolks in the large bowl of an electric mixer and mix on medium speed

*continued*

### To Freeze and Defrost the Cake

Unroll the cake onto a piece of plastic wrap. Remove the parchment paper. Roll up the cake in the plastic wrap to keep it from sticking. Carefully wrap heavy aluminum foil around the roll. Freeze up to 2 months. Defrost the wrapped cake at room temperature.

### To Freeze the Bark

After the chocolate hardens, peel away the wax paper. Put the chocolate strips in a long plastic or metal container lined with plastic wrap. Cover the chocolate with plastic wrap. Cover tightly and freeze up to 1 month. The bark can be used while it is still frozen.

### To Serve

Defrost the wrapped cake overnight in the refrigerator. Before serving the cake, let it sit at room temperature, loosely covered with plastic wrap, until the buttercream softens, about 1 hour. Cut the cake with a large sharp knife. Dip the knife in hot water and dry it. The warm knife will cut through the cake without breaking the chocolate. If the chocolate begins to break, dip and dry the knife again. Cover leftover cake with plastic wrap and refrigerate up to 4 days.

just to break up the yolks. Add ¼ cup of the sugar and beat for 5 minutes until the mixture thickens, the color lightens to pale yellow, and the egg mixture looks like softly whipped cream. Mix in the vanilla and almond extract. Put the egg whites and cream of tartar in another clean large bowl and with clean dry beaters beat on low speed until the egg whites are foamy and the cream of tartar is dissolved. Increase the speed to medium and beat the egg whites to soft peaks. Slowly beat in the remaining ½ cup sugar, 1 tablespoon at a time. Sprinkle half of the flour mixture over the egg yolk mixture and use a rubber spatula to fold it in. The mixture will be thick and some of the flour will not be completely incorporated. With the same rubber spatula, fold a third of the whites into the egg yolk and flour mixture. Fold in the remaining whites. Sprinkle the remaining flour mixture over the batter, folding it in as you add it. Continue folding just until no white streaks of flour remain.

3. Pour the batter into the prepared pan and gently smooth the top. Bake until a toothpick inserted in the center of the cake comes out clean, about 15 minutes. Cool the cake in the pan for 10 minutes. Use a small sharp knife to loosen the cake from the sides of the pan. Invert the cake onto a clean dish towel. Carefully peel off the parchment paper and place it back on the cake. Roll up the cake in the dish towel. Let the cake cool in the towel for 1 hour. The cake can be frozen before it is filled and frosted.

## Prepare the syrup

4. Put the water and sugar in a small saucepan and mix over low heat just until the sugar dissolves. Remove from the heat, stir in the rum, and cool the syrup. The syrup may be covered and stored in the refrigerator up to 1 week.

## Prepare the chocolate bark

5. Preheat the oven to 175°F. Put the semisweet chocolate in a small ovenproof container and the white chocolate in another small nonreactive ovenproof container and melt both in the oven, 8 to 10 minutes. Remove the chocolate from the oven when melted and stir each until smooth. Cut 2 pieces of wax paper 14 inches long and from these pieces cut three 1½-inch- and four 2-inch-wide strips of paper. Line a baking sheet with 1-inch-high sides with wax paper and place another 15-inch-long piece of wax paper next to the baking sheet. The 15-inch paper is just to keep the kitchen counter clean. Lay the wax paper strips on the large piece of wax paper. Drizzle a quarter of the white chocolate on a strip of wax paper, either width is fine. Use a thin metal spatula to spread a thin, even layer of dark chocolate over the white chocolate, leaving a 1-inch plain edge at each end of the paper for easier handling. No wax paper should show through the chocolate. Place the chocolate-coated strip on the baking sheet, chocolate side up. Repeat with 3 more strips, placing two of the strips over the edge of the baking sheet to curve them slightly. Choose either width strip as they will be used randomly. Coat the 3 remaining strips of wax paper with semisweet chocolate and place them on the baking sheet. Let the strips sit at room tem-

perature or in the refrigerator until the chocolate is hard. This makes more bark than is needed to cover the cake but allows for damaged pieces.

## Finish the cake roll

6. Unroll the sponge cake and remove the parchment paper. Or defrost the frozen cake and remove the plastic wrap. Use a pastry brush to lightly brush the top of the cake with the rum syrup. Spread 2 cups of the chocolate buttercream evenly over the cake. Roll up the cake like a jelly-roll. Place the cake, seam side down, on a 16-inch-long narrow platter or piece of cardboard covered with heavy aluminum foil. Spread the remaining 2 cups of buttercream over the cake, including the ends. Break off pieces of chocolate bark 5 to 8 inches long. Begin on either side of the cake roll and cover the cake with overlapping strips of chocolate placed lengthwise on the cake. Place the smooth side of the chocolate bark (the side that was touching the wax paper) facing out. Alternate dark and white and dark strips. The buttercream will hold the chocolate bark in place. Do not cover the frosted ends of the cake with chocolate bark.

## Good Advice

- Beat the egg yolks and sugar for the cake until they are as thick as softly whipped cream. Aerating the eggs thoroughly and dissolving the sugar thoroughly help the cake form a desirable structure.
- I add part of the flour mixture to the yolk mixture before adding the beaten egg whites. This prevents some of the deflation of the beaten egg whites when the flour is added to them.
- Beat the filling just until it thickens to the consistency of soft whipped cream. It is better to beat the cream less rather than more. Overbeating causes a grainy texture. The chocolate cream firms up quickly and should be used immediately.

## Doubling the Recipe

Mix two batches of the sponge cake batter. Double the ingredients for the filling and glaze.

## To Freeze and Defrost the Cake

Invert the cooled cake onto plastic wrap. Wrap the cake with the plastic wrap then heavy aluminum foil. Label with date and contents. Freeze up to 2 months. Defrost the wrapped cake at room temperature. Fill and glaze the cake as soon as it is thawed enough to cut.

Rigó Jancsi

# Hungarian Chocolate Cake

**Serves 12**

Rigó Jancsi, the inspiration for this cake, is a classic Hungarian cake. Two thin chocolate cake layers are filled with a thick layer of chocolate cream and covered with a chocolate glaze. The flavor of each layer comes from pure chocolate—chocolate cake, chocolate cream, chocolate glaze. Traditional Rigó Jancsi has a very dense cake and cream filling, and it is so rich that it is served in small squares. My version is made with a light sponge cake prepared with melted chocolate and cocoa; the chocolate gives the cake a deep chocolate taste, which is often lacking in cocoa-only sponge cakes. The one-inch-thick chocolate cream filling has a high ratio of cream to chocolate. It is a light filling with great chocolate flavor but not overly rich. I feel these variations justify serving slices of cake rather than tiny squares. Since it is still rather rich, I cut the nine-inch cake into twelve slices.

### Dark Chocolate Sponge Cake

**2 ounces unsweetened chocolate, in 1-ounce pieces**
**½ cup cake flour**
**2 tablespoons cornstarch**
**¼ cup unsweetened Dutch process cocoa powder**
**6 large eggs, separated**
**¾ cup sugar**
**1 teaspoon vanilla extract**
**⅛ teaspoon almond extract**
**½ teaspoon cream of tartar**

### Chocolate Cream Filling

**2 cups whipping cream**
**12 ounces semisweet chocolate, chopped**
**2 tablespoons unsweetened Dutch process cocoa powder**
**1 teaspoon vanilla extract**
**1 recipe Shiny Chocolate Glaze (page 172)**

1. Position a rack in the middle of the oven. Preheat the oven to 175°F. Butter the inside of a 9-inch cake pan with 1¾ to 2-inch-high sides. Line the bottom of the pan with parchment or wax paper and butter the paper.

## Prepare the cake

2. Put the unsweetened chocolate in a heatproof container and melt it in the oven, 8 to 10 minutes. As soon as the chocolate is melted, remove it from the oven and raise the oven temperature to 350°F. Set the chocolate aside to cool slightly.

### To Freeze

Freeze the cake, uncovered, to firm the chocolate glaze and filling, about 1 hour. Use a small sharp knife to loosen the cake from the sides of the springform pan. Release the sides of the pan and remove the cake. Use the knife to smooth the sides of the cake. Leave the cake on the springform bottom or use a wide metal spatula to slide the cake onto a cardboard cake circle or platter. Wrap tightly with plastic wrap. Gently press heavy aluminum foil around the cake. Label with date and contents. Freeze up to 1 month.

### To Serve

Defrost the wrapped cake overnight in the refrigerator. Unwrap the cake and let it sit at room temperature about 1 hour before serving. It is important that the cake be served at room temperature to bring out the flavor of the chocolate and let the glaze and filling become soft and creamy. Leftover cake can be covered with plastic wrap and refrigerated up to 4 days.

3. Sift the flour, cornstarch, and cocoa together and set aside. Put the egg yolks in the large bowl of an electric mixer and mix on medium speed just to break up the yolks. Add ¼ cup of the sugar and beat for about 5 minutes, until the mixture thickens and the color lightens to pale yellow. Add the vanilla and almond extract. Use a rubber spatula to fold in the melted chocolate and set aside. Put the egg whites and cream of tartar in another clean large bowl and with clean dry beaters beat on low speed until the cream of tartar is dissolved. Increase the speed to medium and beat the egg whites to soft peaks. Slowly beat in the remaining ½ cup sugar, 1 tablespoon at a time. Sprinkle half of the flour mixture over the chocolate mixture and use a rubber spatula to fold it into the chocolate mixture. The mixture will be thick and some of the flour will not be completely incorporated. With the same rubber spatula, fold a third of the whites into the chocolate mixture. Fold in the remaining whites. Sprinkle the remaining flour mixture over the batter, folding it in as you add it. Continue folding just until no white streaks of flour remain.

4. Pour the batter into the prepared pan and gently smooth the top. Bake until a toothpick inserted in the center of the cake comes out clean, about 20 minutes. Cool the cake in the pan for 5 minutes. Use a small sharp knife to loosen the cake from the sides of the pan and invert onto a cake rack to cool thoroughly. Remove the wax paper. The cake can be frozen before it is filled and glazed.

## Prepare the chocolate cream

5. Put the cream in a medium saucepan and heat until the mixture is hot and measures about 150°F. on a food thermometer. Remove the pan from the heat. Add the chopped chocolate and cocoa and stir until the chocolate is melted and the mixture is smooth. Stir in the vanilla. Pour the chocolate cream into a large mixing bowl, cover, and refrigerate until it is chilled thoroughly, about 2 hours. The edges of the chocolate cream should just begin to harden.

## Assemble the cake

6. Use a serrated knife to cut the cooled cake into 2 layers. Use the removable bottom of a tart pan to slide the bottom of the cake layer on the bottom of a 9-inch springform pan with at least 2¾-inch-high sides. Have the chocolate glaze ready at a pouring consistency. Beat the chilled chocolate cream with an electric mixer on medium speed until the cream thickens and lines just begin to form from the movement of the beaters, about 15 to 45 seconds. The colder the chocolate cream, the less time it will take to beat. Immediately spread the chocolate cream evenly over the cake layer. Use the bottom of the tart pan to slide the remaining cake layer, top side up, onto the chocolate cream. Pour the chocolate glaze over the cake and tilt the pan to spread it evenly. A little glaze will run between the edges of the cake and the springform. This will glaze the top edge of the cake with a neat, finished border.

# White Chocolate and Orange Double Decadence

Serves 8

In recent years, the word *decadence* has taken on a new meaning. It often refers to a sophisticated-looking cake containing little or no flour and a large quantity of chocolate. White Chocolate and Orange Double Decadence meets these criteria plus a few additional ones. The cake, which has the consistency of soft fudge, is prepared with a pound of white chocolate and flavored three different ways with orange—juice, zest, and glazed peel. Definitely double decadence.

White Chocolate Torte

**1 pound white chocolate, chopped, Callebaut preferred**
**6 tablespoons (¾ stick) unsalted butter, cut into 6 pieces**
**4 large eggs**
**1 tablespoon sugar**
**1 tablespoon grated orange zest**
**2 tablespoons fresh orange juice**
**1 teaspoon vanilla extract**
**1 tablespoon Grand Marnier**
**3 tablespoons sifted unbleached all-purpose flour**

Semisweet Chocolate Glaze

**6 ounces semisweet chocolate, chopped**
**6 tablespoons (¾ stick) unsalted butter, cut into 6 pieces**
**2 tablespoons light corn syrup**
**1 teaspoon vanilla extract**

Glazed Orange Peel

**2 oranges, rind only**
**⅔ cup water**
**½ cup sugar**
**3 tablespoons cider vinegar**

1. Preheat the oven to 400°F. Position an oven rack in the middle of the oven. Line the bottom of an 8-inch springform pan with 2¾-inch-high sides with heavy aluminum foil. Butter the pan and aluminum foil. Wrap a piece of heavy aluminum foil under the bottom and halfway up the outside of the springform pan.

## Prepare the torte

2. Put the white chocolate and butter in a large heatproof container set over, but not touching, a saucepan of barely simmering water. Stir constantly until the chocolate and butter melt and the mixture is smooth. Transfer the white chocolate mixture to a large bowl and set aside. Put the eggs and

### Good Advice

- White chocolate burns easily and should be melted slowly with the butter. Stir the mixture constantly as it melts.
- Since there are only three tablespoons of flour in this cake, much of the cake's structure comes from the protein in the eggs rather than the flour. The foam produced when air is beaten into the eggs leavens and lightens the cake. Whisking the eggs with sugar over hot water before beating makes them yield more foam.
- After baking, the cake is chilled overnight, so that it will be firm enough to handle and easy to glaze.
- This method for glazing orange peel, which I learned at La Varenne cooking school in France, makes a brightly colored, not-too-sweet glazed peel.

### Doubling the Recipe

Double the ingredients for the cake and bake it in two pans. Double the ingredients for the chocolate glaze and glazed peel.

### To Freeze and Defrost the Torte

Follow the directions in Step 5 for leveling the top of the cake and removing the cake and foil from the springform pan. Invert the cooled cake onto plastic wrap. Wrap the cake tightly with plastic wrap then heavy aluminum foil. Label with date and contents. Freeze up to 2 months. Defrost the wrapped cake in the refrigerator overnight.

### To Freeze the Cake

Freeze the cake, uncovered, until the glaze is firm. Wrap the cake tightly with plastic wrap. Gently press heavy aluminum foil around the cake. Label with date and contents. Freeze up to 1 month.

### To Serve

Defrost the wrapped cake overnight in the refrigerator. Unwrap the cake and place a border of drained glazed orange peel on the top of the cake. Let the unwrapped cake soften at room temperature for about 1 hour before serving. Leftover cake can be covered with plastic wrap and refrigerated for up to 3 days.

sugar in a large heatproof mixing bowl and set it over, but not touching, the saucepan of barely simmering water. Whisk the mixture until it is warm to the touch and reaches 100°F. on a food thermometer. Remove from over the water. Using an electric mixer, beat the egg mixture at medium-high speed until it is thick, fluffy, and light yellow, about 4 minutes. Stir the grated orange zest, orange juice, vanilla, and Grand Marnier into the melted white chocolate mixture. Sprinkle the flour over the white chocolate mixture and use a rubber spatula to fold the flour in. Fold a quarter of the egg mixture into the white chocolate mixture. Fold in the remaining egg mixture just until all of the ingredients are mixed thoroughly.

3. Pour the batter into the prepared pan. Bake 25 minutes. The cake will still be soft in the center. Cool the cake in the pan on a wire cooling rack for 30 minutes at room temperature. Cover and refrigerate at least 8 hours or preferably overnight. The torte can be frozen without the glaze.

## Prepare the chocolate glaze

4. Put the chocolate, butter, and corn syrup in a large heatproof container and set it over a saucepan of barely simmering water. Stir until the chocolate melts and the mixture is smooth. Remove from over the water. Stir in the vanilla. Cool the glaze at room temperature until it thickens and feels barely warm to the touch, about 30 minutes.

## Glaze the cake

5. Remove the chilled cake from the refrigerator. Use a small sharp knife to loosen the sides of the cake from the springform pan. With the back of a spoon press down the edges of the cake to level the top of the cake. The cake will not be completely level. Remove the aluminum foil wrapping the pan and the sides of the pan. Invert the cake onto a cake rack. Remove the bottom of the springform pan. Peel off the aluminum foil. Put a piece of wax paper under the rack to catch and "recycle" any glaze that drips off the cake. Pour the warm glaze over the cake, spreading the glaze over the sides with a thin metal spatula. Slide a wide metal spatula under the cake and transfer it to a serving plate or cardboard cake circle.

## Glaze the orange peel

6. Using a vegetable peeler and a slight sawing motion, remove the orange rind from the orange in large strips. Trim off any white pith. Cut the rind into matchstick-size strips. Discard any uneven pieces. Put the orange strips in a small saucepan and cover with water. Bring to a boil. Drain the orange strips in a strainer and rinse them with cold water. Put the water, sugar, and vinegar into the small saucepan. Bring to a simmer over medium heat, stirring to dissolve the sugar. As soon as the sugar is dissolved, add the orange rind. Simmer 10 minutes. If using the orange peel immediately, drain the peel and cool it. Or refrigerate the peel in its syrup up to 1 week.

# Chocolate Raspberry Mousse Cake

**Serves 12**

At first glance this may look like a typical chocolate cake, but as soon as you take the first bite you'll know there's nothing ordinary about it. This is a luxurious cake, filled with a dense chocolate mousse and lots of whole raspberries. It's the restaurant's most popular summer cake—it sells out within a couple of hours.

Framboise or Kirsch Syrup

1 tablespoon hot water
1 tablespoon plus 1 teaspoon sugar
3 tablespoons framboise or kirsch

Chocolate Mousse

9 ounces semisweet chocolate, chopped
2 ounces unsweetened chocolate, chopped
¼ cup hot water
¾ cup whipping cream
1 teaspoon vanilla extract
3 large egg whites
¼ teaspoon cream of tartar
½ cup sugar

One 10-inch Chocolate Butter Cake Layer (page 38), cooled or defrosted just until soft enough to split
2 cups raspberries, preferably fresh, or frozen unsweetened raspberries, not defrosted
2 cups Chocolate Truffle Sauce (page 45), defrosted and warmed to spreading consistency
1 cup fresh raspberries, for garnishing the cake (optional)

## Prepare the syrup

1. Put the water and sugar in a small saucepan and mix over low heat just until the sugar dissolves. Remove from the heat, stir in the framboise or kirsch, and cool the syrup. The syrup may be covered and stored in the refrigerator up to 1 week.

## Prepare the chocolate mousse

2. Put the semisweet chocolate, unsweetened chocolate, and water in a heatproof container and place it over, but not touching, a saucepan of barely simmering water. Stir the chocolate and water together until the chocolate melts and the mixture is smooth. Remove the chocolate from over the hot water and set aside to cool slightly. Put the whipping cream and vanilla in the large bowl of an electric mixer. Beat the cream at medium speed until soft peaks form. Cover and refrigerate while you beat the egg whites. Put the egg whites and cream of tartar in the clean large bowl of an electric mixer

### Good Advice

- The mousse contains a high ratio of chocolate to meringue and whipped cream and will firm up quickly. Use it immediately while it's easy to spread on the cake.
- The glaze should be pourable but thick enough not to run off the sides of the cake. Chilling the glaze will firm it quickly.

### Doubling the Recipe

Use two ten-inch chocolate cake layers. Double the ingredients for the syrup, glaze, and the raspberries. Prepare the mousse in two batches, one at a time, and assemble each cake as soon as the mousse for it is ready.

### To Freeze

Chill the cake in the freezer for 1 hour, until the glaze is firm. Wrap tightly with plastic wrap. Gently press heavy aluminum foil around the cake. Label with date and contents. Freeze up to 1 month.

### To Serve

Defrost the wrapped cake overnight in the refrigerator. Unwrap the cake and let it sit at room temperature 30 minutes before serving. If fresh raspberries are available, place a border of raspberries on the top of the cake. Leftover cake can be covered with plastic wrap and stored in the refrigerator up to 3 days.

and with clean dry beaters, beat the egg whites with the cream of tartar on low speed until the egg whites are foamy and the cream of tartar is dissolved. Increase the speed to medium-high, and beat just until soft peaks form. Slowly add the sugar, 1 tablespoon at a time. Whisk about a quarter of the beaten egg whites into the chocolate mixture. Use a rubber spatula to fold the remaining egg whites into the chocolate mixture. Fold the reserved whipped cream into the chocolate mixture. Assemble the cake immediately.

## Assemble the cake

3. Place the chocolate cake layer on a serving plate or cardboard cake circle. With a serrated knife, split the cake into 3 horizontal layers and remove two of the layers. To remove the 2 top layers, slide the removable bottom of a tart pan under each layer and move it to the side. Slide strips of wax paper under the cake to protect the plate. Use a pastry brush to lightly brush each layer with the syrup. Place 1 cup of raspberries evenly on the bottom cake layer. Using a thin metal spatula, spread half of the chocolate mousse over the raspberries. The layer of mousse should be level. Add a second cake layer and repeat with the remaining raspberries and chocolate mousse. Top with the remaining cake layer. Use the metal spatula to smooth the sides of the cake. Chill the cake for 15 minutes. Stir the chocolate sauce to smooth it and pour about 1¼ cups of the sauce over the top of the cake. Use a thin metal spatula to spread the sauce evenly over the top of the cake. Spread the remaining sauce over the sides of the cake, lifting any that drips onto the wax paper back onto the sides of the cake. If the sauce is too soft to remain on the sides of the cake, chill the sauce about 5 minutes to firm it. Carefully remove the wax paper strips. The cake is now ready to serve or to freeze.

# Garden Party Raspberry and White Chocolate Cake

Serves 12

When the Camden Garden Club celebrated its seventy-fifth anniversary, I volunteered to bake the birthday cake. The only problem was that I was going to be at my son's college in Massachusetts for parents' weekend and would not arrive home until late on the night before the party. The cake had to be baked, decorated, and frozen before I left, and that is how this cake, worthy of any party, garden or otherwise, was created. I decided to put large white chocolate curls to suggest spring flower petals on top of the cake.

Buttercream

- 1½ cups fresh raspberries, or unsweetened frozen raspberries, defrosted and drained
- 8 ounces white chocolate, chopped, Callebaut preferred
- ¾ cup plus 2 tablespoons sugar
- ¼ cup water
- 1 tablespoon light corn syrup
- 5 large egg whites
- ½ teaspoon cream of tartar
- ½ pound plus 2 tablespoons (2¼ sticks) unsalted butter, softened to about the same temperature as the cooled meringue, about 72° to 78°F. if tested with a food thermometer
- 1 teaspoon vanilla extract
- One 10-inch Yellow Butter Cake Layer (page 36), cooled or defrosted just until soft enough to split
- Framboise or Kirsch Syrup (page 140)
- 4 cups (4 to 5 ounces) white Chocolate Curls (page 47), Callebaut preferred
- 1 cup fresh raspberries (optional)

## Prepare the raspberry puree and buttercream

1. Puree the raspberries in a food processor. Use the back of a spoon to press the raspberries through a strainer to remove the seeds. Measure 6 tablespoons of strained puree to add later to the buttercream and set aside. Save any additional puree for another use.

2. Preheat the oven to 175°F. Put the white chocolate in a small nonreactive ovenproof container and melt it in the oven, 8 to 10 minutes. Remove the white chocolate from the oven as soon as it is melted and stir until smooth. Set aside to cool while you prepare the buttercream. Put the ¾ cup sugar, water, and corn syrup in a small saucepan. Cover the saucepan and cook the syrup over low heat until all of the sugar is dissolved, stirring occasionally to help the sugar dissolve. Do not let the syrup boil until the sugar dissolves. Uncover the saucepan, increase the heat to high, and boil the mixture without stirring until the syrup measures 240°F. on a candy ther-

### Good Advice

- For Good Advice about Italian meringue, see page 86. The base for this buttercream is Italian meringue.
- Make the white chocolate curls before chopping the white chocolate for the buttercream so that you have a large piece of chocolate to work with. Or use white chocolate curls that have been prepared ahead, stored in the freezer, and are still frozen.

### Doubling the Recipe

Use two ten-inch Yellow Butter Cake Layers. Double the ingredients for the buttercream and use a heavy-duty mixer with a five-quart bowl. Beat the Italian meringue for eight to ten minutes rather than five minutes. If you don't have a five-quart bowl, prepare two batches of buttercream. Double the syrup ingredients and white chocolate curls.

### To Freeze

Chill the frosted cake, uncovered, in the freezer for 1 hour. Wrap tightly with plastic wrap. Gently press heavy aluminum foil around the cake. Label with date and contents. Freeze up to 1 month.

## To Serve

Defrost the wrapped cake overnight in the refrigerator. Unwrap the cake and allow it to sit at room temperature about 1 hour before serving, until the buttercream softens. Fresh raspberries can be scattered over the cake or on individual plates. Leftover cake can be covered with plastic wrap and stored in the refrigerator up to 3 days.

mometer. Wipe down the sides of the pan with a pastry brush dipped in hot water to dissolve any sugar crystals that form on the side of the pan.

3. Begin beating the egg whites when the sugar syrup starts to boil. Put the egg whites and cream of tartar in the clean large bowl of an electric mixer and beat with clean dry beaters on low speed until the egg whites are foamy and the cream of tartar is dissolved. Increase the speed to medium-high and beat the egg whites to soft peaks. Add the remaining 2 tablespoons of sugar, 1 tablespoon at a time. As soon as the syrup reaches 240°F., with the mixer on low speed, slowly pour the hot syrup in a thin stream onto the softly beaten egg whites. If the syrup reaches 240°F. before the egg whites are ready, remove the syrup from the heat for a few seconds and finish beating the egg whites. Pour the syrup in the space between the beaters and the sides of the bowl to prevent as much sugar syrup as possible from splashing onto the sides of the bowl and the beater. Continue beating the meringue at medium-low speed for 5 minutes. The outside of the bowl will be lukewarm and the meringue will be stiff and have a temperature of 72 to 78°F. measured with a food thermometer.

4. Beat in the softened butter 2 tablespoons at a time. The meringue will deflate slightly. Stop the mixer and scrape the bowl once, but do not scrape any sugar syrup that may have splashed onto the side of the bowl and hardened. On low speed, mix in the slightly cooled melted white chocolate and the vanilla. Transfer 2 cups of the buttercream to a small bowl, add the reserved raspberry puree to the small bowl, and stir to combine thoroughly. You now have a raspberry buttercream and a white chocolate buttercream. If the buttercreams seem too soft to spread, refrigerate them for about 20 minutes to firm slightly, then whisk each buttercream for a few seconds until smooth. The buttercreams can be covered and refrigerated up to 1 week in tightly covered plastic containers. If the buttercreams have been chilled, bring them back to room temperature and whisk each buttercream until smooth and spreadable.

## Assemble the cake

5. Place the cake on a serving plate or cardboard cake circle. With a serrated knife, split the cake into 3 thin layers and remove the 2 top layers. Slide the removable bottom of a tart pan under each layer and move it to the side. Slide strips of wax paper under the bottom layer to keep the cake plate clean. Using a pastry brush, lightly brush each of the layers with syrup. Use a thin metal spatula to spread half the raspberry buttercream over the bottom layer. Slide the bottom of the tart pan under the middle cake layer and carefully place it on the bottom cake layer. Spread the remaining raspberry buttercream over this layer. Slide the bottom of the tart pan under the top cake layer and carefully place it on the cake. Spread a thin layer of white chocolate buttercream on the top and sides of the cake to help the crumbs adhere to the cake. Spread the remaining buttercream over the top and sides of the cake. Spoon white chocolate curls over the top of the cake, then use the spoon to press curls onto the sides of the cake. Gently remove the wax paper strips from under the cake.

# Pistachio and White Chocolate Buttercream Cake

**Makes 12 servings**

The subtle flavors of pistachio nuts and white chocolate complement each other, nowhere more so than in this pistachio sponge cake, which is filled and covered with a delicate white chocolate buttercream. Glazed pistachio nuts dusted with powdered sugar cover the top of the cake for a dazzling finish.

### Pistachio Sponge Cake

**⅔ cup shelled pistachio nuts, roasted and unsalted**
**8 large egg yolks**
**⅔ cup sugar**
**1 teaspoon vanilla extract**
**½ teaspoon almond extract**
**5 large egg whites**
**⅔ cup cake flour**
**¼ cup cornstarch**

### Liqueur Syrup

**5 tablespoons water**
**3 tablespoons sugar**
**3 tablespoons framboise or kirsch liqueur**

### White Chocolate Buttercream

**2 cups whole milk**
**3 large egg yolks**
**½ cup sugar**
**¼ cup cornstarch, sifted**
**6 ounces white chocolate, chopped, Callebaut preferred**
**2 teaspoons vanilla extract**
**2 tablespoons kirsch**
**¾ pound (3 sticks) soft unsalted butter**

**1¼ cups glazed pistachio nuts (page 50), for garnishing the cake**
**Powdered sugar, for dusting the top of the cake**

1. Position a rack in the upper third of the oven. Preheat the oven to 300°F. Butter the bottom and sides of two 9-inch cake pans with at least 1½-inch-high sides. Line the bottom of each pan with parchment or wax paper and butter the paper.

## Prepare the cake

2. Spread the pistachio nuts on a baking sheet and discard any nuts that are dark and wrinkled. Toast the nuts for 5 minutes. Cool the nuts and rub off any loose skins. Put the nuts in the workbowl of a food processor fitted with the metal blade. Begin with a few on/off pulses, then process the nuts just until they are finely ground, about 15 seconds.

## Good Advice

- Remove the sponge cake from the baking pan and cool it on a cake rack to prevent it from absorbing too much moisture from the hot pan as it cools.
- This cake crumbs easily, so the top and sides of the cake should be spread with a thin coating of buttercream to help the crumbs adhere. Then a final thicker coating of buttercream is applied.
- Top the cake with the glazed nuts the day the cake is served so the nuts remain crisp.

## Doubling the Recipe

Double the ingredients for the cake layers, buttercream, syrup, and glazed nuts.

## To Freeze and Defrost the Cake Layers

Wrap each cooled layer tightly in plastic wrap. Stack 2 layers together and wrap in heavy aluminum foil. Freeze up to 2 months. Defrost the layers when ready to use at room temperature, unwrapped but loosely covered with the plastic wrap. The layers are easier to split if they are cold but not frozen.

### To Freeze

Chill the cake in the freezer about 2 hours, until the frosting is firm. Wrap the cake tightly with plastic wrap. Gently press heavy aluminum foil against the cake. Do not stack anything on top of the cake in the freezer. Freeze up to 1 month.

### To Serve

Defrost the wrapped cake in the refrigerator overnight. Remove the glazed pistachio nuts from the freezer and defrost at room temperature in the covered plastic container for 2 hours or overnight. Unwrap the cake and cover the top of the cake with the nuts. Sift about 2 tablespoons powdered sugar over the nuts. The powdered sugar should completely cover the top of the cake. Cover the cake and keep it refrigerated until 30 minutes before serving time. Let the cake stand at room temperature 30 minutes before serving so the buttercream softens and becomes creamy. Cover any leftover cake with plastic wrap and store it in the refrigerator up to 3 days.

3. Increase the oven temperature to 350°F.

4. Put the egg yolks in the large bowl of an electric mixer and mix on medium speed for 15 seconds, just to break up the yolks. Add ⅓ cup of the sugar and beat on medium-high speed for about 3 minutes, until the mixture is thick and light and yellow. Mix in the vanilla and almond extract. Set the yolk mixture aside. Put the egg whites in another clean large bowl and with clean dry beaters beat the egg whites on medium speed to soft peaks. Slowly beat in the remaining ⅓ cup sugar, 1 tablespoon at a time. Use a rubber spatula to fold a third of the whites into the yolk mixture. Fold in the ground nuts. Combine the flour and cornstarch and sift the mixture over the batter. Use one hand to sift and the other to fold the flour mixture into the yolks. Fold in the remaining egg white mixture.

5. Divide the batter evenly between the prepared pans. Smooth the tops. Bake for 18 to 20 minutes, until a toothpick inserted in the center of the cake comes out clean. Cool the cakes in the pan for 5 minutes. Loosen the sides of the cakes from the pan with a small thin knife blade. Place a wire cooling rack on top of each cake and invert onto the rack. Carefully remove the paper liner from the bottom of the cake and discard. Cool thoroughly. The cake layers can be frozen before they are filled.

## Cook the syrup

6. Put the water and sugar in a small saucepan and mix over low heat just until the sugar dissolves. Remove from the heat, stir in the framboise or kirsch, and cool the syrup. The syrup may be covered and stored in the refrigerator up to 1 week.

## Prepare the buttercream

7. Place a strainer over a large bowl. Heat the milk in a medium saucepan until it is hot and reaches 150°F. on a food thermometer. Put the egg yolks in a medium bowl and whisk just to break up the yolks. Add the sugar and whisk the mixture smooth, about 15 seconds. Add the cornstarch and whisk just until it is incorporated. Whisking constantly, slowly pour the hot milk mixture onto the yolks. Return the hot mixture to the saucepan and cook, stirring constantly, over medium heat just until the mixture reaches a boil and thickens. You will see several large bubbles. Stir the mixture often where the sides and the bottom of the pan meet. Immediately strain the hot custard into the large bowl. Add the white chocolate and stir gently until the chocolate melts and the mixture is smooth. Stir in the vanilla and kirsch. Press plastic wrap directly on the custard and refrigerate it until it is cool to the touch but not cold, about 1 hour. Touch the custard and butter, they should feel about the same temperature; if measured with a food thermometer they will be at room temperature, 65 to 75°F. Put the butter in a large mixing bowl and beat at high speed for 1 minute, until the butter lightens slightly in color. Stop the mixer and scrape the sides of the bowl. Decrease the speed to low and mix in the custard in 3 additions. Mix each addition of custard smooth before adding the next.

*continued*

### Assemble the cake

8. Use a serrated knife to split each cake layer into 2 layers. Slide the removable bottom of a tart pan under each layer to separate the layers and move them to the side. Slide the bottom of a cake layer on a plate or cardboard cake circle. Slide wax paper strips under the cake to protect the plate. Use a pastry brush to lightly brush the cake layer with a quarter of the syrup and spread a thin layer, about ¾ cup, of buttercream over the cake layer. Repeat with 2 more cake layers. Top with the remaining cake layer and brush with syrup. Cover the top and sides of the cake with a very thin layer of buttercream to help loose crumbs adhere to the cake. Cover the top and sides of cake with the remaining buttercream. Remove wax paper strips.

## Lemon Velvet Cake

**Serves 10**

White chocolate and lemon play up each other's sweet and tart qualities in this smooth-as-velvet cake. It's a dense cake that is flavored with white chocolate and lemon. Delicate, petal-like white chocolate curls add style and refinement.

#### Lemon and White Chocolate Cake

**10 ounces white chocolate, chopped, Callebaut preferred**
**½ pound (2 sticks) unsalted butter, cut into 12 pieces**
**¾ cup sugar**
**1 teaspoon grated lemon zest**
**3 tablespoons fresh lemon juice**
**¼ teaspoon salt**
**1½ teaspoons vanilla extract**
**½ teaspoon almond extract**
**6 large eggs**
**⅔ cup unbleached all-purpose flour, unsifted**

#### White Chocolate Ganache

**⅔ cup heavy whipping cream**
**2 tablespoons unsalted butter**
**8 ounces white chocolate, chopped, Callebaut preferred**
**1 teaspoon vanilla extract**

**½ cup cold Lemon Curd (page 44)**
**3½ cups (about 4 ounces) white Chocolate Curls (page 47), Callebaut preferred**
**Mint leaves, for garnish (optional)**
**Thin lemon slices, for garnish (optional)**

1. Position a rack in the middle of the oven. Preheat the oven to 350°F. Butter the inside of a 9-inch cake pan with 1¾- to 2-inch-high sides. Line the bottom of the pan with parchment or wax paper and butter the paper.

### Good Advice

- With no leavening and a large quantity of chocolate, the cake has the firm texture of a flourless cake, even though there is some flour.
- Chill the ganache mixture thoroughly prior to beating it and spreading it over the cake.

### Doubling the Recipe

Double the ingredients.

### To Freeze and Defrost the Unfrosted Cake

Invert the cooled cake onto plastic wrap. Wrap the cake tightly with the plastic wrap, then heavy aluminum foil. Label with date and contents. Freeze up to 2 months. Defrost at room temperature.

### To Freeze the Frosted Cake

Freeze the cake, uncovered, for 1 hour. Wrap tightly with plastic wrap. Gently press heavy aluminum foil around the cake. Label with date and contents. Freeze up to 1 month.

## To Serve

Defrost the wrapped cake overnight in the refrigerator. Unwrap and let the cake sit at room temperature before serving to soften the whipped ganache, about 30 minutes. Garnish each slice with mint leaves scattered over thin slices of lemon, if desired. Leftover cake can be covered with plastic wrap and stored in the refrigerator up to 3 days.

## Prepare the cake

2. Melt the white chocolate and butter in a large heatproof container set over, but not touching, a saucepan of barely simmering water, stirring until the chocolate melts and the mixture is smooth. Put the mixture in the large bowl of an electric mixer and beat on low speed until smooth. Add the sugar and mix until the sugar is blended completely into the mixture. The mixture will look lumpy. Add the lemon zest, lemon juice, salt, vanilla, and almond extract and mix until the mixture is smooth again, about 15 seconds. Beat in the eggs, two at a time, beating well after each addition, about 15 seconds. Add the flour and mix just until it is incorporated. Stir any loose flour into the batter.

3. Pour the batter into the prepared pan. Bake 35 to 40 minutes. To test for doneness gently press your fingers on the top of the cake. It should feel firm. If so, insert a toothpick into the center of the cake. When the toothpick comes out clean, the cake is done. Cool the cake in the pan for 10 minutes. Loosen the sides of the cake from the pan with a thin knife blade. Place a wire cooling rack on top of the cake and invert the cake onto the rack. Carefully remove the paper from the bottom of the cake and discard it. Leave the cake bottom side up. The bottom will be the top of the finished cake. Due to the lack of leavening the cake may have several slightly sunken spots, but the Lemon Curd and ganache will fill them. Cool the cake thoroughly. The cake can be frozen before it is frosted.

## Prepare the white chocolate ganache

4. Put the cream and butter in a medium saucepan and heat the mixture until it is hot and measures about 150°F. on a food thermometer. The butter should melt completely. Remove from the heat. Add the chopped white chocolate and stir until it is melted and the mixture is smooth. Stir in the vanilla. Pour the ganache into a large mixing bowl, cover, and refrigerate until chilled thoroughly, about 1 hour 15 minutes. The edges of the ganache should just begin to harden and the mixture should be cold throughout.

## Finish the cake

5. Spread the Lemon Curd over the top of the cake. Freeze the cake until the Lemon Curd is firm, about 30 minutes. Slide the cake onto a cardboard cake circle or plate and slide wax paper strips under the cake to protect the plate. Whisk the chilled white chocolate ganache vigorously for 1 minute. It will thicken slightly. Spread the whipped ganache over the top and sides of the cake. Spoon the White Chocolate Curls on the top and press them onto the sides of the cake. Remove the wax paper strips.

# Orange Poppy Seed Cake with Orange Cream

Serves 8

During the long winter months in Maine, the piles of oranges displayed in the produce section remind me it's time for Orange Poppy Seed Cake with an orange whipped cream topping. Since the orange cream takes only about five minutes to prepare, I whip it the day the cake is served.

### Orange Poppy Seed Cake

**2 cups cake flour**
**1 teaspoon baking powder**
**1 teaspoon baking soda**
**¼ teaspoon salt**
**½ pound (2 sticks) soft unsalted butter**
**1½ cups sugar**
**5 large eggs**
**1 tablespoon grated orange zest**
**¼ cup fresh orange juice**
**1 cup sour cream**
**3 tablespoons poppy seeds**
**1 teaspoon vanilla extract**

### Orange Cream Topping

**1 cup cold heavy whipping cream**
**1 teaspoon vanilla extract**
**1⅛ cups Orange Curd (page 44), defrosted just until spreadable**

1. Position a rack in the middle of the oven. Preheat the oven to 350°F. Butter the bottom, sides, and center tube of an 9½- or 10-inch tube or bundt pan with at least 3¾-inch-high sides. If using a tube pan, line the bottom with parchment or wax paper and butter the paper.

## Prepare the cake

2. Sift the flour, baking powder, baking soda, and salt together and set aside. Put the butter in the large bowl of an electric mixer and mix on low speed for 15 seconds. Add the sugar and beat on medium speed for 2 minutes until the mixture is thick and fluffy. Stop the mixer and scrape the sides of the bowl once during the beating. Mix in the eggs, one at a time. Beat for 2 more minutes. Stop the mixer and scrape the bowl again. The mixture may look curdled. Add the orange zest to the orange juice. Stir in the sour cream, poppy seeds, and vanilla. Decrease the speed to low and add the flour mixture and the sour cream mixture alternately, beginning and ending with the flour mixture (3 flour, 2 sour cream). Stop the mixer and

### Good Advice

- Wash and dry two oranges and finely grate the zest. Grate only the orange part, not the bitter white pith. Squeeze the oranges.
- The Orange Curd must be cold to produce a firm orange cream. Use Orange Curd that has been frozen and only slightly defrosted.

### Doubling the Recipe

Use 1½ teaspoons baking powder and 1½ teaspoons baking soda and double the remaining ingredients for the cake. Mix the cake in a five-quart bowl and bake it in two pans. Double the ingredients for the topping.

### To Freeze

Use a thin sharp knife to loosen the sides of the cooled cake from the sides and the center tube of the pan. Invert the cake onto plastic wrap. Carefully remove and discard any paper liner. Wrap the cake tightly with plastic wrap then heavy aluminum foil. Label with date and contents. Freeze up to 3 months.

## To Serve

Defrost the wrapped cake at room temperature 3 hours or overnight. Unwrap the cake and place it on a serving plate. If you are frosting the cake, slide wax paper strips under the cake to protect the plate.

scrape the sides of the bowl before the last addition of flour. The batter is ready when the final addition of flour is mixed completely into the batter and the mixture is smooth. Stir any flour clinging to the sides of the bowl into the batter.

3. Pour the batter into the prepared pan and smooth the top. Bake for 40 minutes. To check for doneness, gently press your fingers on the top of the cake. It should feel firm. If so, insert a toothpick into the center of the cake. When the toothpick comes out clean, the cake is done. Cool the cake in the pan on a wire cooling rack.

## Variation

Serve the cake plain, without the orange cream topping, but with a scoop each of orange sherbet and vanilla ice cream.

## Prepare the topping

4. Place the whipping cream and vanilla in a large bowl and beat with an electric mixer at medium speed until the cream just begins to thicken. With the mixer running, add the cold Orange Curd and beat until the cream forms soft peaks. The orange cream can be refrigerated up to 2 days. Either cover the entire cake with the orange cream or serve wedges of cake garnished with large spoonfuls of the orange cream. Remove any wax paper strips if used. Leftover cake, without topping, can be stored at room temperature up to 4 days. Frosted cake can be covered with plastic wrap and refrigerated up to 2 days.

# Date Cake with Cream Cheese Frosting

**Serves 12**

Desserts by their nature should be generous—no skimping. So when I put together this cake, I made sure it was laden with dates. Then I used prune juice for part of the liquid, rather than water or milk, partly to intensify the dark color of the cake. The spicy dark brown cake with its contrasting white frosting is perfect for serving on a blustery winter day.

### Date Cake

**1 cup pitted dates, cut into small pieces, about ¼ inch**
**1½ cups pitted dates, cut into large pieces, about ½ inch**
**1 cup boiling water**
**1 teaspoon baking soda**
**2¼ cups unbleached all-purpose flour**
**1 teaspoon baking powder**
**½ teaspoon salt**
**1 teaspoon ground cinnamon**
**½ teaspoon ground nutmeg**
**¼ teaspoon ground cloves**
**¼ pound (1 stick) soft unsalted butter**
**1½ cups (packed) light brown sugar**
**3 large eggs**
**1 teaspoon vanilla extract**
**½ cup sour cream**
**½ cup prune juice**

### Cream Cheese Frosting

**6 ounces cream cheese, softened about 2 hours at room temperature**
**¼ pound (1 stick) soft unsalted butter**
**2 teaspoons vanilla extract**
**3 cups powdered sugar**

1. Position a rack in the middle of the oven. Preheat the oven to 325°F. Butter the bottom, sides, and tube of a 9-inch tube pan. Line the bottom of the pan with parchment or wax paper and butter the paper.

## Prepare the cake

2. Put all of the dates in a medium bowl. Stir in the boiling water. Gently stir in the baking soda. Let the mixture cool about 1 hour until it is lukewarm. Sift the flour, baking powder, salt, cinnamon, nutmeg, and cloves together and set aside. Put the butter in the large bowl of an electric mixer and mix on low speed for 15 seconds. Add the brown sugar and beat on medium speed until the mixture is smooth, about 1 minute. Add the eggs and vanilla and beat until they are blended with the butter mixture, about 30 seconds. Stop the mixer and scrape the sides of the bowl once during this beating. Decrease the speed to low and mix in the date mixture. Stir the sour cream and prune juice together in a small bowl. There will be small pieces of sour

### Good Advice

Cut the dates for the cake in two sizes. The smaller pieces disappear into the cake and add moistness; the larger ones stay nice and chewy.

### Doubling the Recipe

Use 1½ teaspoons baking powder for the cake and bake it in two pans. Double the remaining ingredients.

### To Freeze

Freeze the cake for 1 hour, until the frosting is firm. Wrap tightly with plastic wrap. Gently press heavy aluminum foil around the cake. Label with date and contents. Freeze up to 1 month.

### To Freeze and Defrost the Cake

Wrap the cake tightly with the plastic wrap then heavy aluminum foil. Label with date and contents. Freeze up to 2 months. Defrost the wrapped cake at room temperature.

### To Serve

Defrost the wrapped cake overnight in the refrigerator. Unwrap and let sit at room temperature for 1 hour before serving. Wrap leftover cake with plastic wrap and store it in the refrigerator up to 5 days.

cream. Add the flour mixture and the sour cream mixture alternately, beginning and ending with the flour mixture (3 flour, 2 sour cream). Scrape the sides of the bowl again before the last addition of liquid. The batter is ready as soon as the final addition of flour is mixed completely into the batter. Stir any loose flour into the batter.

3. Pour the batter into the prepared pan. Bake 65 to 70 minutes. To test for doneness, gently press your fingers on the top of the cake. It should feel firm. If so, insert a toothpick into the center of the cake. When the toothpick comes out clean, the cake is done. Loosen the cake from the sides and center tube of the pan with a thin sharp knife. Cool the cake in the pan for 20 minutes. Place a cake rack on top of the cake and invert the cake onto the rack. Carefully remove the paper from the bottom of the cake and discard it. Cool the cake thoroughly, about 2 hours. Place a cake plate or cardboard cake circle on the bottom of the cake and invert the cake so that it is right side up. The cake can be frozen before it is frosted.

## Prepare the frosting

4. Put the cream cheese, butter, and vanilla in the large bowl of an electric mixer and beat on medium-low speed for about 1 minute, until the mixture is smooth and the cream cheese and butter are combined thoroughly. Decrease the speed to low and add the powdered sugar, 1 cup at a time. Beat the mixture until the powdered sugar is incorporated and the frosting is smooth, about 1 minute. Use a thin metal spatula to spread the frosting inside the hole in the center and on the top and sides of the cake. The cake is moist and firm and there should be no problem with crumbs sticking to the frosting. Swirl the top of the frosting with the tip of the spatula.

# Pies *and* Tarts

Pies, with their informal appearance and simple fillings of fruit, nuts, or chocolate, represent the American family dessert to me. Since pies are baked and served in pie tins or individual baking dishes, the pans, rather than the crusts, preserve the pie shape. Crusts can be flaky and delicate. Pie crusts should bake to a light brown color to bring out the flavor of the butter and to toast the flour. Bake some dough scraps to a pale cream color and some others to light brown and taste the difference. I bake pies first at a high temperature to color the crust, then at a lower temperature so the top of the pie doesn't burn before the filling is done.

Most of these pies are baked and then frozen in the baking pan, but several that contain fruit are frozen first and baked later when ready to serve. Baking the fruit for a short time before it is frozen in a dessert prevents the fruit from discoloring. The recipes for the Deep Dish Apple Pie and the fruit crisps include this preliminary baking. Watch fruit pies carefully during the final fifteen minutes of baking. If a pie begins to bubble over and out of the pie crust, it's probably done. If it requires further baking, slide a baking sheet under it to catch any drips.

Tarts are baked in a special tart pan with a fluted edge. Since this pan is removed after baking, the crust must be strong enough to carry the weight of the filling. A crust prepared with butter and no vegetable shortening is a good choice. After tarts cool, the crust becomes firm. The rim of the tart pan can then be easily removed and the tart placed on a cardboard cake circle or platter for freezer storage. When you are ready to serve the tart, place it on an attractive platter that shows off the perfectly fluted edge. With one exception, the Fresh Fruit Tart, the tarts in this chapter are all baked and then frozen.

Generally speaking, the middle of the oven is the best place to bake pies and tarts. The bottom crust will bake properly and the top will not brown too quickly. Fill only one oven rack with pies or tarts to avoid overcrowding the oven and disrupting the circulation of air and heat.

# Maple Apple–Walnut Crunch Pie

**Serves 8**

Many baked fruit pies do not freeze well because the large amount of juice produced by the cooked fruit makes the pie soggy when it defrosts. But this pie is something special. Grated apples and oatmeal flavored with maple syrup bake together with just enough liquid to keep the pie moist but not drenched in juice.

**½ cup (packed) light brown sugar**
**¼ pound (1 stick) unsalted butter, melted**
**¾ cup oatmeal, not quick cooking**
**½ cup pure maple syrup**
**2 large eggs, lightly beaten**
**1 teaspoon vanilla extract**
**4 cups peeled and grated apples (about 7 apples)**
**¼ cup whipping cream**
**1 Easy as Pie Crust (page 32), unbaked and frozen in pie pan**
**1½ cups walnuts, coarsely chopped**

1. Position an oven rack in the middle of the oven. Preheat the oven to 425°F.

2. Put the brown sugar, melted butter, oatmeal, maple syrup, eggs, vanilla, grated apples, and cream in a large bowl and stir the mixture until the ingredients are combined thoroughly. Pour the filling into the frozen pie crust. Sprinkle the walnuts over the top of the pie. Bake 10 minutes. Reduce the heat to 350°F. Bake 30 to 35 minutes more, until the pie looks puffy and the top is golden. Check to see that the pie is set by giving it a gentle shake; the center should remain firm. Cool thoroughly at room temperature.

## Variation

Serve with maple syrup whipped cream: Whip 1 cup cold heavy whipping cream with 1 teaspoon vanilla extract and 1 tablespoon pure maple syrup to soft peaks.

### Good Advice

- Grate the apples on the large holes of a four-sided hand grater.
- Use pure maple syrup for marvelous flavor.

### Doubling the Recipe

Use two pie crusts and double the remaining ingredients.

### To Freeze

Press plastic wrap tightly onto the cooled pie then wrap with heavy aluminum foil, gently pressing the aluminum foil against the pie. Freeze up to 1 month.

### To Serve

Defrost the wrapped pie at room temperature. Unwrap the pie and heat in a preheated 250°F. oven for about 15 minutes. Serve the pie warm.

# Deep Dish Apple Pie

**Serves 6**

Deep dish rather than two-crust is the direction my apple pies take. The sound of the spoon cutting through the crisp top crust signals something good is coming; besides, a deep dish holds an extra-generous amount of apples. And with only a top crust to prepare, the pie is assembled quickly.

The sour cream pastry used for this crust has a flaky texture and a slightly tart flavor, which complements the apples, but Easy as Pie Crust (page 32) can be used instead.

Sour Cream Pastry

**1 cup unbleached all-purpose flour**
**¼ pound (1 stick) cold unsalted butter, cut into 16 pieces**
**¼ cup cold sour cream**

Spiced Apple Filling

**8 cups peeled and cored apples, sliced about ½ inch thick (about 10 medium apples)**
**3 to 4 tablespoons sugar**
**1 tablespoon unsalted butter, melted**
**1 teaspoon fresh lemon juice**
**½ teaspoon ground cinnamon**
**Pinch ground nutmeg**

Egg Wash and Cinnamon Sugar

**1 egg, beaten with 2 tablespoons whipping cream**
**2 tablespoons sugar, mixed with ½ teaspoon ground cinnamon**

**Vanilla ice cream, for serving with the pie (optional)**

## Prepare the pastry

1. Put the flour and butter pieces in a large mixing bowl and mix with an electric mixer, on low speed until the butter and flour pieces are the size of small lima beans, about 20 seconds. Add the sour cream and mix until the mixture holds together and forms a smooth dough, about 15 seconds. Or, use a pastry blender to combine the butter and flour, then add the sour cream and stir with a large spoon for about 2 minutes, until a smooth dough forms. Form the dough into a ball, flatten it into a 6-inch disk, and wrap it in plastic wrap. Chill 2 hours or overnight.

2. Position a rack in the middle of the oven. Preheat the oven to 350°F.

## Prepare the apples

3. Put the apples in a baking container with a 2-quart capacity, such as a 9-inch layer pan with 2-inch-high sides or a shallow baking dish that is

## Good Advice

- Use the freshest apples available. Bake apple pies in the fall when recently harvested apple varieties appear in stores, one after the other. Freshness is a more important consideration than apple variety. Bite into an apple—if it tastes crisp and fresh, it's a good choice for your pie. For apples out of their growing season, I find Granny Smiths the most reliable.
- When adding sugar to the apple filling, add some of the sugar and then taste the filling. The right amount of sugar will bring out the flavor of the apples without overpowering them with sweetness; the correct amount depends on the apples.
- A nine-inch layer pan with two-inch-high sides is a good size for the pie, but a two-quart ceramic baking dish that can safely be placed in the oven straight from the freezer is more attractive.
- Brushing the frozen pie crust twice with the egg wash and cinnamon sugar makes the crust especially crisp.

## Doubling the Recipe

Double the ingredients and use two baking pans.

### To Freeze

Wrap the pie tightly with plastic wrap then heavy aluminum foil, gently pressing the aluminum foil against the crust. Label with date and contents. Freeze up to 1 month.

### To Bake and Serve

Remove the plastic wrap and aluminum foil from the frozen pie. Position an oven rack in the middle of the oven. Preheat the oven to 400°F. Use a pastry brush to brush the top of the pie with the egg wash and sprinkle with half the cinnamon sugar. Use the pastry brush to gently dab the crust with egg wash again and sprinkle with the remaining cinnamon sugar. Cut four 2-inch-long slits in the top of the crust to release steam while the pie bakes. Bake 35 to 40 minutes, until the crust is dark golden brown. Cool 20 minutes. The pie can be also baked early on the day it is served and warmed in a 250°F. oven for 10 minutes. Either way, use a large spoon to cut and serve the pie. Serve the warm pie with vanilla ice cream, if desired.

safe to transfer from freezer to oven. Stir 3 tablespoons of sugar, the melted butter, and lemon juice into the apples. Taste and add another tablespoon of sugar if needed. Bake the apples, uncovered, for 20 minutes, stirring once. Remove the apple mixture from the oven and stir in the cinnamon and nutmeg. Cover loosely and refrigerate until the apples are cold, about 1 hour.

### Prepare the pie

4. Remove the dough from the refrigerator and unwrap it. Lightly flour the rolling surface and rolling pin. Roll the dough from the center out into a circle about 2 inches wider than the top of the baking pan. Don't flip the dough over while rolling but lift and turn it several times to prevent it from sticking to the rolling surface. The dough should be about ¼ inch thick. Roll the dough circle onto the rolling pin, then unroll it over the cold apples. Fold ½ inch of the edge of the crust under itself to form a smooth edge. Use a fork to press the dough onto the edges of the baking pan. The crust will extend a little over the side of the pan. The pie is now ready to freeze.

# Apple Crisp

Serves 6

Apple Crisp was the only food served in the school cafeteria that I ever enjoyed; it was so good I asked my mother to get the recipe from the school. It was probably the only time anyone had ever asked them for a recipe, but they produced it, apologizing that their proportions made two hundred servings. My mom, as usual, worked it out.

My Apple Crisp is modeled after that lunchroom crisp—plenty of juicy apples covered with lots of topping. When fresh apples first appear in the fall, I prepare several pans of apple crisp for the freezer so that I have them ready to bake and serve often.

### Apple Filling

**8 cups peeled, cored, and sliced apples (about 10 medium apples)**
**1 to 2 tablespoons sugar**
**1 tablespoon unsalted butter, melted**
**2 teaspoons fresh lemon juice**
**¼ teaspoon ground cinnamon**

### Oatmeal Crumb Topping

**¾ cup unbleached all-purpose flour**
**½ cup oatmeal, not quick cooking**
**1 cup (packed) light brown sugar**
**1 teaspoon ground cinnamon**
**6 ounces (1½ sticks) cold unsalted butter, cut into 12 pieces**
**Vanilla ice cream, for serving with the crisp**

1. Position a rack in the middle of the oven and preheat to 350°F.

## Prepare the apple filling

2. Put the apples in a 2½-quart shallow baking pan or baking dish that is safe to transfer from freezer to oven or a 10-inch layer pan with 2-inch-high sides. Stir in 1 tablespoon of sugar, the melted butter, and lemon juice. Taste and add another tablespoon of sugar if needed. Bake, uncovered, for 20 minutes, stirring once. Remove from the oven. Add the cinnamon to the apples and stir well. Wipe the edges of the baking dish clean. Cover loosely and refrigerate until cold.

## Mix the crumb topping

3. Put the flour, oatmeal, brown sugar, and cinnamon in a large bowl and stir together. Add the butter pieces and with an electric mixer, pastry blender, or your fingertips mix together until coarse crumbs form, about ½ to ¾ inch in size. Sprinkle the crumbs over the cold apple mixture.

## Good Advice

- As for the Deep Dish Apple Pie, use recently harvested fresh apples.
- Oatmeal adds crunch to the crumbs. Since the crumb topping is sweet, the apples require only a small amount of sugar.

## Doubling the Recipe

Double all ingredients and use two baking pans.

## To Freeze

Wrap the crisp tightly with plastic wrap then heavy aluminum foil, gently pressing the foil against the crisp. Label with date and contents. Freeze up to 1 month. Don't place anything on top of the frozen crisp.

## To Bake and Serve

Position a rack in the middle of the oven. Uncover the frozen crisp. Preheat the oven to 325°F.

Bake the frozen crisp 55 to 60 minutes, until the crumb topping is golden and the apples just begin to bubble. Or defrost the crisp in the refrigerator and bake the cold crisp at 325°F. for about 45 minutes. Let the crisp cool about 15 minutes before serving or warm previously baked crisp in a 250°F. oven for 10 minutes. Spoon the warm crisp onto individual plates and serve with vanilla ice cream.

# Cranberry-Pear Crunch

**Serves 6**

Until I began writing this book, I never considered freezing fruit crunches and crisps. From the very first test crunch, though, I could detect no difference between a crunch that had been frozen unbaked for a month and one that had just been prepared and baked. What a discovery! You can stock your freezer with several dishes of Cranberry-Pear Crunch or Apple Crisp and have them available for baking at a moment's notice.

Cranberry-Pear Filling

**5 cups peeled and cored pears (about 6 medium pears)**
**¼ cup plus 1 tablespoon sugar**
**1 tablespoon unsalted butter, melted**
**2 teaspoons fresh lemon juice**
**1½ cups cranberries, fresh or frozen**
**1 teaspoon ground cinnamon**

Almond Crumb Topping

**1 cup unbleached all-purpose flour**
**1 cup (packed) light brown sugar**
**1 teaspoon ground cinnamon**
**6 ounces (1½ sticks) cold unsalted butter, cut into 12 pieces**
**1 cup sliced or slivered blanched almonds, toasted and cooled (page 6)**
**Vanilla ice cream, for serving with the crunch**

## Prepare the filling

1. Cut the peeled pears into chunks about 1 inch in size. Put the pears in a 2½-quart baking container. Use a 10-inch layer pan with 2-inch-high sides or a shallow baking dish that is safe to transfer from freezer to oven. Mix in ¼ cup of the sugar, the melted butter and lemon juice. Taste the filling and add up to 1 tablespoon more sugar. Mix in the cranberries and cinnamon and stir the mixture to coat the pears evenly with cinnamon. Wipe the edges of the baking dish clean.

## Mix the topping

2. Put the flour, brown sugar, and cinnamon in a large bowl and stir together. Add the butter pieces and with an electric mixer, pastry blender, or your fingertips mix together just until coarse crumbs form, about ½ to ¾ inch in size. Use a spoon to stir in the cooled, toasted almonds. Sprinkle the crumbs over the pear mixture.

### Good Advice

• Use pears that are ripe but still firm. When Bartlett pears are in season, I use them at the half-yellow half-green stage.

• Peel the pears with a vegetable peeler and cut them in half to remove the core and the hard center string.

### Doubling the Recipe

Double the ingredients and use two baking pans.

### To Freeze

Wrap the crunch tightly with plastic wrap then heavy aluminum foil, gently pressing the foil against the crunch. Label with date and contents. Freeze up to 1 month. Don't place anything on top of the frozen crunch.

### To Bake and Serve

Uncover the frozen crunch. Position a rack in the middle of the oven. Preheat the oven to 325°F. Bake the frozen crunch 50 to 55 minutes, until the filling just begins to bubble and the crumb topping is a golden color. Or defrost the crunch in the refrigerator and bake, uncovered, at 325°F. for 40 to 45 minutes. Let the crunch cool about 15 minutes before serving or warm previously baked crunch, uncovered, in a 250°F. oven for 10 minutes. Spoon the warm crunch onto individual plates and serve with a scoop of vanilla ice cream.

# Cranberry-Hazelnut Pie

**Serves 8**

The hazelnuts and cranberries rise to the top of this pie as it bakes, creating a golden topping studded with red berries. A brisk fall day or the annual Thanksgiving pie feast, when fresh cranberries and the new crop of hazelnuts are available, is the perfect occasion for this pie.

Cranberry-Hazelnut Filling

**3 large eggs**
**1 cup (packed) light brown sugar**
**¾ cup pure maple syrup**
**4 tablespoons (½ stick) unsalted butter, melted and cooled**
**¼ teaspoon salt**
**1 teaspoon vanilla extract**
**1½ cups toasted peeled hazelnuts, coarsely chopped (page 6)**
**1 cup fresh or previously frozen and defrosted cranberries, coarsely chopped**

**1 Easy as Pie Crust (page 32), unbaked and frozen in pie pan**

1. Position an oven rack in the middle of the oven. Preheat the oven to 400°F.

2. Put the eggs in a large bowl and with a large spoon or an electric mixer on low speed mix the egg yolks and whites together. Add the brown sugar and stir until the eggs and brown sugar are combined thoroughly. Mix in the maple syrup, melted butter, salt, and vanilla. Stir in the chopped hazelnuts and chopped cranberries.

3. Pour the filling into the frozen pie crust. Bake 10 minutes. Reduce the oven temperature to 350°F. and continue baking until the filling is set, 30 to 35 minutes. Check to see that the pie is set by giving it a gentle shake; the center should remain firm. Cool thoroughly at room temperature.

## Good Advice

- The easiest way to chop the cranberries and hazelnuts is in a food processor using the steel blade and a few quick on/off pulses.
- Buy peeled hazelnuts if possible.
- To prevent filling from seeping under the crust while the pie bakes, make sure there are no holes in the pie crust.
- Use pure maple syrup.

## Doubling the Recipe

Use a pie crust for each recipe and double or triple the filling ingredients for two or three pies.

## To Freeze

Wrap the cooled pie tightly in plastic wrap then heavy aluminum foil. Label with date and contents. Freeze up to 2 months.

## To Serve

Defrost the wrapped pie at room temperature. Uncover the pie and warm in a preheated 250°F. oven for 10 to 12 minutes. Warming the pie makes it taste freshly baked. Serve the pie warm or room temperature.

# Apricot-Almond Puff Pie

Serves 8

The food processor makes quick work of preparing the almond filling for this pie. The filling will puff up nicely as it bakes. Dried apricots are always a good fruit choice for winter desserts.

**1 cup (packed) dried apricots**
**1 cup boiling water**
**2½ cups (about 8 ounces) blanched almonds**
**1 cup sugar**
**2 tablespoons cornstarch**
**2 large eggs**
**1 tablespoon fresh lemon juice**
**¾ teaspoon almond extract**
**1 teaspoon vanilla extract**
**½ teaspoon grated orange zest**
**3 large egg whites**
**1 Easy as Pie Crust (page 32), unbaked and frozen in pie pan**
**Powdered sugar, for dusting**

1. Put the apricots in a small bowl and cover them with the boiling water. Set aside until the water cools, about 30 minutes.

2. Position a rack in the middle of the oven. Preheat the oven to 400°F.

3. Put the almonds in the workbowl of a food processor fitted with the metal blade. Process with 15 on/off bursts to chop the almonds, then process for 10 seconds. Add ¾ cup of the sugar and the cornstarch and process for 1 minute, until the almonds are finely ground. Add the eggs, lemon juice, almond extract, vanilla, and orange zest and process for about 30 seconds, until the mixture is smooth. The ground almonds will make the mixture look grainy. Scrape the mixture into a large bowl. Drain the apricots and pat them dry. Cut the apricots into approximately ½-inch pieces. Stir the apricots into the almond mixture. Put the egg whites in the large bowl of an electric mixer and beat on medium speed until soft peaks form. Slowly beat in the remaining ¼ cup sugar, 1 tablespoon at a time. Use a rubber spatula to fold about a quarter of the egg whites into the almond mixture. Fold in the remaining egg whites.

4. Pour the filling into the frozen pie crust and smooth the top. Bake 10 minutes. Reduce the oven temperature to 350°F. and continue baking until the filling is set and a toothpick inserted into the center of the pie comes out clean or with just a crumb or two clinging to it, about 30 minutes. Check to see that the pie is set by giving it a gentle shake; the center should remain firm. Cool thoroughly at room temperature.

### Good Advice

Grinding the almonds and sugar together in the food processor allows the nuts to be more finely ground without turning into paste.

### Doubling the Recipe

Use two pie crusts and double the ingredients for the filling.

### To Freeze

Wrap the pie tightly with plastic wrap then with heavy aluminum foil, gently pressing the foil against the pie. Label with date and contents. Freeze up to 2 months.

### To Serve

Defrost the wrapped pie at room temperature. Uncover the pie and warm in a 250°F. oven for 10 to 12 minutes. Warming the pie makes it taste freshly baked. Serve the pie warm or at room temperature. Dust the top of the pie with powdered sugar.

# Prizewinning Blueberry Crumb Pie

**Serves 8**

I won my first baking award—first prize—for this blueberry crumb pie. The contest director told me the pie won because it contained more blueberries than he had ever eaten in a blueberry pie. I agree: Good fruit pies should include a lot of fruit.

**1 tablespoon unbleached all-purpose flour, combined with 1 tablespoon sugar**
**1 Easy as Pie Crust (page 32), unbaked and frozen in pie pan**

Blueberry Filling

**6 to 6½ cups blueberries, fresh or frozen unsweetened, not defrosted**
**⅓ cup (packed) light brown sugar**
**4 tablespoons unbleached all-purpose flour**
**1 teaspoon ground cinnamon**

Pecan Crumb Topping

**½ cup unbleached all-purpose flour**
**⅓ cup (packed) light brown sugar**
**⅓ cup sugar**
**2 teaspoons ground cinnamon**
**Pinch salt**
**¼ pound (1 stick) cold unsalted butter, cut into 8 pieces**
**1 cup pecans, coarsely chopped**

1. Sprinkle the flour and sugar mixture evenly over the bottom of the pie crust.

## Mix the filling

2. Put the blueberries, brown sugar, flour, and cinnamon in a large bowl and stir the mixture until the blueberries are coated evenly. Transfer the blueberry mixture to the pie crust, mounding the blueberries slightly toward the center of the pie.

## Mix the pecan crumb topping

3. Put the flour, brown sugar, sugar, cinnamon, and salt in a large bowl and stir together. Add the butter, and use your fingertips, a pastry blender, or an electric mixer on low speed to combine the butter and flour mixture until crumbs form, about ½ inch in size. Mix in the pecans. Sprinkle the crumbs evenly over the blueberry filling.

Bake the pie 20 minutes. If the crumb topping begins to brown unevenly, turn the pie around on the oven rack. Reduce the oven temperature to 325°F.

### Good Advice

- Blueberry season is a good time to prepare and freeze several pies.
- If the pie is not going to be frozen and the blueberries are fresh, reduce the amount of flour in the pie filling to two tablespoons. A pie that has not been frozen will take about ten minutes less to bake.
- A ten-inch pie crust will hold 6½ cups of small wild blueberries and 6 cups of large cultivated blueberries.
- If using frozen blueberries, do not defrost them before assembling the pie.
- Notice, less than half a cup of brown sugar is added to the blueberry filling. Taste the filling before putting it into the pie crust; the blueberry taste should prevail. If the blueberries are tart, another tablespoon of brown sugar can be added. Don't forget, the crumb topping also adds sweetness to the pie.
- Don't serve the pie hot from the oven: The filling in a hot pie will fall apart when it is cut.

### Doubling the Recipe

Use two or three pie crusts and double or triple the filling and crumb ingredients.

### To Freeze

Wrap the pie tightly with plastic wrap then heavy aluminum foil, gently pressing the aluminum foil against the pie. Label with date and contents. Freeze up to 1 month. Do not put anything on top of the pie in the freezer.

### To Bake and Serve

Unwrap the frozen pie. Position a rack in the middle of the oven. Preheat the oven to 400°F.

Bake about 40 to 45 minutes more, until the crumb topping is golden brown and the blueberry filling just begins to bubble. Cool the pie at least 30 minutes.

4. Serve the pie warm, at room temperature, or cold. The pie is best served within 2 days.

## Lemon Cream Pie

**Serves 8**

Once you taste this pie, it won't matter anymore that lemon meringue pie doesn't freeze well and isn't in this book. You'll have a new favorite—Lemon Cream Pie, which tastes like a lemon meringue pie but with a creamy topping.

**2½ cups Lemon Curd (page 44)**
**1 Graham Cracker Crumb Crust (page 34), baked in a 10-inch pie pan, cooled or frozen**
**1 cup cold heavy whipping cream**
**1 teaspoon vanilla extract**

1. Remove 1¾ cups of the Lemon Curd from the freezer and defrost it in the refrigerator at least 5 hours or overnight. Let the defrosted curd sit at room temperature for 15 minutes and stir it smooth. Remove ¼ cup of the room-temperature curd to swirl on the top of the pie and set aside. Carefully spoon 1½ cups of the room-temperature curd over the crumb crust. Freeze the pie 15 minutes to firm the Lemon Curd.

2. Remove another ¾ cup of Lemon Curd from the freezer and soften it at room temperature for 15 minutes. Put the cream and vanilla in the large bowl of an electric mixer and beat at medium speed until the cream begins to thicken. Lines will just begin to form in the cream. Add the cold Lemon Curd and beat until the cream forms soft peaks, about 1 minute. Spread the lemon whipped cream over the Lemon Curd, mounding the lemon cream toward the center. Drizzle the reserved ¼ cup room-temperature curd over the cream topping. With the tip of a knife swirl the curd over the cream topping.

### Good Advice

The Lemon Curd used for the lemon layer is softened so that it can be spread evenly in the crumb crust without disturbing the crumbs. But the portion added to the whipped cream topping should be cold for the lemon cream to whip to firm peaks.

### Doubling the Recipe

Use two graham cracker crumb crusts and double the remaining ingredients.

### To Freeze

Freeze the pie, uncovered, until the topping is firm. Wrap the pie tightly with plastic wrap then heavy aluminum foil. Label with date and contents. Freeze up to 1 month.

### To Serve

Defrost the wrapped pie in the refrigerator 4 hours or overnight. Serve the pie cold. Leftover pie can be covered with plastic wrap and refrigerated up to 2 days.

# Old-Fashioned Lattice-Top Raisin Pie

**Serves 8**

This pie is a sleeper. Don't be fooled by its simple ingredients—this is an extraordinary pie. I learned this easy technique for the diamond-patterned lattice topping at La Varenne cooking school in Paris. Thanksgiving is a good time to serve Raisin Pie. Everyone thinks it's some fabulous and difficult homemade mince pie. I just smile and savor my secret and my raisin pie.

Raisin Filling

**2 large egg yolks**
**1 cup sour cream**
**1 tablespoon fresh lemon juice**
**1 cup (packed) light brown sugar**
**1 teaspoon cornstarch**
**¼ teaspoon salt**
**1¼ teaspoons ground cinnamon**
**½ teaspoon ground nutmeg**
**¼ teaspoon ground cloves**
**2 cups seedless raisins**
**1¼ cups walnuts, toasted in a 300°F. oven for 5 minutes, cooled and coarsely chopped**

Pie Crust

**1½ cups unbleached all-purpose flour**
**½ cup cake flour**
**¾ teaspoon salt**
**1 tablespoon plus 1½ teaspoons sugar**
**¼ pound plus 1 tablespoon (1⅛ sticks) cold unsalted butter, cut into 9 pieces**
**3 tablespoons cold vegetable shortening**
**5½ to 6 tablespoons cold water**
**1 large egg mixed with 1 tablespoon whipping cream, for egg wash**

## Prepare the raisin filling

1. Put the egg yolks in a large bowl and stir the yolks just to them break them up. Set aside. Stir the sour cream, lemon juice, brown sugar, cornstarch, salt, cinnamon, nutmeg, and cloves together in a medium saucepan until the brown sugar is dissolved. Add the raisins. Cook over medium heat, stirring constantly until the mixture boils. Large bubbles should just begin to form. Stir the egg yolks and add ¼ cup of the hot raisin mixture while stirring. Slowly stir in the remaining raisin mixture. Stir in the walnuts. Cover the bowl and refrigerate the mixture just until it is cool to the touch, about 45 minutes. The temperature should measure about 70°F. on a food thermometer. Stir the mixture occasionally as it cools.

### Good Advice

• Since the lattice crust must be pressed onto the edges of the bottom crust, you cannot use a frozen crust for this pie.
• Cool the filling thoroughly before filling the pie. A hot filling would soften the lattice crust, making it difficult to form a neat pattern.

### Doubling the Recipe

Double the ingredients for the pie crust and filling and use two pie pans.

### To Freeze

Wrap the cooled pie tightly in plastic wrap then heavy aluminum foil. Label with date and contents. Freeze up to 2 months.

### To Serve

Defrost the wrapped pie at room temperature for about 5 hours. Serve the pie at room temperature or warm. To serve the pie warm, unwrap the pie and bake it in a preheated 250°F. oven for 10 to 12 minutes.

## Prepare the pie crust

2. Put the flours, salt, and sugar in the large bowl of an electric mixer and mix on low speed just to blend the ingredients, about 10 seconds. Stop the mixer, add the butter and shortening, and mix just until the butter and shortening pieces are the size of small lima beans, about 20 seconds. You will still see loose flour. Slowly add the water, 1 tablespoon at a time. Stop mixing as soon as the mixture begins to hold together, about 20 seconds. You may not need all of the water. The dough will form large clumps and pull away from the sides of the bowl but will not form a ball. Stop the mixer at any time and squeeze a small piece of dough to check if it holds together. Mixing the crust with a hand mixer will take about 30 seconds longer. Turn the dough mixture out onto a lightly floured rolling surface. With the heel of your hand push the dough down and forward against the rolling surface. Fold the dough in half and repeat 6 times. The dough will be smooth. Divide the dough into 2 pieces, one twice as large as the other. Wrap the dough in plastic wrap and chill in the refrigerator 20 minutes or overnight.

3. Position a rack in the bottom third of the oven. Preheat the oven to 400°F. Lightly grease a 10-inch pie pan with vegetable shortening or spray it with a vegetable oil spray.

## Assemble the pie

4. Remove the dough from the refrigerator and unwrap it. If the dough has become cold and hard, let it sit at room temperature for 5 to 10 minutes, until it softens slightly for easier rolling. Lightly flour the rolling surface and rolling pin. Roll the larger piece of dough from the center out into a circle about 4 inches wider than the bottom of the pie pan. Don't flip the dough over while rolling but lift and turn it several times to prevent it from sticking. Roll the dough circle over the rolling pin and unroll it onto the greased pie pan. Press the dough into the pie pan. Trim the edges evenly to overhang ¾ inch over the edge of the pie pan. Pour the cooled raisin filling into the pie crust. Smooth the filling.

5. Roll the smaller piece of dough into a rectangle about 11 × 7 inches. Cut ten 11 inch long and ½ inch wide strips. There will be extra dough to replace any broken strips. Use a long wide metal spatula to move the dough strips onto the top of the pie. Beginning 1 inch from the edge of the pan, place 5 of the strips 1 inch apart over the top of the pie. Trim the strips even with the outer edge of the pie pan. Turn the pie pan an eighth of a revolution. Lay the remaining 5 strips 1 inch apart over the strips on top of the pie. Trim these strips even with the outer edge of the pie pan. The strips will form a diamond pattern. Fold the dough overhanging the edge of the crust toward the inside of the crust, pressing it onto the edge of the pie pan. Crimp the edge by pressing the dough between your thumb and forefinger. Gently brush the dough strips with the egg wash.

6. Bake 10 minutes. Reduce the oven heat to 350°F. and bake about 25 to 30 more minutes, until the top of the pie is golden brown. Cool the pie thoroughly at room temperature, about 2½ hours.

# Maple Syrup Pecan Pie

**Serves 8**

Loaded with pecans and flavored with real maple syrup, this pie ended my search for the perfect pecan pie. What this pie does have in common with the typical pecan pie is that it is quick and easy to prepare.

Pecan Filling

**3 large eggs**
**1 cup (packed) light brown sugar**
**1 cup pure maple syrup**
**4 tablespoons (½ stick) unsalted butter, melted**
**¼ teaspoon salt**
**1 teaspoon vanilla extract**
**2 cups coarsely chopped pecans**
**1 Easy as Pie Crust (page 32), unbaked and frozen in pie pan**
**Whipped cream or vanilla ice cream, for serving with the pie (optional)**

1. Position an oven rack in the middle of the oven. Preheat the oven to 400°F.

## Prepare the filling

2. Put the eggs in a large bowl and use a large spoon or an electric mixer to mix the yolks and whites together. Add the brown sugar and stir until the eggs and sugar are combined thoroughly. Stir in the maple syrup, melted butter, salt, and vanilla. Stir in the pecans.

## Bake the pie

3. Pour the filling into the frozen pie crust. Bake 10 minutes. Reduce the oven temperature to 350°F. and continue baking until the filling is set, 30 to 35 minutes. Check to see that the pie is set by giving it a gentle shake; the center should remain firm. Cool thoroughly at room temperature.

### Good Advice

• To prevent filling from seeping under the crust while the pie bakes, check to see there are no holes in the pie crust. I once baked this pie and found the crust in the middle. It dawned on me that there must have been a hole in the crust. It tasted fine, but it sure was a strange-looking pie.

• Since the ingredients for the filling need only to be stirred together, it is not necessary to use an electric mixer for this pie.

### Doubling the Recipe

Using a pie crust for each recipe, double or triple the ingredients for two or three pies.

### To Freeze

Wrap the cooled pie tightly in plastic wrap then heavy aluminum foil, gently pressing the aluminum foil against the pie. Label with date and contents. Freeze up to 2 months.

### To Serve

Defrost the wrapped pie at room temperature. Uncover the pie and warm in a preheated 300°F. oven for 10 minutes. The warming makes the pie taste freshly baked. Serve the pie warm, at room temperature, or cold—it tastes good served at any temperature. Whipped cream or vanilla ice cream make a good accompaniment.

# Fudge Pie

Serves 8

These two words, *fudge* and *pie*, send a clear message. Here is a chocolate pie with the satin smooth consistency of fudge candy but with the taste of pure chocolate, not sugar.

**1 Easy as Pie Crust (page 32), unbaked and frozen in pie pan**
**8 ounces semisweet chocolate, chopped**
**1 ounce unsweetened chocolate, chopped**
**½ pound (2 sticks) unsalted butter**
**4 large eggs**
**¾ cup sugar**
**1 teaspoon decaffeinated instant coffee granules**
**1 teaspoon vanilla extract**
**2 teaspoons dark rum**
**½ cup whipping cream, at room temperature**
**Whipped cream, for serving with the pie**

1. Position an oven rack in the middle of the oven. Preheat the oven to 400°F.

2. Press a piece of heavy aluminum foil into the frozen pie crust and over the edges. Fill the foil with raw rice, dried beans, or metal pie weights, about 3½ cups of rice or beans. Check to see that the weights cover the entire bottom of the crust. Bake the pie for 10 minutes. Carefully remove the aluminum foil and pie weights. Prick the pie crust in several places with a fork. Bake for 5 more minutes. Let the crust cool while you prepare the filling. Reduce the oven temperature to 350°F.

3. Put the semisweet chocolate, unsweetened chocolate, and butter in a heatproof container and place it over, but not touching, a saucepan of barely simmering water. Stir the chocolate and butter together until they are melted. Remove the chocolate mixture from over the water and set aside to cool slightly. Put the eggs in the large bowl of an electric mixer and mix on low speed just to blend the yolks and whites together. Add the sugar, coffee, vanilla, and rum and beat for 2 minutes. Add the chocolate mixture and beat just until the chocolate and eggs are mixed together completely. Mix in the whipping cream.

4. Slowly pour the filling into the partially baked pie crust. The filling will come up to the top of the pie crust. Bake for 35 minutes. The pie will look crackly on the top and feel soft, but it will firm as it cools. Cool the pie thoroughly.

## Good Advice

- Before it is filled, the pie crust is partially baked. This forms a barrier between the filling and pie crust and produces a crisper crust.
- Baking the pie crust while still frozen helps keep it from shrinking as it bakes, though the sides may still shrink slightly. A good way to repair this is to press a piece of the reserved pie crust scraps onto any edge that has shrunk before you add the pie filling.

## Doubling the Recipe

Use two pie crusts and double the filling ingredients.

## To Freeze

Wrap the cooled pie tightly with plastic wrap then heavy aluminum foil. Label with date and contents. Freeze up to 2 months.

## To Serve

Defrost the covered pie at room temperature or in the refrigerator for 6 hours. Serve the pie at room temperature or chilled. The chocolate will have a more intense taste at room temperature, but the pie has a firmer, fudge-like texture when chilled. Serve with whipped cream. Cover with plastic wrap and store leftover pie in the refrigerator up to 5 days.

# Candy Bar Pie

**Serves 8 to 10**

A slice of this pie is candy bar heaven. When he first tasted it, my husband, Jeff, gave Candy Bar Pie his ultimate accolade—*Deluxe!*

**1 Easy as Pie Crust (page 32), unbaked and frozen in pie pan**

Fudge Brownie Layer

**6 tablespoons unbleached all-purpose flour**
**½ teaspoon baking powder**
**⅛ teaspoon salt**
**4 ounces semisweet chocolate, chopped**
**1 ounce unsweetened chocolate, chopped**
**¼ pound (1 stick) unsalted butter, cut into 8 pieces**
**1 large egg**
**1 large egg yolk**
**½ cup sugar**
**1 teaspoon vanilla extract**
**2 cups (about 8 ounces) Snickers candy bars cut into ½-inch pieces**

Cream Cheese Layer

**10 ounces cream cheese, softened about 3 hours at room temperature**
**⅓ cup sugar**
**1 large egg**
**1 teaspoon vanilla extract**

Milk Chocolate Glaze

**½ cup whipping cream**
**2 teaspoons light corn syrup**
**8 ounces good quality milk chocolate, chopped, Callebaut or milk chocolate Dove Bar preferred**

**Bite-size Snickers candy bars, for garnish (optional)**

1. Position an oven rack in the middle of the oven. Preheat the oven to 400°F.

## Partially bake the pie crust

2. Press a piece of heavy aluminum foil into the frozen pie crust and over the edges of the crust. Fill the aluminum foil with raw rice, dried beans, or metal pie weights, about 3½ cups of rice or beans. Check to see that the weights cover the entire bottom of the crust. Bake the pie crust for 10 minutes. Carefully remove the aluminum foil and pie weights. Prick the pastry in several places with a fork. Bake for 5 more minutes. Remove the crust from the oven and set aside while preparing the brownie layer.

### Good Advice

• Since this pie is definitely rich, I cut the slices smaller than average.

• Don't be put off by the length of the recipe. It looks difficult, but it's not. The layers are simple to prepare and assemble. I usually do two pies at a time; they can be put together almost as quickly as a single pie.

### Doubling the Recipe

Use two pie crusts and double the ingredients for each of the filling layers.

### To Freeze

Chill the pie, uncovered, in the freezer until the glaze is firm. Wrap the pie tightly with plastic wrap then heavy aluminum foil, gently pressing the aluminum foil against the pie. Label with date and contents. Freeze up to 2 months.

### To Serve

Defrost the wrapped pie in the refrigerator overnight. Serve the pie cold. For an amusing garnish, serve the pie with bite-size Snickers candy bars. Leftover pie can be covered with plastic wrap and refrigerated up to 4 days.

## Mix the brownie layer

3. Sift the flour, baking powder, and salt together and set aside. Put the semisweet chocolate, unsweetened chocolate, and butter in a heatproof container set over, but not touching, a saucepan of simmering water. Stir the chocolate and butter together until they are melted and the mixture is smooth. Remove from over the water and cool slightly. Put the egg and egg yolk in the large bowl of an electric mixer and beat just to break up the yolks. Add the sugar and vanilla and beat on medium-low speed until the mixture thickens slightly, about 1 minute. Mix in the slightly cooled chocolate mixture. Add the flour mixture and mix on low speed just until the flour is incorporated.

4. Transfer the batter to the partially baked pie crust. Bake 17 minutes. Cool 10 minutes.

5. Gently place the Snickers bar pieces evenly over brownie layer.

## Mix the cream cheese layer

6. Put the cream cheese and sugar in the large bowl of an electric mixer. Beat on low-medium speed until the mixture is smooth, about 30 seconds. Add the egg and vanilla and mix just until the mixture is smooth.

7. Use a thin metal spatula to spread the cream cheese mixture evenly over the Snickers bar pieces. Bake 15 minutes. Cool the pie 1 hour, until the cream cheese layer is firm.

## Prepare the glaze and glaze the pie

8. Heat the cream and corn syrup in a medium saucepan and over medium-low heat until the mixture is hot and the butter is melted. The mixture will form tiny bubbles and measure about 175°F. on a food thermometer. Do not let the mixture boil. Remove the saucepan from the heat and stir in the milk chocolate pieces. Stir gently until the chocolate is melted and the mixture is smooth. Cool the glaze 15 minutes until it thickens slightly. Pour the glaze over the cooled pie. Tip the pie gently in several directions to spread the glaze evenly. Use a thin metal spatula to spread the glaze completely over the pie.

# Chocolate Ganache Tart

**Serves 12**

Ganache is a satin-smooth chocolate mixture of chocolate, cream, and butter. It can be used as a glaze or even as a fudge sauce over ice cream. It can also be chilled and lightly whipped for ganache cream or ganache soufflé. That melt-in-your-mouth filling in candy truffles is ganache cream. Eating this Chocolate Ganache Tart is like biting into a big chocolate truffle—a very nice sensation indeed.

### Hazelnut Pastry Crust

**¾ cup (about 3 ounces) hazelnuts, peeled and toasted (page 6)**
**1¼ cups cake flour**
**¼ teaspoon baking powder**
**¼ pound plus 2 tablespoons (1¼ sticks) soft unsalted butter**
**⅔ cup sugar**
**1 large egg yolk**
**½ teaspoon vanilla extract**

### Chocolate Ganache

**3 tablespoons unsalted butter**
**1½ cups whipping cream**
**3 tablespoons sugar**
**1½ pounds bittersweet chocolate, chopped**
**1½ teaspoons vanilla extract**

## Prepare the crust

1. Put the hazelnuts and 2 tablespoons of the flour in the workbowl of a food processor fitted with the steel blade and process until the nuts are finely ground. Mix the remaining flour and baking powder together and set aside. Put the butter and sugar in the large bowl of an electric mixer and beat on medium speed until the mixture looks creamy, about 30 seconds. Mix in the egg yolk and vanilla. Mix in the nut mixture. Add the flour mixture and mix on low speed just until the flour is incorporated. The dough will be soft. Press the dough into an 8-inch disk. Wrap the dough in plastic wrap and chill until firm, at least 1 hour or overnight. Butter an 11-inch tart pan with a removable bottom. Place the chilled dough between 2 pieces of plastic wrap. Roll into a 13-inch circle, about ⅜ inch thick. The dough will extend a little out from the edges of the plastic wrap. Remove the top layer of plastic wrap. Invert the dough over the tart pan and remove the remaining piece of plastic wrap. Press the dough evenly onto the bottom and sides of the tart pan. The dough on the sides of the pan should be ¼ inch thick. Place the crust in the freezer and freeze firm, about 2 hours.

## Good Advice

- The hazelnut pastry for the crust is a cookie-type dough. Because it is soft and sticky, it must be chilled before rolling. Even the cold dough can stick to a rolling surface, so I roll it between large pieces of plastic wrap.
- Carefully press the dough up the sides of the pan and check the crust for any thin spots. Handling the dough to form an even crust will not hurt it; the cookie-like dough doesn't toughen from handling.
- When the weights and paper are removed from the crust after its initial baking, a little dough may stick to the paper. Just scrape the dough from the paper with a thin metal spatula and replace it in the pan.
- Use top quality bittersweet chocolate for the ganache, such as Callebaut or Guittard.

## Doubling the Recipe

Use two tart pans and double the ingredients for the crust and filling.

### To Freeze the Crust

Wrap the crust tightly with plastic wrap, then heavy aluminum foil. Label with date and contents. Freeze up to 2 months.

### To Freeze

Refrigerate the tart to firm the topping, about 1 hour. Once the tart is cold, remove the tart pan: Use a small sharp knife to carefully loosen the crust from each indentation in the sides of the pan. Set the pan on a shallow bowl, such as a soup bowl, and let the rim slide down. With a long wide metal spatula, slide the tart onto a serving platter or 12-inch cardboard cake circle. Wrap the tart tightly with plastic wrap then heavy aluminum foil, gently pressing the foil against the tart. Freeze up to 2 months.

### To Serve

Defrost the wrapped tart in the refrigerator overnight. Uncover the tart and let it sit at room temperature for 1 hour before serving to give the tart a soft consistency and bring out the flavor of the chocolate. Leftover tart can be covered with plastic wrap and stored in the refrigerator up to 4 days.

2. Position a rack in the middle of the oven. Preheat the oven to 400°F.

3. Butter a piece of regular weight foil or parchment paper and place it, buttered side down, on the frozen dough. Fill with raw rice, dried beans, or pie weights. Push some of the weights against the edges of the pan to ensure the sides are supported. Place pan on a baking sheet. Bake 15 minutes. Reduce the oven heat to 350°F. Carefully remove the paper and weights and prick the crust with a fork every 3 inches. Replace any dough that sticks to the paper. Bake 10 to 12 minutes more, until the crust is golden brown. Cool the crust before filling it.

## Prepare the ganache

4. Put the butter, cream, and sugar in a medium saucepan and heat just until the cream is hot and the butter is melted. The mixture will form tiny bubbles and measure about 150°F. on a food thermometer. Do not let the mixture boil. Remove the pan from the heat and add the chopped chocolate. Let the chocolate melt in the cream for a minute. Add the vanilla and stir the sauce until it is smooth and all of the chocolate is melted. Remove 1¼ cups of ganache and set it aside at room temperature. Pour the remaining ganache into a large mixing bowl and press plastic wrap onto the surface. Refrigerate the ganache until it is cold to the touch and just beginning to harden around the edges, about 1 hour. Stir occasionally to ensure the mixture chills throughout. Whisk the cold ganache until it changes from dark to a medium chocolate color and thickens slightly, about 2 minutes. Or beat the ganache with an electric mixer on medium speed, about 30 seconds. Immediately spread the ganache cream evenly in the crust, using a thin metal spatula. Chill 10 minutes to firm the ganache. Spread the reserved unwhipped ganache over the whipped ganache.

# Chocolate–Coconut Macaroon Tart

Serves 12

This is quite an amazing tart. As it cools, it sinks slightly in the center. This slight hollow is filled with glaze, leaving a golden border around the edge.

Coconut Filling

**4 large eggs, separated**
**¼ teaspoon salt**
**1½ cups sugar**
**2 cups shredded sweetened coconut**
**⅓ cup whipping cream**
**3 tablespoons unsalted butter, melted**
**1½ teaspoons fresh lemon juice**
**2 teaspoons vanilla extract**
**½ teaspoon almond extract**
**½ teaspoon cream of tartar**

Shiny Chocolate Glaze

**4 tablespoons (½ stick) unsalted butter, softened**
**⅓ cup whipping cream**
**2 tablespoons light corn syrup**
**6 ounces semisweet chocolate, chopped**

**1 Tart Pastry Crust (page 35), unbaked and frozen**

1. Position a rack in the middle of the oven. Preheat the oven to 375°F.

## Prepare the coconut filling

2. Put the egg whites in a clean large bowl and set aside. Put the egg yolks in the large bowl of an electric mixer and beat with the salt just to break up the yolks. Add 1¼ cups of the sugar and beat on medium speed about 1 minute, until the mixture thickens and lightens slightly in color. Decrease the speed to low and stir in the coconut, cream, melted butter, lemon juice, vanilla, and almond extract. Set aside. Use clean dry beaters to beat the egg whites with the cream of tartar at low speed until the egg whites are foamy. Increase the speed to medium-high and beat until soft peaks form. Slowly add the remaining ¼ cup of sugar, 1 tablespoon at a time. Fold about half of the egg white mixture into the coconut mixture, then fold in the remaining egg white mixture.

3. Pour the coconut filling into the tart crust. The mixture will fill the pastry. Place the pan on a baking sheet. Bake about 40 minutes until the top of the tart is golden and the center remains set if you give the tart a gentle shake. Cool the tart thoroughly, about 1 hour at room temperature. The center will sink slightly.

### Good Advice

The tart will be quite moist, so it is unnecessary to check it with a toothpick.

### Doubling the Recipe

Use two unbaked tart shells and double the remaining ingredients.

### To Freeze

Chill the tart until the glaze is set. Use a small sharp knife to loosen the sides of the crust from the pan. Set the pan on a shallow bowl, such as a soup bowl, and let the rim slide down. Slide the tart onto a serving plate or 12-inch cardboard cake circle. Wrap tightly with plastic wrap then heavy aluminum foil. Label with date and contents. Freeze up to 2 months.

### To Serve

Place the wrapped tart in the refrigerator overnight to defrost. Uncover the tart and let it sit at room temperature 15 minutes before serving. The glaze should soften slightly, but the filling should be cold. Cover leftover tart with plastic wrap and store in the refrigerator up to 5 days.

## Prepare the glaze

4. Put the butter, cream, and corn syrup in a medium saucepan and stir over medium heat, until the mixture is hot and the butter is melted. The mixture will form tiny bubbles and measure about 175°F. on a food thermometer. Do not let the mixture boil. Add the chopped chocolate and let it melt for about 30 seconds. Gently stir the sauce until all of the chocolate is melted and the glaze is smooth. Let the glaze cool 10 minutes and thicken slightly. Gently pour the glaze over the center of the cooled tart. Using a thin metal spatula, spread the glaze over the tart, leaving a 1-inch border without glaze.

## Variations

- One cup of warmed Chocolate Truffle Sauce (page 45) can be substituted for the chocolate glaze.
- Omit the chocolate glaze and serve the tart with whipped cream and sliced strawberries.

# Caramel-Cashew Tart

Serves 12

You would be shocked if you saw my work area when I'm baking at the restaurant. Unfinished desserts and ingredients are spread everywhere, but there is order in this chaos. And it's often the inspiration for other desserts, like the bag of cashew nuts resting against a bowl of caramel sauce that gave me the idea for the caramel cashew filling in this tart.

**1 Tart Pastry Crust (page 35), unbaked and frozen**

Caramel Cashew Filling

**1¼ cups whipping cream**
**2 tablespoons unsalted butter**
**1 cup sugar**
**1 teaspoon vanilla extract**
**2 cups roasted unsalted whole cashew nuts**

**1 ounce white chocolate, Callebaut preferred**

1. Position the oven rack in the bottom third of the oven. Preheat the oven to 400°F.

## Prebake the crust

2. Use a fork to prick the bottom of the crust at 2-inch intervals. Line the crust with heavy aluminum foil and fill with raw rice, dried beans, or pie weights. Push some of the weights against the edges of the pan to ensure the sides are supported. Place pan on a baking sheet. Bake 15 minutes. Reduce the oven heat to 350°F., remove the foil and weights, and prick the crust lightly with a fork. Bake 5 more minutes, until the crust is golden brown. Repair any cracks in the crust with reserved pastry scraps. Leave the oven temperature at 350°F.

## Prepare the filling

3. Heat the cream and butter in a small saucepan and keep the mixture hot, about 150°F. if measured with a food thermometer, without boiling it. Put the sugar in a 2-quart heavy-bottomed saucepan and melt it over medium-low heat. Increase the heat to medium and cook the sugar to a light amber color, stirring occasionally with a wooden spoon to melt the sugar evenly. Remove the caramelized sugar from the heat. Slowly and carefully add the warm cream mixture. The mixture will bubble up, so be careful. Return the saucepan to medium heat and cook the mixture, stirring with the wooden spoon, until the caramel is dissolved in the cream and the sauce is smooth. Cool the caramel for 30 minutes at room temperature, then stir in the vanilla and cashew nuts.

### Good Advice

If there are cracks in the pastry after it is prebaked (unlikely but possible), patch them with reserved pastry scraps to prevent the caramel sauce from leaking through the pastry crust.

### Doubling the Recipe

Use two unbaked Tart Pastry Crusts. Double the remaining ingredients. Use a four-quart saucepan to cook the sugar.

### To Freeze

Once the tart is cold the pan can be removed. Set the pan on a shallow bowl, such as a soup bowl, and let the rim slide down. Use a long wide metal spatula to slide the tart onto a serving platter or 12-inch cardboard circle covered with heavy aluminum foil. Wrap the tart tightly with plastic wrap then heavy aluminum foil. Freeze up to 2 months.

### To Serve

Defrost the wrapped tart in the refrigerator overnight. Bring to room temperature to serve. Any leftover tart can be covered with plastic wrap and stored in the refrigerator up to 4 days, but be sure to bring it to room temperature before serving, so the caramel can soften.

4. Pour the mixture into the partially baked crust and bake 20 minutes. The caramel will be bubbling. Remove from the oven and cool the tart thoroughly.

5. Cool the oven to a temperature of 175°F. Put the white chocolate in a small nonreactive heatproof container; a ceramic or glass baking dish works well. Melt the white chocolate in the oven, 8 to 10 minutes. Remove the white chocolate from the oven as soon as it is melted. Dip a fork into the melted white chocolate and wave it over the tart to form thin lines of white chocolate. Working quickly, wave the fork in a random pattern, crisscrossing back and forth over the tart. Keep dipping the fork and sprinkling the white chocolate until all of the white chocolate is used. Try to sprinkle the chocolate quickly to create thin lines. Use a small sharp knife to loosen the crust from the sides of the pan but do not remove the rim. Chill the tart in the refrigerator to firm the white chocolate.

# Almond Tart with Raspberry Sauce.

**Serves 12**

The filling in this tart has the flavor of marzipan, but with the emphasis on almonds rather than sugar. A good dose of amaretto (almond liqueur) gives it a boost.

Double Almond Filling

- 2 large eggs
- 1 large egg white
- 1/4 teaspoon salt
- 3/4 cup sugar
- 1 teaspoon vanilla extract
- 3/4 teaspoon almond extract
- 2 tablespoons amaretto
- 1 1/4 cups blanched almonds, ground
- 4 tablespoons (1/2 stick) unsalted butter, melted and cooled

1 Tart Pastry Crust (page 35), unbaked and frozen

Raspberry Sauce

- Two 10-ounce packages frozen raspberries in syrup, defrosted and drained with juice reserved
- 6 tablespoons raspberry jam
- 2 tablespoons reserved juice drained from raspberries
- 2 teaspoons lemon juice

Powdered sugar, for dusting the top of the tart

1. Position an oven rack in the middle of the oven. Preheat oven to 400°F.

## Prepare and bake the filling

2. Put the eggs, egg white, and salt in the workbowl of a food processor fitted with the steel blade and process just to combine the eggs. With the machine running, add the sugar and process for 2 minutes. Add the vanilla, almond extract, amaretto, and ground almonds.

Process for 30 seconds. Add the melted butter and process just to combine the butter.

3. Pour the almond filling into the frozen pastry shell. Place pan on a baking sheet. Bake for 10 minutes. Reduce the oven heat to 350°F. and bake for another 10 to 12 minutes, until the filling is light brown and firm. Check to see that the tart is set by giving it a gentle shake; the center should remain firm. Cool the tart completely and dust the top with powdered sugar.

### Good Advice

• To make the almond filling even faster, grind the almonds in the food processor, remove them, and add the filling ingredients to the workbowl without washing it.

### Doubling the Recipe

Use two crusts and double the filling and sauce ingredients.

### To Freeze

Use a small sharp knife to loosen the sides of the crust from the pan. Set the pan on a shallow bowl, such as a soup bowl, and let the rim slide down. Use a long wide metal spatula to slide the tart onto a serving plate or 12-inch cardboard cake circle. Wrap the tart tightly with plastic wrap then heavy aluminum foil. Label with date and contents. Freeze up to 2 months.

### To Serve

Defrost the wrapped tart at room temperature. Dust with additional powdered sugar if there are any bare spots. Slice the tart and spoon raspberry sauce around one or both sides of each slice.

Cover with plastic wrap and store leftover tart at room temperature up to 3 days. Cover with plastic wrap and store leftover raspberry sauce in the refrigerator up to 3 days.

## Prepare the raspberry sauce

4. Put all of the sauce ingredients in a food processor fitted with the steel blade. Process until the ingredients form a puree. Strain the sauce into a plastic freezer container. Press plastic wrap onto the sauce and cover tightly. The sauce can be stored in the refrigerator up to 3 days or frozen up to 1 month. Defrost frozen sauce in the refrigerator 6 hours or overnight. Stir the sauce to smooth it and serve with the tart.

# Lemon Crumb Tart

**Serves 8**

The crust for this tart is an easy press-in butter crumb mixture. Raspberries or blueberries can be added to the filling. Thin lemon slices, fresh mint leaves, or fresh raspberries or blueberries, if berries have been included, make a nice garnish for the tart. This recipe was adapted from a Lemon Crumb Tart that my friend Helen Hall, a co-founder with Susan Winokur of Class Cooking in Bryn Mawr, Pennsylvania, taught in their cooking classes.

### Good Advice

- Press the crust carefully up the sides of the pan so the filling does not leak out as the tart bakes.
- Grate the lemon zest from the two lemons then squeeze the juice.
- This tart is baked in a springform pan which makes smooth rather than fluted edges.

### Doubling the Recipe

Double the ingredients. When preparing two tarts, make one with lemon and one with lemon and berries.

### To Freeze

Wrap the cooled tart tightly with plastic wrap then heavy aluminum foil. Label with date and contents. Freeze up to 2 months.

### To Serve

Defrost the wrapped tart in the refrigerator. Serve the tart cold or at room temperature. Store the tart up to 4 days in the refrigerator.

Crumb Crust

**1¼ cups cake flour**
**⅓ cup powdered sugar**
**¼ pound plus 2 tablespoons (1¼ sticks) cold unsalted butter, cut into 8 pieces**

Crumb Topping

**⅓ cup unbleached all-purpose flour**
**⅓ cup (packed) light brown sugar**
**4 tablespoons (½ stick) cold unsalted butter, cut into 4 pieces**

Lemon Filling

**1½ cups sugar**
**4 large eggs**
**¼ cup fresh lemon juice**
**1 teaspoon baking powder**
**¼ cup unbleached all-purpose flour**
**2 teaspoons grated lemon zest**

**Powdered sugar, for dusting over the tart**

1. Position an oven rack in the middle of the oven. Preheat the oven to 350°F. Butter a 9-inch springform pan.

## Prepare the crumb crust

2. Put the flour, powdered sugar, and butter in the small bowl of an electric mixer. Mix on low speed just until pea-size crumbs form. Transfer the crust mixture to the prepared springform pan and press it evenly over the bottom and 1 inch up the sides of the pan. Bake for 15 minutes. The crust will shrink slightly.

## Mix the crumb topping

3. Put the flour, brown sugar, and butter for the crumb topping in the same small bowl of the electric mixer that was used to mix the crust. It is not necessary to wash the bowl. Mix on low speed just until crumbs the size of lima beans form. Set aside.

## Prepare the filling

4. Put the sugar, eggs, and lemon juice in a large mixing bowl. Mix on low speed with an electric mixer or by hand with a whisk just until the mixture is smooth, about 30 seconds. Sift the baking powder and flour together. Stir the lemon zest and flour mixture into the egg mixture and mix until smooth, about 30 seconds.

5. Gently pour the lemon mixture over the partially baked crust. The lemon mixture should come just to the top of the crust. Bake 20 minutes. Gently sprinkle the crumb topping over the lemon filling. Bake 20 to 25 minutes longer, until the tart looks set. Give the tart a gentle shake; if the filling looks firm, it is done. Remove the tart from the oven and cool thoroughly. Run a small sharp knife around the sides of the pan to loosen the tart. Release the sides of the pan and remove the tart. To remove the bottom of the springform pan, use a sharp knife to loosen the tart from the bottom of the pan and a wide metal spatula to slide the tart onto a platter or cardboard cake circle. Sprinkle the cooled tart with powdered sugar.

## Variation

Gently place 1½ cups fresh or frozen unsweetened raspberries or blueberries evenly on the lemon mixture after pouring it into the crust in Step 5. The berries will sink to the bottom of the tart. Proceed with the baking.

# Fresh Fruit Tart

**Serves 10**

Classic desserts, like the Fresh Fruit Tart, earn their reputation for good reasons, usually because they taste good and appeal to most people. The only negative feature about a Fresh Fruit Tart is that it's best served the day it's prepared and thus involves last-minute preparation—not my idea of fun. But with a Tart Pastry Crust and Pastry Cream in the freezer, a spectacular fruit tart can be assembled very quickly. Tarts can be baked in any shaped pan—round, heart, or oblong.

**1 Tart Pastry Crust (page 35), unbaked and frozen**
**¼ or ½ cup cold whipping cream**
**1 cup cold Pastry Cream (page 42)**
**Fresh fruit, such as 1½ pints strawberries cut in half lengthwise; 3½ cups blueberries, raspberries, or blackberries; 8 peeled kiwi fruit sliced ¼ inch thick; or a combination**
**2 tablespoons seedless jam or jelly, strawberry or raspberry jam to glaze strawberries or raspberries; apricot jam for blueberries, blackberries, or kiwi fruit**

1. Position an oven rack in the middle of the oven. Preheat the oven to 400°F.

### Bake the crust

2. Press a piece of heavy aluminum foil into the frozen tart crust and over the edges of the pan. Fill the aluminum foil with raw rice, dried beans, or metal pie weights, about 2½ cups of rice or beans. Check to see that the weights cover the entire bottom of the crust. Place pan on a baking sheet. Bake the tart for 10 minutes. Carefully remove the aluminum foil and pie weights. Prick the pastry in several places with a fork. Bake for 5 more minutes. Reduce the oven temperature to 350° F. Bake the crust until it is an even golden brown, about 20 minutes. Cool the crust completely.

### Prepare a tart using sliced fruit

3. Put the ¼ cup whipping cream in a small bowl and beat with a hand mixer on high speed until soft peaks form. Put the Pastry Cream in a medium bowl and whisk until smooth, about 15 seconds. Use a rubber spatula to fold the whipped cream into the Pastry Cream. Spread the cream mixture evenly over the bottom of the cooled pastry crust. Beginning at the rim, arrange the halved strawberries or kiwi slices in a circular pattern on top. For a strawberry tart, place strawberry halves with the point of each strawberry overlapping the bottom of the strawberry in front of it for snug rows. For a kiwi tart, place each kiwi slice in the middle of the preceding slice to overlap. Heat strawberry or raspberry jam for a strawberry tart or apricot jam for a kiwi tart in a small saucepan over low heat just until melted. Strain

### Good Advice

Bake the crust up to one day before filling it.

### Doubling the Recipe

Use two baked Tart Pastry Crusts and double the remaining ingredients.

### To Serve

Set the pan on a shallow bowl, such as a soup bowl, and let the rim slide down. Use a long wide metal spatula to slide the tart onto a serving plate. Use a large sharp knife to cut the tart. Serve the tart the same day it is assembled.

the jam into a small bowl. Using a pastry brush, lightly brush the fruit with the jam.

## Prepare a berry tart using whole berries

4. Put the ½ cup whipping cream in a small bowl and beat with a hand mixer on high speed until soft peaks form. Put the Pastry Cream in a medium bowl and whisk until smooth, about 15 seconds. Use a rubber spatula to fold the whipped cream into the pastry cream. Spread the cream mixture evenly over the bottom of the cooled pastry crust. Gently spoon the blueberries, raspberries, or blackberries evenly on top. The fruit should completely cover the cream. Or arrange rings of a combination of blueberries, blackberries, or raspberries over the top. Heat strawberry or raspberry jam for a raspberry tart or apricot jam for a blueberry or blackberry tart in a small saucepan over low heat just until melted. Strain the jam into a small bowl. Using a pastry brush, lightly dab the fruit with the jam. The fruit will not be completely covered with jam.

## Variation

Spread 1 cup Pastry Cream, without the whipped cream addition, in the bottom of the baked pastry crust. Top with fruit.

# Frozen Terrines, Mousses, *and* Mousse Pies

I think of these terrines and pies as party desserts—the best kind since they are made and frozen long before party day.

Most of them are prepared from either an Italian meringue, a French parfait, or a mousse. Even when frozen, these desserts have a light, creamy texture.

Iced Pistachio Praline Mousse and Mile High Peach, Strawberry, and Toasted Almond Soufflé are prepared with an Italian meringue. For an Italian meringue, a hot sugar syrup is beaten into whipped egg whites; the firm meringue is then mixed with whipped cream and flavorings.

For the French parfait base, used for the Hazelnut, Chocolate, and Espresso Terrine, a hot sugar syrup is beaten into whole eggs. Again whipped cream and flavorings are added, but since the parfait is made with whole eggs, the result is creamier and more dense than when egg whites alone are used. The other desserts in this chapter are made with a straightforward mousse.

All these desserts are frozen in either a long narrow loaf pan (terrine pan) or a springform pan. They unmold easily and the pans take care of shaping the desserts into neat shapes.

# Lemon Meringue Terrine

**Serves 10**

This terrine gives new meaning to lemon meringue. Lemon mousse is layered with toasted almond meringues in a long narrow loaf pan for a fancy looking shape. After it is unmolded, the entire terrine is covered with crushed meringue.

Toasted Almond Meringues

**5 large egg whites**
**½ teaspoon cream of tartar**
**1 cup sugar**
**½ teaspoon vanilla extract**
**½ teaspoon almond extract**
**1 tablespoon cornstarch**
**1¼ cups ground toasted blanched almonds (page 6)**

Lemon Mousse

**½ cup heavy whipping cream**
**½ cup fresh lemon juice**
**4 large eggs**
**1 cup sugar**
**2 tablespoons grated lemon zest**
**1¼ cups cold heavy whipping cream**
**1 teaspoon vanilla extract**

**Thin slices of lemon, for garnish (optional)**

1. Preheat the oven to 275°F. Line two large baking sheets with aluminum foil. Butter the aluminum foil and lightly coat it with powdered sugar. Using the bottom of a loaf pan, preferably a long one about 12 × 4 inches, as a guide, mark 2 rectangles on each baking sheet with a dull knife.

## Prepare the meringues

2. Put the egg whites and cream of tartar in the large bowl of an electric mixer and beat on low speed until the egg whites are frothy. Increase the speed to medium-high and beat until soft peaks form. Reduce the speed to medium and slowly beat in the sugar, 1 tablespoon every 30 seconds. Mix in the vanilla and almond extract. Mix the cornstarch and ground almonds in a large bowl and fold the egg white mixture into the nut mixture in 2 additions.

3. Use a thin metal spatula to spread the meringue mixture over the 4 marked rectangles. Smooth the edges with the metal spatula. Or, fit a pasty bag with a ½-inch plain tip, fill the pastry bag with the meringue and pipe it onto the rectangles. Bake 65 to 75 minutes, until the meringues are crisp and dry. Remove from the oven. Place the bottom of the loaf pan on the

### Good Advice

- The meringues will spread slightly as they bake. If they need trimming, do it while they are still warm and soft. When you are ready to remove them from the baking sheet, peel the aluminum foil from the meringues rather than the meringues from the foil.
- Take care not to let the lemon custard boil, as this will cause it to curdle.
- While any loaf pan with a seven- or eight-cup capacity will work, I prefer the sophisticated look that a long narrow pan gives this dessert.

### Doubling the Recipe

Double the meringue and mousse ingredients. The meringues will need four baking sheets.

### To Freeze the Meringues

Cut a rectangular piece of cardboard an inch larger than the meringues. Cover the cardboard with aluminum foil. Stack the meringues on the cardboard, placing plastic wrap between each layer. Carefully cover the stack of meringues with plastic wrap, then heavy aluminum foil. The meringues may be frozen up to 1 month. Do not defrost before using.

meringues and trim them while still warm. If the pan is slant-sided, use the top of the pan as a guide to trim two of the meringues. Cool the meringues on the baking sheet. Peel the aluminum foil from the meringues. The meringues can be frozen.

### Prepare the mousse

4. Have ready a strainer set over a bowl. Put the ½ cup of heavy whipping cream in a medium saucepan and heat over medium-low heat until the cream is hot, about 150°F. if measured on a food thermometer. Put the lemon juice, eggs, and sugar in a large bowl and whisk smooth. Whisking constantly, slowly pour the hot cream over the egg mixture. Return the mixture to the saucepan and cook over medium heat, stirring until the mixture reaches 160°F. on a food thermometer, thickens, and coats a spoon. This will take about 4 minutes. Do not let the custard boil. Immediately strain the custard into the bowl and stir in the lemon zest. Press plastic wrap onto the custard and refrigerate until cold. Put the cold heavy whipping cream and vanilla in the large bowl of an electric mixer and beat on medium speed to firm peaks. Use a rubber spatula to fold a third of the whipped cream into the cold lemon mixture to lighten it. Fold in the remaining whipped cream.

### Assemble the terrine

5. Do this 1 day or up to 1 week before serving. Cut a strip of parchment paper to fit the bottom and extend over the ends of the loaf pan used to measure the meringues. Lightly oil the pan and press the parchment paper strip onto the bottom and over the ends of the pan. Spread a ½-inch layer of mousse in the bottom of the pan. Choose the 3 best looking meringues to layer with the mousse. If a meringue breaks, place the pieces on the mousse; the mousse will hold it together. Place a meringue on top of the mousse. Spread about ¾ inch of mousse on the meringue. Add another meringue and spread on the remaining mousse. Top with the third meringue.

### To Freeze the Terrine

Crush the remaining meringue, seal it in a plastic freezer bag or freezer container and keep it frozen until you unmold the terrine. Wrap the loaf pan tightly with plastic wrap then heavy aluminum foil. Freeze the terrine overnight or up to 1 week.

### To Serve

On the day of serving, remove the terrine from the freezer and loosen the sides of mousse with a sharp knife. Place a serving plate on top of the terrine and invert. Release the terrine from the loaf pan by pulling on the parchment paper. Remove the parchment paper. Press the reserved crushed meringue on the top and sides of the terrine. Wrap with plastic wrap and return to the freezer until serving time. Remove the terrine from the freezer 10 minutes before serving time. Cut into slices and serve. For a nice garnish place 2 thin slices of lemon overlapping each other on each plate.

# Hazelnut, Chocolate, and Espresso Terrine

Serves 12

The base of this terrine is French parfait, a preparation made by beating a hot sugar syrup into eggs. It lends itself to a variety of flavorings and remains creamy when frozen. I use the term French parfait rather than simply parfait to distinguish it from American parfaits, which consist of layers of ice cream and sauce. For this terrine one recipe of French parfait mixture is divided into thirds and each portion is flavored differently. I won't try to hide it—this recipe takes a lot of bowls.

**4 ounces white chocolate, chopped**
**6 ounces semisweet chocolate, chopped**
**⅓ cup hot water**
**⅔ cup sugar**
**1 tablespoon light corn syrup**
**2 large eggs**
**4 large egg yolks**
**1¾ cups cold whipping cream**
**1 teaspoon vanilla extract**
**2 teaspoons instant decaffeinated coffee, dissolved in 1 tablespoon whipping cream**
**¼ cup ground hazelnut praline (page 48)**

**1½ cups Cold Chocolate Sauce (page 46), for serving with the terrine**

1. Cut a long piece of parchment paper to fit the bottom and overlap the ends of a long, narrow loaf or terrine pan with a 7- to 8-cup capacity, preferably 12 × 4 × 2¾ inches.

2. Preheat the oven to 175°F. Place the white chocolate in a small nonreactive ovenproof container and the semisweet chocolate in another small ovenproof container. Melt each chocolate, about 8 minutes. Remove each chocolate from the oven as soon as it is melted, stir it smooth, and set aside to cool slightly.

3. Put the hot water, sugar, and corn syrup in a small saucepan. Cover and cook over low heat until all of the sugar is dissolved, stirring occasionally to help the sugar dissolve. Increase the heat to medium-high and boil without stirring until the syrup reaches 240°F. Brush the sides of the pan with a brush dipped in hot water to dissolve any sugar crystals that form.

4. Have ready a large bowl half filled with ice. Put the eggs and egg yolks in a large bowl of an electric mixer and beat at high speed until the eggs lighten in color and become fluffy, about 2 minutes. Decrease the speed to low and pour the hot syrup in a thin stream onto the beaten egg yolks.

### Good Advice

Adding melted white chocolate to the coffee and hazelnut mixtures enriches them and makes them creamier. To prevent any discoloration of the white chocolate, melt it in a nonreactive container.

### Doubling the Recipe

Double the ingredients but use large mixing bowls. When adding the hot sugar syrup to the eggs, use a five-quart mixing bowl.

### To Freeze

Wrap tightly with plastic wrap then heavy aluminum foil. Label with date and contents. Freeze up to 1 month.

### To Serve

Remove the terrine from the freezer and loosen the sides of the mousse with a small sharp knife. Place a long serving plate on top of the terrine and invert the terrine onto the plate. Release the dessert from the pan by pulling on the ends of the parchment paper. Slice the frozen terrine with a sharp knife and spoon Cold Chocolate Sauce around 1 side of each slice.

Try to pour the syrup in the space between the beaters and egg yolks to prevent as much sugar syrup as possible from splashing onto the sides of the bowl and the beater. Increase the speed to medium-high and beat for 1 minute. Put the egg mixture in a stainless steel bowl or nonreactive saucepan and place it over, but not touching, a saucepan of barely simmering water. Stirring constantly, cook just until the mixture reaches 160°F. on a food thermometer, thickens, and coats a spoon. Stir often where the bottom and the sides of the container meet. The cooking will take about 4 to 5 minutes. Immediately pour the hot mixture into a large bowl and place it in the ice-filled bowl. The egg mixture will be thick and smooth. Cool the mixture, stirring occasionally, until it is cool to the touch and measures about 75°F. on a food thermometer, about 5 minutes.

5. While the egg mixture cools, put the cream and vanilla in the large bowl of an electric mixer and beat at medium speed to soft peaks. Use a rubber spatula to fold half the whipped cream into the cooled egg mixture, then fold in the remaining cream. Divide the mixture among 3 medium bowls. Each bowl will contain about 2 cups. Fold the melted semisweet chocolate into 1 bowl; fold the dissolved coffee and half of the melted white chocolate into the second bowl; and fold the hazelnut praline and remaining melted white chocolate into the third bowl. Cover and refrigerate the hazelnut and coffee mixtures. Spread the chocolate layer in the bottom of the prepared pan and smooth the top. Freeze for 10 minutes. Spread the hazelnut mixture over the chocolate layer and smooth the top. Freeze for 30 minutes, until the hazelnut mixture is firm. Spread the coffee mixture over the hazelnut layer and smooth the top.

# Pistachio Praline Mousse with Strawberry Sauce

**Serves 12**

This elegant dessert is based on Italian meringue. Pistachio praline adds nice crunch and a bit of color to the white mousse.

### Pistachio Praline Mousse

**⅓ cup hot water**
**1 cup sugar**
**1 tablespoon light corn syrup**
**4 large egg whites**
**½ teaspoon cream of tartar**
**1¾ cups whipping cream**
**1 teaspoon vanilla extract**
**½ teaspoon almond extract**
**¾ cup pistachio praline, finely crushed (page 48)**
**½ cup shelled roasted unsalted pistachio nuts, coarsely chopped**

### Strawberry Sauce

**1 pint fresh strawberries or 2½ cups unsweetened frozen strawberries, defrosted and drained**
**4 to 5 tablespoons strawberry jam, depending on the sweetness of the strawberries**
**1 tablespoon fresh lemon juice**

1. Cut a long piece of parchment paper to fit the bottom and overhang the ends of a long narrow loaf pan with an 8-cup capacity, preferably 12¾ × 4¼ × 2½ inches.

## Prepare the mousse

2. Put the hot water, ¾ cup plus 2 tablespoons sugar, and corn syrup in a small clean saucepan. Cover the saucepan and cook over low heat until all of the sugar is dissolved, stirring occasionally to help the sugar dissolve. Do not let the syrup boil until the sugar dissolves. Increase the heat to high and boil without stirring until the syrup reaches 240°F. measured on a candy thermometer. Brush the sides of the pan with a brush dipped in hot water to dissolve any sugar crystals that form.

3. When the syrup begins to boil, start beating the egg whites. Put the egg whites and cream of tartar in a clean large bowl of an electric mixer. Beat on low speed for 30 seconds to dissolve the cream of tartar. Increase the speed to medium-high and beat the egg whites to soft peaks. Add the remaining 2 tablespoons of sugar, 1 tablespoon at a time. As soon as the syrup reaches 240°F., and with the mixer on low speed, slowly pour the hot

### Good Advice

Italian meringue requires careful attention while the sugar syrup boils and when beating the hot syrup into the egg whites. All bowls, pots, and utensils should be clean and greasefree.

• I prefer fresh strawberries for the sauce, but frozen strawberries are quite acceptable.

### Doubling the Recipe

Double all ingredients. Use a five-quart mixing bowl for preparing the Italian meringue.

### To Freeze the Mousse

Wrap the loaf pan tightly with plastic wrap, then heavy aluminum foil. Label with date and contents. Freeze overnight or up to 3 weeks.

### To Freeze the Strawberry Sauce

Place the sauce in a plastic freezer container and press plastic wrap onto the sauce. Label with date and contents. Cover the container and freeze up to 1 month. Defrost the sauce in the refrigerator for 5 hours or overnight. Stir the sauce with a whisk to smooth it.

## To Serve

Remove the mousse from the freezer. Unwrap the mousse and loosen the sides from the pan with a small sharp knife. Place a long narrow serving plate on top of the mousse and invert it onto the plate. Release the mousse from the pan by pulling on the ends of the parchment paper and removing the pan. Discard the parchment paper. Cut the frozen mousse into slices with a large sharp knife. Spoon the strawberry sauce around 1 side of each slice of mousse.

syrup in a thin stream onto the egg whites. If the syrup reaches 240°F. before the egg whites are whipped, remove the syrup from the heat for a few seconds and finish beating the egg whites. Try to pour the syrup in the space between the beaters and egg whites to prevent as much sugar syrup as possible from splashing onto the sides of the bowl and the beater. Increase the speed to medium and beat the meringue for 5 minutes. The outside of the bowl will be lukewarm and the meringue will be stiff and have a temperature of about 72 to 78°F. measured with an instant-read food thermometer.

4. Put the cream, vanilla, and almond extract in the large bowl of an electric mixer. Beat the cream on medium speed to soft peaks. Use a large rubber spatula to fold half of the whipped cream into the meringue. Fold the remaining whipped cream, the praline, and pistachio nuts into the meringue. Pour the mousse into the prepared pan. Smooth the top of the terrine.

## Prepare the strawberry sauce

5. Wash and hull fresh strawberries. Place fresh or defrosted frozen strawberries, 4 tablespoons of the strawberry jam, and lemon juice in a food processor fitted with the steel blade. Process the mixture to a puree and taste for sweetness. Add up to 1 more tablespoon of strawberry jam. Strain the sauce into a serving bowl, cover, and chill until serving time. The sauce can be refrigerated up to 3 days or frozen.

# Mile High Peach, Strawberry, and Toasted Almond Soufflé

**Serves 10 to 12**

Frozen soufflés are the foolproof kind of soufflé. I freeze this one in a springform pan; when the sides of the pan are removed, the beautiful colored layers are revealed. The height of the dessert makes a big impression on people, but with the springform it's easy to achieve.

**1 pint fresh strawberries, washed and hulled**
**1½ cups (7 ounces) dried peaches (about 10 large halves)**
**¾ cup fresh orange juice**
**9 ounces white chocolate, chopped, Callebaut preferred**
**½ cup hot water**
**1½ cups plus 2 tablespoons sugar**
**2 tablespoons light corn syrup**
**9 large egg whites**
**¾ teaspoon cream of tartar**
**3 cups cold whipping cream**
**1½ teaspoons vanilla extract**
**2 teaspoons fresh lemon juice**
**2 teaspoons Grand Marnier**
**1 cup ground toasted blanched almonds**
**½ teaspoon almond extract**
**Fresh strawberries with stems, for garnish**

1. Cut a strip of wax paper or parchment paper 28 × 8 inches. Fold the paper in half lengthwise and wrap it tightly around the top of an 8-inch springform pan. Tape the overlapping ends together. The paper should extend at least 3 inches above the rim of the pan.

2. Puree the strawberries in a food processor until smooth. You will have about 1¼ cups puree. Place the peaches in a small saucepan and add the orange juice. Cover and bring to a simmer. Small bubbles will form around the edges. Simmer for 5 minutes. Remove from the heat and let the covered peaches sit for 10 minutes. Puree the peach mixture in a food processor. The peaches will be chunky, not smooth. Cover the mixture and set aside.

3. Preheat the oven to 175°F. Place the white chocolate in a small nonreactive heatproof container. Melt the chocolate in the oven, 8 to 10 minutes. Remove it from the oven as soon as it is melted and stir it smooth.

4. Put the hot water, 1½ cups of sugar, and corn syrup in a small grease-free saucepan. Cook, covered, over low heat until all of the sugar is dissolved, stirring occasionally. Do not let the syrup boil until the sugar dissolves. Increase the heat to high and boil, without stirring, until the syrup reaches 240°F. measured on a candy thermometer. Brush the sides of the pan with a brush dipped in hot water to dissolve any sugar crystals that form.

### Good Advice

- Beat a small amount of sugar into the egg whites for the meringue before adding the hot sugar syrup to them. This stabilizes the egg whites in case they have to wait for the sugar syrup to reach the proper temperature.
- Dried peaches reconstituted in fresh orange juice give an intense peach flavor to the soufflé. Dried peaches are usually available at health food stores or specialty food shops. Hadley Fruit Orchards, listed in the mail order information on page 245, ships dried peaches.

### Doubling the Recipe

There is too much Italian meringue (the sugar syrup and egg whites) in this recipe to double it and beat it properly even in a large mixing bowl; make separate recipes of the Italian meringue. The melted white chocolate, whipped cream, and flavoring additions can be doubled. A five-quart bowl will be just large enough to whip six cups of cream.

### To Freeze

Gently press plastic wrap on the top of the soufflé. Freeze overnight. Remove the parchment paper collar. Wrap the soufflé tightly with plastic wrap, then heavy aluminum foil. Label with date and contents. Freeze up to 3 weeks.

Once the soufflé is frozen, you may remove the springform pan. Dip a dish towel in hot water and wring out the water. Hold the hot towel around the sides of the pan for 15 seconds. Release the sides of the springform. Either leave the pie on the springform bottom or transfer it to a serving plate. Rewrap the soufflé with the plastic wrap and foil.

### To Serve

Remove the soufflé from the freezer. Let sit 10 minutes, unwrap, and cut into wedges to serve. Garnish with fresh strawberries.

5. When the syrup begins to boil, start beating the egg whites. Put the egg whites and cream of tartar in the large bowl of an electric mixer and beat on low speed for 30 seconds to dissolve the cream of tartar. Increase the speed to medium-high and beat the egg whites to soft peaks. Add the remaining 2 tablespoons of sugar, 1 tablespoon at a time. As soon as the syrup reaches 240°F. on a candy thermometer, and with the mixer on low speed, slowly pour the hot syrup in a thin stream onto the softly beaten egg whites. If the syrup reaches 240°F. before the egg whites are whipped, remove the syrup from the heat for a few seconds and finish beating the egg whites. Try to pour the syrup in the space between the beaters and egg whites to prevent as much sugar syrup as possible from splashing onto the sides of the bowl and the beater. Beat the meringue at medium speed for about 5 minutes. The outside of the bowl will be lukewarm and the meringue will be stiff and have a temperature of about 72° to 78°F. if measured with a food thermometer. Decrease the speed to low and mix in the melted white chocolate. The meringue will deflate slightly when the white chocolate is added. Cover and chill 15 minutes.

6. Put the cream and vanilla in a large bowl of an electric mixer and beat on medium speed to soft peaks. Fold half of the whipped cream into the cooled meringue mixture, then fold in the remaining whipped cream. Divide the mixture among 3 large bowls. There will be about 12 cups of soufflé mixture. Remove ¼ cup of the cream mixture from 1 bowl and stir it into the peach puree to lighten it and separate the peach pieces. Fold the peach puree back into this bowl. Fold the strawberry puree, lemon juice, and Grand Marnier into the second bowl of the soufflé mixture. Fold the toasted almonds and almond extract into the third bowl. Refrigerate the strawberry and almond mixtures. Pour the peach mixture into the springform pan and smooth the top. Freeze 45 minutes, until firm. Carefully pour the strawberry mixture into the springform pan and smooth the top. Freeze 45 minutes, until firm. Pour the almond mixture into the springform pan and smooth the top. The soufflé will be about 1½ inches above the top of the springform pan.

### Variation

Substitute raspberries for the strawberries and dried apricots for the dried peaches.

# Key Largo Lemon Crunch Pie

**Serves 10 to 12**

Naming this pie was easy. Key Largo reminds me of the classic Humphrey Bogart romantic adventure movie and Florida Key lime pie. With similar ingredients and the same easy preparation that typifies Key lime pie, this pie replaces the hard-to-find Key limes with lemons. The pie is served frozen, but never freezes hard. Cold, creamy, lemony—this is as refreshing as a pie gets.

**Lemon Filling**

**4 large eggs, separated**
**Two 14-ounce cans sweetened condensed milk**
**1 teaspoon grated lemon zest**
**1 cup fresh lemon juice (4 to 5 large lemons)**
**½ teaspoon cream of tartar**

**1 Graham Cracker Crumb Crust (page 34), baked in a 9-inch springform pan, cooled or frozen**

**Lemon Buttercrunch**

**½ pound (2 sticks) unsalted butter**
**1⅓ cups sugar**
**1 tablespoon light corn syrup**
**3 tablespoons water**
**1½ teaspoons grated lemon zest**

**Whipped cream, for serving with the pie**
**Thin lemon slices, for garnish**

## Prepare the lemon filling

1. Put the egg yolks in a large bowl and mix with a whisk just to break up the egg yolks. Add the condensed milk and mix with the whisk. Add the lemon zest and lemon juice and whisk until the mixture is smooth. In the large bowl of an electric mixer, beat the egg whites with the cream of tartar on low speed until the egg whites are foamy. Increase the speed to medium-high and beat just until soft peaks form. Use a rubber spatula to fold about a quarter of the egg whites into the lemon mixture. Fold in the remaining egg whites. Pour the filling into the crust.

## Prepare the buttercrunch

2. Line a 13 × 9 × 2-inch baking pan with heavy aluminum foil. Do not butter the foil. Put the butter in a medium saucepan and melt over low heat. Add the sugar, corn syrup, and water. Stir with a wooden spoon over medium heat until the mixture reaches 320°F. on a candy thermometer. The mixture will turn a light caramel color then a darker caramel color as it

### Good Advice

- Wash the lemons and grate 2½ teaspoons lemon zest, then squeeze a cup of lemon juice. One teaspoon of zest will be for the pie filling and the remainder for the buttercrunch.
- When it is cooking, the lemon buttercrunch mixture is very hot so be careful not to splash any on yourself.
- Once the lemon buttercrunch is added to the pie, it will become soft. It loses its crunch in about three days, so wait until the day the pie is served to add the topping.

### Doubling the Recipe

Use two baked Graham Cracker Crumb Crusts and double the ingredients for the pie filling. The lemon buttercrunch recipe makes enough for three pies.

### To Freeze the Pie

Freeze the pie, uncovered, for about 2 hours, until it is cold and firm. Wrap the springform pan tightly with plastic wrap then heavy aluminum foil. Label with date and contents. Freeze at least overnight or up to 3 weeks.

Once the pie is frozen, you can remove the springform pan. Dip a dish towel in hot water and wring out the water. Hold the hot towel around the sides of the pan for 15 seconds. Release the sides of the springform. Either leave the pie on the springform bottom or slide it onto a serving plate. Rewrap the pie with the plastic wrap and foil.

### To Freeze the Buttercrunch

Put the buttercrunch in a plastic freezer container and press plastic wrap onto the buttercrunch. Cover the container. Or put the buttercrunch in a plastic freezer bag and seal tightly. Label with date and contents. Freeze up to 2 months.

### To Serve

Remove the pie from the freezer and sprinkle 1 cup of the crushed lemon buttercrunch over the top. Let the pie sit 10 minutes at room temperature. Cut into wedges and serve with whipped cream. Garnish with thin lemon slices. Return leftover pie to the freezer. If the buttercrunch softens on leftover pie, top with more buttercrunch.

reaches 320°F. Stir constantly toward the end of the cooking time to prevent any burning. As soon as the mixture reaches 320°F. remove it from the heat and stir in the lemon zest. Immediately pour into the foil-lined pan. Be careful not to splash any of the hot mixture on yourself. Cool completely until hard. Remove the buttercrunch from the pan and peel off the foil. Place the buttercrunch between 2 pieces of wax paper or heavy aluminum foil and crush with a rolling pin or the flat side of a mallet into pieces about ½ inch in size.

# Raspberry and White Chocolate Mousse Pie

Serves 12

This mousse pie and the two that follow are all prepared the same easy way. Egg whites are beaten with sugar until stiff, then combined with a chocolate or white chocolate mixture. Whipped cream is folded in and the mixture is poured into a chocolate crumb crust and frozen in a springform pan so it is easy to unmold and to serve.

**1½ cups fresh raspberries or frozen sweetened raspberries in syrup**
**9 ounces white chocolate, chopped, Callebaut preferred**
**¼ cup hot water**
**3 large eggs, separated**
**¼ teaspoon cream of tartar**
**½ cup sugar**
**2 cups cold whipping cream**
**1 teaspoon vanilla extract**
**2 tablespoons white crème de cacao**
**1 Chocolate Wafer Cookie Crumb Crust (page 34), baked in a 9-inch springform pan, cooled or frozen**
**Fresh raspberries and mint leaves, for garnish (optional)**

1. If using fresh raspberries, crush them slightly and set aside. If using frozen raspberries, defrost, drain, and crush slightly.

2. Put the white chocolate and hot water in a heatproof container and place it over, but not touching, a saucepan of gently simmering water. Stir the white chocolate and water together until the white chocolate is melted and smooth. Remove the saucepan from the heat and whisk in the egg yolks. Place the mixture back over the simmering water, and, stirring constantly, cook just until the temperature reaches 160°F. on a food thermometer, about 5 minutes. The white chocolate mixture will thicken when the egg yolks are added, then become shiny and smooth as it reaches 160°F. Immediately transfer the white chocolate mixture to a large bowl and refrigerate the mixture until it is cool to the touch, about 15 minutes.

3. Put the egg whites and cream of tartar in the clean large bowl of an electric mixer and with clean dry beaters, beat on low speed until the egg whites are foamy. Increase the speed to medium-high and beat just until soft peaks form. Slowly add the sugar, 1 tablespoon at a time. Remove the cooled white chocolate mixture from the refrigerator, and whisk about a quarter of the beaten egg whites into the white chocolate mixture. Use a rubber spatula to fold in the remaining beaten egg whites.

4. Put the cream, vanilla, and crème de cacao in the clean bowl of an electric mixer. Beat the cream at medium speed until soft peaks form. Fold the whipped cream into the white chocolate mixture. Fold in the raspberries. Pour the mousse into the crumb crust. Smooth the top with a metal spatula.

## Good Advice

Either fresh raspberries or frozen *sweetened* raspberries can be used for the mousse. Frozen unsweetened raspberries tend to freeze too hard in the mousse.

## Doubling the Recipe

Use two baked crumb crusts and double the filling ingredients.

## To Freeze

Freeze the mousse pie, uncovered, about 2 hours, until it is cold and firm. Wrap the springform pan with plastic wrap then with heavy aluminum foil. Label with date and contents. Freeze at least overnight or up to 3 weeks. Once the pie is frozen, you can remove the springform pan. Dip a dish towel in hot water and wring out the water. Hold the hot towel around the sides of the pan for 15 seconds. Release the sides of the pan. Either leave the pie on the pan bottom or transfer it to a serving plate. Rewrap the pie with the plastic wrap and foil.

## To Serve

Let the wrapped pie soften for 10 minutes at room temperature. Use a large sharp knife to slice the pie. You can scatter a few fresh raspberries and fresh mint leaves on each plate for a pretty garnish.

# White Mocha Mousse Pie

**Serves 12**

This white chocolate and coffee mousse pie is quickly prepared by flavoring half of a recipe of white chocolate mousse with coffee. Swirling some of the coffee mousse over the white chocolate mousse creates an attractive marbleized look.

**9 ounces white chocolate, chopped, Callebaut preferred**
**¼ cup hot water**
**3 large eggs, separated**
**¼ teaspoon cream of tartar**
**½ cup sugar**
**2 cups cold whipping cream**
**1 teaspoon vanilla extract**
**1 tablespoon instant decaffeinated coffee granules, dissolved in 1 tablespoon hot water**
**1 Chocolate Wafer Cookie Crumb Crust (page 34), baked in a 9-inch springform pan, cooled or frozen**

1. Put the white chocolate and hot water in a heatproof container and place it over, but not touching, a saucepan of gently simmering water. Stir the white chocolate and water together until the white chocolate is melted and smooth. Remove the saucepan from the heat and stir in the egg yolks. Place the mixture back over the simmering water, and stirring constantly, cook just until the temperature reaches 160°F. on a food thermometer, about 5 minutes. The chocolate mixture will thicken when the egg yolks are added, then become shiny and smooth as it reaches 160°F. Immediately transfer the white chocolate mixture to a large bowl and refrigerate it until it is just cool to the touch, about 15 minutes.

2. Put the egg whites and cream of tartar in the large clean bowl of an electric mixer and with clean dry beaters beat on low speed until the egg whites are foamy. Increase the speed to medium-high and beat just until soft peaks form. Slowly add the sugar, 1 tablespoon at a time. Remove the cooled white chocolate mixture from the refrigerator and whisk about a quarter of the beaten egg whites into the white chocolate mixture. Use a rubber spatula to fold in the remaining whites.

3. Put the cream and vanilla in the clean large bowl of an electric mixer. Beat the cream at medium speed until soft peaks form. Fold the whipped cream into the white chocolate mixture. Transfer half of the white chocolate mousse to a large mixing bowl and fold in the dissolved coffee. Reserve ¼ cup of the coffee-flavored mousse and pour the remaining coffee mousse into the crust. Spread evenly. Gently pour the white chocolate mousse on top of the coffee mousse. Spread it evenly over the coffee mousse. Spoon the reserved coffee mousse on top and with the tip of a knife swirl the 2 mousses together.

### Good Advice

I use decaffeinated instant coffee in my desserts since the taste is indistinguishable from coffee with caffeine, which some people are bothered by.

### Doubling the Recipe

Use two baked crusts and double the filling ingredients.

### To Freeze

Freeze the mousse, uncovered, for about 2 hours, until it is cold and firm. Wrap the springform pan tightly with plastic wrap then heavy aluminum foil. Label with date and contents. Freeze at least overnight or up to 3 weeks. Once the pie is frozen, you can remove the springform pan. Dip a dish towel in hot water and wring out the water. Hold the hot towel around the sides of the pan for 15 seconds. Release the sides of the springform pan. Either leave the wrapped pie on the springform bottom or slide it onto a serving plate. Rewrap with the plastic wrap and foil.

### To Serve

Let the wrapped pie soften for 10 minutes at room temperature. Use a large sharp knife to slice the pie.

# Chocolate–Hazelnut Praline Mousse Pie

Serves 12

Hazelnut praline adds a little crunch and a lot of flavor to this frozen chocolate mousse pie.

**9 ounces semisweet chocolate, chopped**
**2 ounces unsweetened chocolate, chopped**
**¼ cup sugar**
**¼ cup hot water**
**3 large eggs, separated**
**¼ teaspoon cream of tartar**
**½ cup sugar**
**2 cups cold whipping cream**
**1 teaspoon vanilla extract**
**½ cup hazelnut praline powder (page 48)**
**1 Chocolate Wafer Cookie Crumb Crust (page 34), baked in a 9-inch springform pan, cooled or frozen**
**Hazelnut praline powder, for garnish**

1. Put the semisweet chocolate, unsweetened chocolate, sugar, and hot water in a heatproof container and place it over, but not touching, a saucepan of gently simmering water. Stir the chocolate and water together until the chocolate is melted and the mixture is smooth. Remove the saucepan from the heat and whisk in the egg yolks. Place the chocolate mixture back over the simmering water and, stirring constantly, cook just until the temperature reaches 160°F. on a food thermometer, about 5 minutes. The chocolate mixture will thicken when the egg yolks are added, then become shiny and smooth as it reaches 160°F. Transfer the chocolate mixture to a large bowl and refrigerate until it is cool to the touch, about 15 minutes.

2. Put the egg whites and cream of tartar in the clean large bowl of an electric mixer and with clean dry beaters, beat on low speed until the egg whites are foamy. Increase the speed to medium high, and beat just until soft peaks form. Slowly add the sugar, 1 tablespoon at a time. Remove the chocolate mixture from the refrigerator and whisk about a quarter of the beaten egg whites into the chocolate mixture. Fold in the remaining whites.

3. Put the cream and vanilla in the clean large bowl of an electric mixer. Beat the cream at medium speed until soft peaks form. Use a rubber spatula to fold the whipped cream and the hazelnut praline powder into the chocolate mixture. Pour the mousse into the chocolate crumb crust. Smooth the top of the mousse with a metal spatula.

### Good Advice

Prepare this and all mousse pies at least one day ahead so they have time to freeze firm.

### Doubling the Recipe

Use two baked crusts and double the filling ingredients.

### To Freeze

Freeze the mousse pie, uncovered, for about 2 hours, until it is cold and firm. Wrap the springform pan tightly with plastic wrap then heavy aluminum foil. Label with date and contents. Freeze at least overnight or up to 3 weeks. Once the pie is frozen, you can remove the springform pan. Dip a dish towel in hot water and wring out the water. Hold the hot towel around the sides of the pan for 15 seconds. Release the sides of the springform. Either leave the wrapped pie on the springform bottom or transfer it to a serving plate. Rewrap the pie with the plastic wrap and foil.

### To Serve

Let the wrapped pie soften for 10 minutes at room temperature. Use a large sharp knife to slice the pie. For a garnish, sprinkle more praline powder on top of the pie.

# Ice Cream Pies

After my children were born, I realized I was going to have to cook to the tune of an easygoing drummer or never have grown-ups to dinner again. The ice cream pie was my dessert solution. I started with Peppermint–Chocolate Crunch Ice Cream Pie and went on and on, dreaming up new combinations. I think it fitting that my first magazine article, in *Bon Appétit,* featured ice cream pies.

Ice cream pies have the advantages of quick preparation and simple ingredients. But because ice cream pies are served frozen, they need to have crusts that taste good frozen. Cookie crumb crusts fit the bill perfectly.

Most of the pies are prepared in a springform pan. This type of pan makes it possible to construct a pie that is almost three inches high and that is easy to remove from the pan and cut.

With the exception of the Cold Fudge Ice Cream Pie, I use a good quality ice cream rather than a premium ice cream. Federal government regulations state ice cream must have a minimum milkfat content of 10 percent. Good quality ice cream has about 12 percent milkfat; it also most likely contains better quality ingredients than a less expensive 10 percent milkfat ice cream. Economy supermarket brands of ice cream often have the minimum milkfat content; I do not recommend them for these ice cream pies. Buy a nice creamy ice cream that tastes good to you. A higher milkfat content also retards ice crystal formation when the ice cream freezes hard after its slight softening during preparation. Premium ice cream has a milkfat content of 14 to 18 percent. I suggest premium ice cream for some desserts but find it unnecessarily rich for ice cream pies.

Some of the additions that make these pies into such pull-out-all-the-stops desserts are crunchy cookies, chewy dates or brownies, and thick fudge sauces. Some of the cookies are storebought and some are homemade. Each ice cream pie has its extras added to the middle and top of the pie.

When preparing the pie, soften the ice cream just until it is easy to scoop and spread. The less the ice cream melts, the better it will taste after it freezes firm again. One good method is to soften the ice cream in the refrigerator for about 30 minutes, so that it softens evenly without melted spots. Since Grandma Tillie's Date Nut Ice Cream Pie has dates and nuts stirred into the ice cream, there is some additional softening from the stirring, but the liquor lowers the freezing temperature of the ice cream slightly, helping it to stay creamy. But even for this pie, you should try to let the ice cream soften as little as possible. When adding sauces to ice cream pies, the sauce should be soft and spreadable, but not warm. Warm sauce would melt the ice cream.

As soon as the ice cream pie is assembled, return it to the freezer and follow the wrapping instructions carefully. I recommend storing ice cream pies up to two weeks in the freezer. After that, they will still be edible but not at their best. The longer the pie remains in the freezer, the more likely it is that cookies and crunches will begin to soften, that sauces begin to dissolve into the ice cream, and that frost will form.

When serving an ice cream pie, soften it at room temperature until it is easy to cut. Since the temperature of your freezer and kitchen affect how the ice cream pie will react, there is no hard-and-fast rule as to how long to let the pies sit out of the freezer. Ten minutes is usually about right, but the best advice is to check the pie and serve it when it cuts easily and before any melting occurs.

# Pecan Turtle Sundae Ice Cream Pie

Serves 10 to 12

This pie is reminiscent of a pecan turtle candy, sweet and chewy.

Simple Caramel Sauce

**1 cup whipping cream**
**1 cup sugar**

**1 Graham Cracker Crumb Crust (page 34), baked in a 9-inch springform pan, cooled or frozen**
**½ gallon good quality vanilla ice cream, softened until spreadable but not melted**
**3 cups toasted pecan halves (page 6)**
**¾ cup Chocolate Truffle Sauce (page 45), warmed just until spreadable**

## Prepare the caramel sauce

1. Heat the cream in a small saucepan and keep it hot, about 150°F. if measured with a food thermometer, without boiling it. Put the sugar in a medium heavy-bottomed saucepan and cook over low heat until the sugar begins to melt. Increase the heat to medium-high and cook until the sugar melts, caramelizes, and turns a dark golden color. Watch the sugar carefully and stir it with a wooden spoon occasionally to ensure it cooks evenly. Remove from the heat. Slowly add the hot cream to the hot sugar. The mixture will bubble up, so be careful. Return the saucepan to medium heat and cook the mixture, stirring with the wooden spoon, until the caramel is completely dissolved and the sauce is smooth. Cool the sauce about 30 minutes at room temperature before using it. Or cover the sauce and refrigerate it up to 2 weeks or freeze it. To use the sauce, reheat it gently in a heatproof container placed over warm water just until the sauce is spreadable.

## Assemble the ice cream pie

2. Drizzle 3 tablespoons of the caramel sauce over the crumb crust. Use an ice cream spade to spread half of the softened ice cream over the crust. Sprinkle 1 cup of the pecans evenly over the ice cream. Spoon half of the remaining caramel sauce over the pecans, then half the chocolate sauce over the caramel sauce. Spread the remaining ice cream over the chocolate sauce. Spread the remaining 2 cups of pecans on top of the pie. Spoon the remaining caramel sauce over the pecans, then drizzle with the remaining chocolate sauce.

### Good Advice

The simple caramel sauce is prepared with just whipping cream and sugar, no vanilla.

### Doubling the Recipe

Use two crusts and double the remaining ingredients.

### To Freeze

Freeze the pie 15 minutes to firm the chocolate sauce. Wrap the pie tightly with plastic wrap then with heavy aluminum foil, gently pressing the foil against the pie. Label with date and contents. Freeze overnight or up to 2 weeks. Once the pie is frozen, you can remove the springform pan. Dip a dish towel in hot water and wring out the water. Hold the hot towel around the sides of the pan for 15 seconds. Release the sides of the pan. Either leave the pie on the springform bottom or slide it onto a serving plate. Rewrap the pie with plastic wrap and foil and return to the freezer.

### To Serve

Remove the ice cream pie from the freezer and let it soften at room temperature for about 10 minutes. Use a large sharp knife to cut the pie into wedges.

# Caramel Fudge Brownie Ice Cream Pie

Serves 10 to 12

Offered the choice between a hot fudge sundae and a hot caramel sundae, I have a hard time making a decision. I solved my predicament by combining both sundae ideas in an ice cream pie. Now, I don't have to make a difficult decision, and everyone else is happy besides.

**2 pints good quality chocolate ice cream, softened until spreadable but not melted**
**1 Oreo Cookie Crumb Crust (page 34) or Chocolate Wafer Cookie Crumb Crust (page 34), baked in a 9-inch springform pan, cooled or frozen**
**Half 8 × 8 × 2-inch pan Fudge Bars (page 76), defrosted but still cold, cut into ½-inch pieces**
**1 recipe Simple Caramel Sauce (page 199), warmed just until spreadable**
**½ cup Chocolate Truffle Sauce (page 45), warmed just until spreadable**
**2 pints good quality vanilla ice cream, softened until spreadable but not melted**

Use an ice cream spade to spread the softened chocolate ice cream over the crumb crust. Sprinkle half the Fudge Bar pieces evenly over the ice cream. Spoon ½ cup of the Caramel Sauce over the Fudge Bar pieces. Spoon ¼ cup of the Chocolate Truffle Sauce over the top, spooning the chocolate sauce in the spaces where there is no caramel sauce. Spread the vanilla ice cream over the chocolate sauce. Sprinkle the remaining Fudge Bar pieces evenly over the ice cream. Drizzle the Fudge Bar pieces first with the remaining Chocolate Truffle Sauce then with the remaining Caramel Sauce. Try to spoon the Caramel Sauce in the spaces where there is no chocolate sauce.

## Variation

Substitute coffee ice cream for the chocolate or the vanilla ice cream.

## Good Advice

- The caramel sauce is the last sauce added to the ice cream pie; it gives the top of the pie a nice shine.
- Fudge Bars are especially good in an ice cream pie because they are moist and won't dry out or freeze too hard.

## Doubling the Recipe

Use two crusts and double the remaining ingredients.

## To Freeze

Freeze the pie 15 minutes to firm the caramel sauce. Wrap the pie tightly with plastic wrap then with heavy aluminum foil, gently pressing the foil against the pie. Label with date and contents. Freeze overnight or up to 2 weeks. Once the pie is frozen, you can remove the springform pan. Dip a dish towel in hot water and wring out the water. Hold the hot towel around the sides of the pan for 15 seconds. Release the sides of the pan. Either leave the wrapped pie on the springform bottom or slide it onto a serving plate. Rewrap with plastic and foil and return the pie to the freezer.

## To Serve

Remove the ice cream pie from the freezer and let it soften at room temperature for about 10 minutes. Use a large sharp knife to cut the pie into wedges.

# Raspberry–Chocolate Shell Ice Cream Pie

Serves 10 to 12

The ice cream in this pie is layered with a chocolate coating similar to that on an ice cream pop. The chocolate forms thin, crisp shards in the middle throughout the pie, which is then covered with the same coating. The pie is like a giant raspberry ice cream pop.

Chocolate Coating

**10 ounces semisweet chocolate, chopped, or semisweet chocolate chips**
**3 tablespoons vegetable oil**

**2 pints good quality raspberry sherbet, softened until spreadable but not melted**
**1 Oreo Cookie Crumb Crust (page 34) or Chocolate Wafer Cookie Crumb Crust (page 34), baked in a 9-inch springform pan, cooled or frozen**
**2 pints good quality vanilla ice cream, softened until spreadable but not melted**

## Prepare the chocolate coating

1. Put the chocolate and vegetable oil in a heatproof container and place it over, but not touching, a saucepan of barely simmering water. Stir the mixture over the hot water until the chocolate is melted and the mixture is smooth. Remove the chocolate coating from over the hot water.

## Assemble the pie

2. Use an ice cream spade to spread the softened raspberry sherbet over the crumb crust. Spoon ½ cup of the chocolate coating evenly over the raspberry sherbet. The coating will not cover the sherbet completely. Spread the vanilla ice cream over the chocolate coating. Drizzle the remaining chocolate coating over the vanilla ice cream. The coating will cover most of the ice cream but not all of it. Immediately use a large chef's knife to cut through the coating on the top of the pie and mark 10 to 12 servings.

### Good Advice

Since the chocolate coating forms a hard shell over the top of the pie, cut through the chocolate coating and mark the slices as soon as you've drizzled the coating over the top.

### Doubling the Recipe

Use two crusts and double the remaining ingredients.

### To Freeze

Freeze the pie 15 minutes to firm the chocolate coating. Wrap the pie tightly with plastic wrap then heavy aluminum foil, gently pressing the foil against the pie. Label with date and contents. Freeze overnight or up to 2 weeks. Once the pie is frozen, you can remove the springform pan. Dip a dish towel in hot water and wring out the water. Hold the hot towel around the sides of the pan for 15 seconds. Release the sides of the pan. Either leave the pie on the springform bottom or slide it onto a serving plate. Rewrap with plastic wrap or foil and return the pie to the freezer.

### To Serve

Remove the ice cream pie from the freezer and let it soften at room temperature for about 10 minutes. Dip a large sharp knife in hot water and dry it. Cut the pie into slices with the warm knife.

## Good Advice

Form rounded spoonfuls of peanut butter in the pie so that there are thick chunks of chocolate-covered peanut butter in each slice of pie.

## Doubling the Recipe

Use two crusts and double the remaining ingredients.

## To Freeze

Wrap the pie tightly with plastic wrap, then with heavy aluminum foil, gently pressing against the pie. Label with date and contents. Freeze overnight or up to 2 weeks. Once the pie is frozen, you may remove the springform pan. Dip a dish towel in hot water and wring out. Hold the hot towel around the sides of the pan for 15 seconds. Release the sides of the pan. Either leave the pie on the springform bottom or slide it onto a serving plate. Rewrap with plastic wrap and foil and return to the freezer.

## To Serve

Remove the ice cream pie from the freezer and let it soften at room temperature for about 10 minutes. Use a large sharp knife to cut the pie into wedges.

# Peanut Butter–Fudge Ice Cream Pie

**Serves 10 to 12**

Chocolate and peanuts are the flavors in this ice cream pie. Chocolate Truffle Sauce is spooned over peanut butter and instantly forms pockets of homemade peanut butter cups throughout the pie.

**½ gallon good quality chocolate ice cream, softened until spreadable but not melted**
**1 Oreo Cookie Crumb Crust (page 34) or Chocolate Wafer Cookie Crumb Crust (page 34), baked in a 9-inch springform pan, cooled or frozen**
**1 cup smooth peanut butter**
**1 cup Chocolate Truffle Sauce (page 45), warmed just until spreadable**
**½ cup coarsely chopped unsalted peanuts**

Use an ice cream spade to spread half of the softened chocolate ice cream over the crumb crust. Drop the peanut butter in rounded teaspoonfuls evenly over the chocolate ice cream. Spread ½ cup of the Chocolate Truffle Sauce over the peanut butter pieces. Spread the remaining chocolate ice cream over the peanut butter pieces. Drizzle the remaining Chocolate Truffle Sauce over the ice cream. The sauce will not form a solid layer. Sprinkle the peanuts evenly over the top of the pie.

# Cold Fudge Ice Cream Pie

**Serves 8**

Since this pie is frozen in a pie pan, it has a thinner layer of ice cream than the other ice cream pies, which are frozen in springform pans. Each bite of pie will have a good thick layer of fudge to go with every mouthful of ice cream.

**3 pints good quality or premium ice cream softened until spreadable but not melted, such as peppermint, cherry vanilla, coffee, or raspberry**
**1 Oreo Cookie Crumb Crust (page 34) or Chocolate Wafer Cookie Crumb Crust (page 34), baked in a 10-inch pie pan, cooled or frozen**
**1⅓ cups Chocolate Truffle Sauce (page 45), warmed just until spreadable**

Spread the ice cream evenly in the crumb crust. Smooth the top. Cover the pie and freeze it until the ice cream is firm, about 30 minutes. Uncover pie and pour the chocolate sauce evenly over it. Use a thin metal spatula to spread the sauce smooth. Cover the ice cream completely with sauce.

## Good Advice

- Use either good quality or premium ice cream for this ice cream pie. Slices are smaller and thinner than usual, so premium ice cream is not too rich.
- Flavors that contrast with the chocolate topping are best.

## Doubling the Recipe

Use two crumb crusts and double the remaining ingredients.

## To Freeze

Freeze the pie 15 minutes to firm the chocolate sauce. Wrap the pie tightly with plastic wrap then with heavy aluminum foil, gently pressing the foil against the pie. Label with date and contents. Freeze overnight or up to 2 weeks.

## To Serve

Remove the ice cream pie from the freezer and let it soften at room temperature for about 10 minutes. Use a large sharp knife to cut the pie.

# Cookies and Cream Ice Cream Pie

**Serves 10 to 12**

When I want to create a new ice cream pie, I think about all my favorite things and fill it with them. Let's see—graham crackers and chocolate chips, vanilla and chocolate ice cream, Oreos and chocolate chip cookies, and chocolate fudge sauce. Sounds great to me.

Graham Cracker and Chocolate Chip Crumb Crust

**1½ cups graham cracker crumbs**
**¼ teaspoon ground cinnamon**
**5 tablespoons unsalted butter, melted**
**½ cup (3 ounces) miniature semisweet chocolate chips**

**2 pints good quality chocolate ice cream, softened until spreadable but not melted**
**1½ cups ½-inch pieces Oreo cookies (about 12 cookies)**
**2 cups ½-inch pieces homemade Big Chocolate Chip Cookies (page 81) (about six 3-inch cookies)**
**½ cup Chocolate Truffle Sauce (page 45), warmed just until spreadable**
**2 pints good quality vanilla ice cream, softened until spreadable but not melted**

**1½ cups Chocolate Truffle Sauce (page 45), for serving with the ice cream pie**

1. Position a rack in the center of the oven. Preheat the oven to 325°F. Butter a 9-inch springform pan with sides at least 2¾-inches high.

## Make the crumb crust

2. Mix the cracker crumbs with the cinnamon in a large bowl. Add the melted butter and stir together until the crumbs are evenly moistened with butter. Stir in the chocolate chips. Transfer the crumbs to the springform pan. With the back of your fingers or a spoon, press the crumbs evenly over the bottom and ¾ inch up the sides of the pan. Bake the crust for 6 minutes. Cool the crust completely before filling it with the ice cream. The crust can be baked 1 day ahead, covered with plastic wrap, and stored at room temperature.

### Good Advice

• Use homemade chocolate chip cookies from your freezer or good cookies from a bakery; a good cookie makes a difference. The cookie measurements are approximate; a few extra cookie pieces will not be a problem (notice, I did not say *a few less*). Break up the cookies by hand.

• Defrost two cups of Chocolate Truffle Sauce from the freezer. Use some when preparing the ice cream pie and refrigerate the rest for up to two weeks to use when the pie is served.

### Doubling the Recipe

Use two baked crumb crusts and double the remaining ingredients.

### To Freeze

Freeze the pie 15 minutes to firm the chocolate sauce. Wrap the pie tightly with plastic wrap then with heavy aluminum foil, gently pressing the foil against the pie. Label with date and contents. Freeze overnight or up to 1 week. The pie can be frozen up to 2 weeks, but the chocolate chip cookies will soften slightly. Once the pie is frozen, you can remove the springform pan. Dip a dish towel in hot water and wring out the water. Hold the hot towel around the sides of the pan for 15 seconds. Release the sides of the pan. Either leave the pie on the springform bottom or slide it onto a serving plate. Rewrap the pie with plastic and foil and return it to the freezer.

### To Serve

Remove the ice cream pie from the freezer and let its often at room temperature for about 10 minutes. Warm the 1½ cups of Chocolate Truffle Sauce in a medium saucepan over low heat, stirring frequently. Use a large sharp knife to cut the pie into wedges and pass the warm Chocolate Truffle Sauce.

### Assemble the ice cream pie

3. Use an ice cream spade to spread the softened chocolate ice cream over the crumb crust. Sprinkle half the crumbled Oreos and chocolate chip cookies evenly over the ice cream. Drizzle about 6 tablespoons of Chocolate Truffle Sauce over the cookies. Spread the softened vanilla ice cream over the cookies. Sprinkle the remaining Oreo and chocolate chip cookies pieces evenly over the ice cream. Drizzle with 2 tablespoons of Chocolate Truffle Sauce.

# Peppermint–Chocolate Crunch Ice Cream Pie

Serves 10 to 12

This was my first successful ice cream pie, and I still make it. I'm particularly proud of the chocolate crunch, which remains crisp even after two weeks in the freezer.

Chocolate Crunch

**2 cups (9-ounce package) finely crushed chocolate cookie crumbs, Nabisco Famous Chocolate Wafers preferred**
**6 ounces semisweet chocolate, chopped, or semisweet chocolate chips**
**1 tablespoon plus 1 teaspoon vegetable oil**

**½ gallon good quality peppermint ice cream, softened until spreadable but not melted.**
**1 Oreo Cookie Crumb Crust (page 34) or Chocolate Wafer Cookie Crumb Crust (page 34), baked in a 9-inch springform pan, cooled or frozen**
**1½ cups Chocolate Truffle Sauce (page 45), defrosted, for serving with the pie**

### Good Advice

The Chocolate Crunch is also good simply sprinkled over a dish of ice cream.

• Use chocolate wafers, not sandwich cookies, for the Chocolate Crunch.

### Doubling the Recipe

Use two crusts and double the remaining ingredients.

*continued*

## Prepare the chocolate crunch

1. Put the chocolate cookie crumbs in a large mixing bowl. Put the chocolate and oil in a heatproof container over, but not touching, a saucepan of barely simmering water. Stir the mixture over the hot water until the chocolate is melted and the mixture is smooth. Pour the chocolate mixture over the cookie crumbs and stir until the cookie crumbs coated evenly with chocolate. The mixture will look shiny and pea-size pieces of crunch that crisp as they cool will form.

## Assemble the ice cream pie

2. Use an ice cream spade to spread half of the softened peppermint ice cream over the crumb crust. Sprinkle half of the chocolate crunch evenly over the ice cream. Spread the remaining ice cream over the crunch. Sprinkle the remaining chocolate crunch evenly over the ice cream.

### To Freeze the Crunch

Spread the Chocolate Crunch in a single layer on a baking sheet to keep the crunch from freezing into a hard block. Freeze the crunch, then pour it into a plastic freezer bag. Seal the bag tightly and label it with date and contents. Freeze the crunch up to 1 month.

### To Freeze

Wrap the pie tightly with plastic wrap then heavy aluminum foil, gently pressing the foil against the pie. Label with date and contents. Freeze overnight or up to 2 weeks. Once the pie is frozen, you may remove the springform pan. Dip a dish towel in hot water and wring out the water. Hold the hot towel around the sides of the pan for 15 seconds. Release the sides of the pan. Either leave the pie on the springform bottom or slide it onto a serving plate. Rewrap with plastic wrap and foil and return the pie to the freezer.

### To Serve

Remove the ice cream pie from the freezer and let it soften at room temperature for about 10 minutes. Warm the Chocolate Truffle Sauce in a medium saucepan over low heat, stirring frequently. Use a large sharp knife to cut the pie into wedges and pass the warm Chocolate Truffle Sauce to pour over the ice cream pie.

# Mocha Mud Ice Cream Pie

**10 to 12 servings**

I used to make mud pies when I was a little girl and name them after my favorite desserts. Now I take some of my favorite ingredients like ice cream, Oreos, and chocolate sauce and name them after my mud pies.

**2 pints good quality chocolate ice cream, softened until spreadable but not melted**
**1 Oreo Cookie Crumb Crust (page 34), baked in a 9-inch springform pan, cooled or frozen**
**3½ cups ½-inch pieces Oreo cookies**
**1 cup Cold Chocolate Sauce (page 46), defrosted if frozen**
**2 pints good quality coffee ice cream, softened until spreadable but not melted**

Use an ice cream spade to spread the softened chocolate ice cream over the crumb crust. Sprinkle half of the cookie pieces evenly over the ice cream. Spoon ½ cup of the Cold Chocolate Sauce over the cookies. Spread the coffee ice cream evenly over the cookies. Sprinkle the remaining cookie pieces over the ice cream. Spoon the remaining ½ cup of Cold Chocolate Sauce over the cookies.

## Variation

Defrost an additional cup of Cold Chocolate Sauce to serve with the pie.

### Good Advice

Don't make the cookie pieces too large, or the frozen cookies will make the pie difficult to cut.

### Doubling the Recipe

Use two crumb crusts and double the remaining ingredients.

### To Freeze

Freeze the pie, uncovered, for 15 minutes to firm the sauce. Wrap the pie tightly with plastic wrap then with heavy aluminum foil, gently pressing the foil against the pie. Label with date and contents. Freeze overnight or up to 2 weeks. Once the pie is frozen, you may remove the springform pan. Dip a dish towel in hot water and wring out the water. Hold the hot towel around the sides of the pan for 15 seconds. Release the sides of the pan. Either leave the pie on the springform bottom or transfer it to a serving plate. Rewrap with plastic wrap and foil and return the pie to the freezer.

### To Serve

Remove the ice cream pie from the freezer and let it sit at room temperature for about 10 minutes to soften slightly. Using a large sharp knife cut the pie into wedges.

# Heavenly Haystack Ice Cream Pie

Serves 10 to 12

I call these crisp chunks of white chocolate and toasted coconut haystacks. That's what they look like to me as they sit on a chocolate ice cream field. See if you don't agree.

White Chocolate Haystacks

**1 cup shredded sweetened coconut**
**6 ounces white chocolate, Callebaut preferred**
**1 tablespoon plus 1 teaspoon vegetable oil**

**½ gallon good quality chocolate ice cream, softened until spreadable but not melted**
**1 Oreo Cookie Crumb Crust (page 34) or Chocolate Wafer Cookie Crumb Crust (page 34), baked in a 9-inch springform pan, cooled or frozen**

1. Position a rack in the middle of the oven. Preheat the oven to 300°F.

## Prepare the haystacks

2. Spread the coconut on a baking sheet. Toast for about 10 minutes until the coconut becomes golden, stirring once during baking. Cool thoroughly. Put the toasted coconut in a medium bowl. Put the white chocolate and oil in a heatproof container and place it over, but not touching, a saucepan of barely simmering water. Stir the mixture over the hot water until the chocolate is melted and the mixture is smooth. Pour the white chocolate mixture over the coconut and mix until all of the coconut is coated.

## Assemble the ice cream pie

3. With an ice cream spade, spread half of the softened chocolate ice cream over the crumb crust. Using half of the white chocolate and coconut mixture, drop rounded teaspoonfuls of the mixture evenly over the chocolate ice cream. Spread the remainder of the ice cream over the haystack pieces. Drop rounded teaspoonfuls of the remaining white chocolate and coconut mixture evenly over the top of the pie. The haystacks will harden quickly as they cool on top of the ice cream.

### Good Advice

For easier cutting, use a large knife warmed in hot water and dried to cut through the haystacks.

### Doubling the Recipe

Use two crumb crusts and double the remaining ingredients.

### To Freeze

Freeze the pie 15 minutes to firm the haystacks completely. Wrap the pie tightly with plastic wrap then with heavy aluminum foil, gently pressing the foil against the pie. Label with date and contents. Freeze overnight or up to 2 weeks. Once the pie is frozen, you can remove the springform pan. Dip a dish towel in hot water and wring out the water. Hold the hot towel around the sides of the pan for 15 seconds. Release the sides of the pan. Either leave the pie on the springform bottom or slide it onto a serving plate. Rewrap the pie with plastic wrap and foil and return it to the freezer.

### To Serve

Remove the ice cream pie from the freezer and let it soften at room temperature for about 10 minutes. Dip a large sharp knife in hot water and dry it. Cut the pie into slices with the warm knife, dipping the knife in the hot water as needed.

# Butterscotch Praline Ice Cream Pie

Serves 10 to 12

Which came first, the cookie or the pie? In this case, I used one of my favorite cookies to create a butterscotch extravaganza. These praline cookies consist of a simple sauce of butter, brown sugar, and pecans baked on graham crackers.

Praline Cookies

**12 whole graham crackers, 4¾ × 2¼-inch size**
**½ pound (2 sticks) unsalted butter**
**1 cup (packed) light brown sugar**
**2 cups pecans, coarsely chopped**

**1¾ cups Butterscotch Sauce (page 110), softened at room temperature until spreadable**
**1 Graham Cracker Crumb Crust (page 34), baked in a 9-inch springform pan, cooled or frozen**
**½ gallon good quality vanilla ice cream, softened until spreadable, but not melted**

1. Position a rack in the middle of the oven and preheat the oven to 350°F. Line a 15 × 10 × 1-inch baking sheet with heavy aluminum foil. Butter the aluminum foil.

## Prepare the cookies

2. Place the 12 graham crackers in a single layer on the prepared baking sheet. Melt the butter and brown sugar in a medium saucepan over medium heat, stirring until the mixture boils. Boil 2 minutes without stirring. Remove from the heat and stir in the chopped pecans. Slowly pour the mixture evenly over the graham crackers. Spread the nuts evenly over the graham crackers. Bake 10 to 12 minutes, until the praline is bubbling on top of the cookies. Cool the cookies 5 minutes on the pan. Remove the cookies from the foil and transfer them to a rack to cool completely. Break half of the cookies into irregular ¾-inch pieces for the pie. Break the remaining cookies into larger pieces to serve as cookies or freeze them.

## Assemble the ice cream pie

3. Spoon ½ cup of the Butterscotch Sauce over the crumb crust. Use an ice cream spade to spread half of the softened ice cream over the crust. Spoon ½ cup of the remaining butterscotch sauce over the ice cream and sprinkle half of the cookie pieces evenly over the sauce. Spread the remaining ice cream over the cookies and sprinkle the remaining cookie pieces evenly over the ice cream. Spoon the remaining ¾ cup of Butterscotch Sauce over the cookies.

### Good Advice

The recipe makes enough praline cookies for two pies.

### Doubling the Recipe

Use two graham crumb crusts and the whole recipe of cookies and double the remaining ingredients.

### To Freeze the Cookies

Wrap cookies in plastic wrap and place them in a metal or plastic freezer container and cover tightly. Label with date and contents. Freeze up to 3 months.

### To Freeze

Freeze the pie, uncovered, for 15 minutes to firm the sauce. Wrap the pie tightly with plastic wrap, then with heavy aluminum foil, gently pressing against the pie. Label with date and contents. Freeze overnight or up to 2 weeks. Once the pie is frozen, you can remove the springform pan. Dip a dish towel in hot water and wring out. Hold the hot towel around the sides of the pan for 15 seconds. Release the sides of the pan. Either leave the pie on the springform bottom or transfer to a serving plate. Rewrap the pie with plastic wrap and foil and freeze or serve it.

### To Serve

Remove the ice cream pie from the freezer and let it sit at room temperature for about 10 minutes. Use a large sharp knife to cut the pie into wedges.

# Grandma Tillie's Date Nut Ice Cream Pie

**Serves 10 to 12**

Grandma Tillie, Jeff's grandmother, had a knack for making something special from whatever ingredients she had on hand. Her recipes were seldom written down, but she was happy to have you watch her in the kitchen anytime. I was lucky enough to watch her make this ice cream pie many years ago and to share this recipe with you now.

**½ gallon plus 1 pint good quality vanilla ice cream**
**10 ounces (about 2 cups) pitted dates cut in ½-inch pieces**
**1 cup coarsely chopped toasted walnuts (page 6)**
**½ cup white crème de cacao liqueur**
**1 Graham Cracker Crumb Crust (page 34), baked in a 9-inch springform pan, cooled or frozen**
**2 tablespoons graham cracker crumbs for sprinkling over top of pie**

Scoop the ice cream into a large bowl. Add the dates, walnuts, and crème de cacao. Use an ice cream spade or wooden spoon to stir and mash the mixture together just until the ingredients are mixed together. Work quickly so the ice cream melts as little as possible. It will look like soft custard ice cream but will not be completely melted. Spoon the ice cream mixture into the crust. If there's a small amount of melted ice cream in the bottom of the bowl, discard it. Press plastic wrap on the surface of the ice cream pie and freeze it for 1 hour to firm the ice cream. Remove the pie from the freezer and discard the plastic wrap. Sprinkle the graham cracker crumbs evenly over the top of the pie.

### Good Advice

Use whole pitted dates, not date pieces that may have been rolled in sugar.

### Doubling the Recipe

Use two crumb crusts and double the remaining ingredients.

### To Freeze

Wrap the pie tightly with plastic wrap then with heavy aluminum foil, gently pressing the aluminum foil against the pie. Label with date and contents. Freeze overnight or up to 2 weeks. Once the pie is frozen, you can remove the springform pan. Dip a dish towel in hot water and wring out the water. Hold the hot towel around the sides of the pan for 15 seconds. Release the sides of the pan. Either leave the pie on the springform bottom or slide it onto a serving plate. Rewrap the pie with plastic and foil and return to the freezer.

### To Serve

Remove the ice cream pie from the freezer and let it soften at room temperature for about 10 minutes. Use a large sharp knife to cut the pie into wedges.

# Lemon Ripple Ice Cream Pie

Serves 10 to 12

In this ice cream pie, Lemon Curd freezes to the consistency of a dense lemon fudge. I like the way it ripples through the creamy vanilla ice cream.

Lemon Almond Crumb Crust

**¾ cup graham cracker crumbs**
**1¼ cup ground toasted almonds (page 6)**
**2 teaspoons grated lemon zest**
**6 tablespoons (¾ stick) unsalted butter**
**½ teaspoon almond extract**

**½ gallon good quality vanilla ice cream, softened until spreadable but not melted**
**1½ cups cold Lemon Curd (page 44)**

1. Position a rack in the center of the oven. Preheat the oven to 325°F. Butter a 9-inch springform pan with sides at least 2¾ inches high.

## Prepare the crust

2. Put the graham cracker crumbs, almonds, and grated lemon zest in a medium bowl and mix together. In a small saucepan melt the butter with the almond extract. Pour the melted butter mixture over the crumb mixture and stir until the crumbs are evenly moistened. Transfer the crumb mixture to the springform pan. With the back of your fingers or a spoon, press the crumbs evenly over the bottom and 1 inch up the sides of the pan. Bake the crust for 6 minutes. Cool the crust completely before filling it. The crust can be baked 1 day ahead, covered with plastic wrap, and stored at room temperature.

## Assemble the ice cream pie

3. Use an ice cream spade to spread half of the softened ice cream over the crust. Spread ¾ cup of the Lemon Curd over the ice cream. Spread the remaining ice cream over the curd. Spread the remaining ¾ cup of Lemon Curd over the ice cream. Use the tip of a small sharp knife to swirl the curd topping in a marbleized pattern.

### Good Advice

Defrost the Lemon Curd just enough so it spreads easily.

### Doubling the Recipe

Use two crumb crusts and double the remaining ingredients.

### To Freeze

Freeze the pie 15 minutes to firm the Lemon Curd completely. Wrap the pie tightly with plastic wrap then with heavy aluminum foil, gently pressing the foil against the pie. Label with date and contents. Freeze overnight or up to 2 weeks. Once the pie is frozen, you can remove the springform pan. Dip a dish towel in hot water and wring out the water. Hold the hot towel around the sides of the pan for 15 seconds. Release the sides of the pan. Either leave the pie on the springform bottom or slide it onto a serving plate. Rewrap with plastic and foil and return to the freezer.

### To Serve

Remove the ice cream pie from the freezer and let it soften at room temperature for about 10 minutes. Use a large sharp knife to cut the ice cream pie into wedges.

# Double Strawberry Ice Cream Meringue Sandwiches

Serves 10

"Pretty in pink," I say to myself whenever I serve these meringue sandwiches filled with strawberry ice cream and sauced with slightly sweetened strawberries. For Valentine's Day, you might want to pipe the meringues into heart shapes instead of circles.

**Vanilla Meringues**

**5 large egg whites**
**½ teaspoon cream of tartar**
**½ cup granulated sugar**
**1 teaspoon vanilla**
**1 cup powdered sugar, sifted**

**4 pints strawberry ice cream**
**Powdered sugar, for dusting**

**Chopped Strawberry Sauce**

**1 pint fresh strawberries, stemmed and chopped into ½-inch pieces**
**2 to 4 teaspoons sugar**

1. Position 2 oven racks in the middle and upper third of the oven. Preheat the oven to 200°F. Line 2 large baking sheets with aluminum foil. Butter the aluminum foil and lightly coat it with powdered sugar. Mark ten 3¼-inch circles on each piece of foil with the tip of a dull knife. A clean tuna fish can works well as a marking guide.

## Prepare the meringues

2. Put the egg whites and cream of tartar in the large bowl of an electric mixer and beat on low speed for about 30 seconds, until the egg whites are frothy. Increase the speed to medium-high and beat until soft peaks form. Decrease the speed to medium and gradually beat in the granulated sugar, 1 tablespoon every 30 seconds. Add the vanilla. Use a rubber spatula to fold the powdered sugar into the egg whites. Fit a large pastry bag with a ⅜-inch plain tip and fill the pastry bag no more than two-thirds full with the meringue mixture. Pipe the meringue onto the marked circles. Use your finger to smooth out the little tail that forms when the pastry bag is lifted from each meringue. The meringues will be ⅜ inch thick. Bake about 2 hours, until the meringues are crisp and dry. Turn off the oven and cool the meringues in the oven for 1 hour. The meringues will be a light golden color. Remove the meringues from the oven. Carefully lift the meringues from the aluminum foil to release them, and cool the meringues thoroughly on the baking sheets.

### Good Advice

- Meringues prepared with granulated and powdered sugar are more tender and delicate than those prepared with only granulated sugar.
- Once the meringues are filled with ice cream, they will soften quickly and must be used within two days. It's best to fill only as many meringues as you need at one time and leave the rest frozen.

### Doubling the Recipe

Double the ingredients. Use four baking sheets.

### To Freeze the Meringues

Carefully layer the meringues in a shallow metal or plastic freezer container. Place wax paper between the layers and plastic wrap over the top layer. Cover tightly. Label with date and contents. Freeze up to 1 month. Do not defrost the meringues before using them.

### To Freeze

Carefully wrap each meringue sandwich in plastic wrap. Place the meringue sandwiches in a single layer in a metal or plastic freezer container. Do not crowd the meringues in the container. Cover tightly. Label with date and contents. Freeze up to 2 days.

### To Serve

Unwrap the meringue sandwiches and serve immediately. Spoon some strawberry sauce beside each meringue.

### Fill the meringues

3. Soften the strawberry ice cream about 20 minutes in the refrigerator, just until it is spreadable but not melted. Put a baking sheet in the freezer. Turn 10 cooled meringues bottom (flat) side up. Spread 2 meringues with about ⅔ cup strawberry ice cream. The ice cream will be about ¾ inch thick. Smooth the edges of the ice cream with a thin metal spatula. Top the ice cream with another meringue, flat side of the meringue facing down. Put the filled meringues on the baking sheet in the freezer. Continue filling and freezing the remaining meringues. You will have a little bit of ice cream left over. Let the meringues and ice cream freeze firm in the freezer, about 1 hour. Sift a thin layer of powdered sugar over the top of the meringues.

### Prepare the strawberry sauce

4. Mix the chopped strawberries with 2 teaspoons of sugar. Taste the strawberries and add up to 2 more teaspoons of sugar. Cover and refrigerate at least 1 hour or up to 6 hours. The strawberries will release juice as they chill.

# Bombes, Parfaits, *and* Sundaes

Beyond the Hot Fudge Sundae might be a more appropriate title for this chapter. I know that I wasn't the first person to serve ice cream with a sauce or pack several flavors into a mold, but I have spent no small part of my dessert life finding new ways to embellish ice cream. A worthy endeavor as far as I'm concerned.

Inspiration comes from many sources—tasting a Tartufo Bombshell while traveling, combining several favorite flavors to make a Coffee Toffee Parfait, or brainstorming with friends to come up with a brownie sundae swimming in caramel sauce. The Raspberry Rhubarb Sundae over Buttery Pound Cake came about when my friend at work, Deb Martin, told me about a rhubarb sauce she had served for years over pound cake. We decided to add ice cream and make it a knock-out sundae.

Many of the easiest desserts I know appear in this chapter. With the exception of the Hot Caramel Sundae with Caramel Vanilla Ice Cream, all the ice cream is storebought. The Easy Nutella Ice Cream Cups are just a matter of assembling ice cream and a purchased sauce.

Dress up any of the sundaes or parfaits by serving them in crystal goblets or china dishes. But don't worry about dressing up either of the two impressive ice cream bombes. Presented whole as a perfect dome, then sliced into colorful wedges, these bombes would be quite at home at the grandest of state dinners.

Let the ice cream soften before serving. At the right temperature, bombes will be easy to slice, parfaits easy to dig a spoon into, and ice cream easy to scoop for sundaes.

## Chocolate Chestnut Bombe

**Serves 8 to 10**

A bombe is a dome-shaped frozen dessert composed of several layers of ice cream and sauce. Much of the appeal of a bombe is in its contrasting flavors, colors, and textures. In this simple yet elegant bombe, store-bought sweetened chestnuts in syrup are mixed with vanilla ice cream for the outer layer with Chocolate Truffle Sauce and chocolate ice cream forming a dark, fudgy center. Serve this festive bombe during the winter holiday season.

**1½ pints premium vanilla ice cream, softened until spreadable but not melted**
**1 cup chestnut pieces in syrup or glazed chestnuts, chopped**
**1 cup Chocolate Truffle Sauce (page 45), warmed just to spreading consistency**
**1 pint premium chocolate ice cream, softened until spreadable but not melted**

**1 cup Chocolate Truffle Sauce (page 45), warmed, for serving with the bombe**

### Good Advice

- Use a premium ice cream with a high butterfat content, like Häagen-Dazs or Ben & Jerry's.
- *Marron* is the French word for chestnut, and jars containing chestnuts are often labeled *marron* rather than chestnut. Raffetto brand *marron* pieces in syrup are a good choice for the chestnuts. Glazed chestnuts (*marrons glacés*), a French confection usually available during the Christmas holidays, can also be used.

## Doubling the Recipe

Double the ingredients and make two bombes.

## To Freeze

Wrap the bombe tightly with plastic wrap then heavy aluminum foil. Label with date and contents. Freeze overnight or up to 2 weeks.

## To Serve

Unmold the bombe the day before serving or at least 1 hour before serving. Chill a serving plate that is large enough to hold the bombe for about 15 minutes. Remove the bombe from the freezer and unwrap it. Dip a dish towel in hot water and wring out the water. Press the hot towel onto the sides of the bowl or mold for about 20 to 30 seconds. Place the chilled serving plate on top of the bombe and invert it onto the plate. Discard the paper liner. If the bombe does not release easily, repeat the process with the hot towel. Return the bombe to the freezer for 30 minutes to firm the ice cream. If the bombe is going to be stored overnight in the freezer, wrap it tightly with plastic wrap. When the bombe is served, drizzle 1/4 cup warm Chocolate Truffle Sauce over the top of the bombe. Use a large sharp knife to cut the bombe into wedges. Serve with the remaining Chocolate Truffle Sauce.

Chill a round, deep 1½-quart bowl or metal mold in the freezer for 15 minutes. Cut a small piece of parchment or wax paper to fit the bottom of the bowl and line it with the paper. Put the softened vanilla ice cream in a medium bowl and use a large spoon to quickly mash the chestnut pieces into the ice cream. Use an ice cream spade to line the bottom and sides of the chilled bowl with about a 1-inch-thick layer of the vanilla ice cream mixture. Use all of the ice cream. Press plastic wrap over the ice cream and freeze until firm, about 1 hour. Remove from the freezer and discard the plastic wrap. Use the back of a spoon to smooth the ice cream. This gives the vanilla layer a smooth looking edge when the bombe is cut. Pour ¾ cup Chocolate Truffle Sauce over the ice cream and tilt the bowl to spread the sauce evenly over the ice cream. Freeze until firm, about 15 minutes. Fill the center of the bombe with half of the chocolate ice cream. Pour ¼ cup Chocolate Truffle Sauce over the ice cream. Spread the remainder of the chocolate ice cream over the sauce. Smooth the top of the bombe.

# Orange and Vanilla Ice Cream Bombe

**Serves 8 to 10**

When the Good Humor ice cream truck called us children with its bell, my choice would usually be a cup filled with vanilla ice cream and orange sherbet. This dessert reminds me of those ice cream cups. The outer layer of the bombe is vanilla ice cream; it's spread with a thin layer of Orange Curd and filled with more curd whipped with cream. With its refreshing taste and pastel shades, it's a fine spring or summer dessert. Grandmother Sophie's Butter Cookies (page 53) make a good accompaniment.

**½ gallon premium vanilla ice cream, softened until spreadable but not melted**
**1⅛ cups cold Orange Curd (page 44), defrosted until spreadable but not melted**
**½ cup cold heavy whipping cream**
**1 teaspoon vanilla extract**
**3 tablespoons ground almond praline (page 48), for topping the bombe**

1. Chill a round, deep 2-quart bowl or metal mold in the freezer for 15 minutes. Cut a small piece of parchment or wax paper to fit the bottom of the bowl and line it with the paper. Use an ice cream spade to line the bottom and sides of the chilled bowl with about a 1¼-inch-thick layer of vanilla ice cream. Use all of the ice cream. Press plastic wrap over the ice cream and freeze until the ice cream is firm, about 1 hour. Remove the bowl from the freezer and discard the plastic wrap. Use the back of a spoon to smooth the vanilla ice cream layer for a smooth looking edge when the bombe is cut. Spread ¼ cup of the Orange Curd evenly over the vanilla ice cream and return the bowl to the freezer while you whip the filling.

2. Put the cream and vanilla in the large bowl of an electric mixer and beat with an electric mixer at medium speed until the cream just begins to thicken. With the mixer running, add the remaining cold Orange Curd and beat just until the cream forms soft peaks. Pour the whipped mixture into the center of the bombe. Smooth the top.

### Good Advice

The Orange Curd should be very cold when beaten into the cream. If the curd has been frozen, defrost it just until it is spreadable.

### Doubling the Recipe

Double the ingredients and use two bowls.

### To Freeze

Wrap the bombe tightly with plastic wrap then heavy aluminum foil. Label with date and contents. Freeze overnight or up to 2 weeks.

### To Serve

Unmold the bombe the day before serving or at least 1 hour before serving. Chill a serving plate for about 15 minutes. Remove the bombe from the freezer and uncover it. Dip a dish towel in hot water and wring it out. Press the hot towel onto the sides of the bowl for 20 to 30 seconds. Invert the bombe onto the chilled serving plate. Discard the paper liner. If the bombe does not release easily, repeat the process with the hot towel. Sprinkle the top of the bombe with the almond praline. Return the bombe to the freezer for 30 minutes to firm the ice cream. If the bombe is going to be stored overnight in the freezer, wrap it tightly with plastic wrap. Cut the bombe into wedges to serve.

# Tartufo Bombshells

**Serves 8**

Tre Scalini, a café situated on the Piazza Navona in Rome, is renowned for its truffle-shaped ball of rich chocolate ice cream covered with shaved chocolate. In the center is a liqueur-soaked cherry; "For a little surprise," say the waiters. The idea is remarkably simple, but reproducing the dessert was not. I had no trouble finding premium chocolate ice cream or quality semisweet chocolate, but I was never satisfied with the cherries. Finally I hit upon the idea of placing a chocolate-covered cherry in the center.

**4 ounces semisweet chocolate, in 1 piece**
**2 pints premium chocolate ice cream, softened until it can be scooped easily but not melted**
**8 dark chocolate–covered cherries**
**Sweetened whipped cream, for serving with the bombshells**

1. Using the large holes of a box grater, grate the chocolate. To prevent scraped fingers, grate from a large piece of chocolate. There will be a piece left over that is too small to grate; save this for another use. Spread the grated chocolate on a plate and set aside. Line a shallow pan large enough to hold the 8 bombshells with parchment or wax paper and place it in the freezer.

2. Fill a round ice cream scoop with chocolate ice cream. Use a teaspoon to press a hole in the center of the ice cream. Press a chocolate-covered cherry, flat side up, into the hole. Add more ice cream, using the teaspoon to mound it into a round ball. Check to see that the cherry is covered completely. Drop the ball of ice cream onto the baking sheet in the freezer. Repeat to form 7 more balls. Each ball will use about ½ cup of ice cream. Freeze the balls for 15 minutes to firm them. Quickly roll each ball in the grated chocolate, pressing gently on the grated chocolate to cover the ice cream completely. Freeze for 30 minutes to firm the ice cream again.

### Good Advice

- I grate Dove Bar dark chocolate bars for the chocolate coating.
- Get dark chocolate–covered cherries from a good candy shop for the cherry centers.

### Doubling the Recipe

Double the ingredients.

### To Freeze

Wrap each bombshell tightly with plastic wrap. Place in a single layer in a metal or plastic freezer container and cover tightly. Label with date and contents. Freeze up to 2 weeks.

### To Serve

Unwrap the bombshells and place in individual shallow bowls. Serve with sweetened whipped cream.

# Coffee Toffee Parfait

**Serves 6**

Here is an up-to-date rendition of the ice cream parfaits popular in the fifties, actually do-ahead frozen sundaes. I always picture June Cleaver in "Leave It to Beaver" making parfaits for her family. In this sophisticated parfait, a coffee-cognac caramel syrup is layered with coffee ice cream and crushed toffee. Try this, June Cleaver!

Caramel Syrup

**⅔ cup sugar**
**⅓ cup boiling water**
**¼ teaspoon vanilla extract**
**¾ teaspoon cognac or brandy**
**¼ teaspoon instant decaffeinated coffee granules, dissolved in ½ teaspoon warm water**

**3 pints coffee ice cream, softened until spreadable but not melted**
**½ cup crushed toffee candy, such as Almond Roca, Skor, or Heath Bars**

1. Put the sugar in a small heavy-bottomed saucepan and cook over low heat until the sugar begins to melt. Increase the heat to medium-high and cook until the sugar melts completely, caramelizes, and turns a dark golden color, about 4 minutes. Watch the sugar carefully and stir it with a wooden spoon occasionally to ensure it cooks evenly. Remove the caramel from the heat. Slowly add the boiling water to the hot sugar. The mixture will steam and bubble up so be careful. Return the saucepan to medium heat and cook the mixture, stirring with the wooden spoon, until the caramel is completely dissolved and the sauce is smooth. Set the sauce aside to cool for 5 minutes. Stir in the vanilla, cognac, and dissolved coffee. Cool the sauce completely before using it. The sauce can be covered and refrigerated up to 1 week.

2. Have ready 6 parfait or sundae glasses of at least 10-ounce capacity. Prepare 3 parfaits at a time to prevent the ice cream from melting during preparation. Half fill 3 of the glasses with coffee ice cream. Drizzle about 2 teaspoons of cooled caramel syrup over the ice cream. Drizzle the caramel syrup near the edges so that it shows through the glass. Sprinkle 2 teaspoons of crushed toffee over the caramel syrup. Fill each glass with coffee ice cream, mounding the ice cream and leaving space around the edge for more syrup to drip into the glass. Drizzle each parfait with 1 teaspoon of caramel syrup and sprinkle with 2 teaspoons of crushed toffee. Drizzle ½ teaspoon of caramel sauce over the toffee. Freeze the parfaits until the syrup is firm, about 30 minutes. Repeat to prepare the 3 remaining parfaits.

## Variation

The caramel syrup can be spooned over ice cream as a sundae sauce. It's good with butter pecan, chocolate, or vanilla ice cream.

### Good Advice

Sugar is easy to caramelize. Take care to cook the sugar slowly and not to burn yourself or the sugar.

### Doubling the Recipe

Double the ingredients. Use a medium saucepan to cook the caramel syrup.

### To Freeze

Wrap each parfait with plastic wrap. Gently press heavy aluminum foil around each parfait. Label with date and contents. Freeze up to 1 week.

### To Serve

Unwrap the parfaits and let sit at room temperature for 5 to 10 minutes to soften the ice cream slightly.

# Easy Nutella Ice Cream Cups

**Serves 8**

When I travel to foreign countries, I always visit the markets and grocery stores. It's a great way to learn about the food of a country and also to find interesting local products to take home. Browsing in an Italian *supermercato* a few years ago, I noticed a jar labeled nutella, which looked like milk chocolate sauce even though the label pictured the sauce being spread on bread. But the ingredient list contained the magic chocolate word so I bought a jar to give my son, who loves chocolate as much as I do. Nutella turned out to be a thick milk chocolate sauce flavored with hazelnuts. The Italians use it as we would use peanut butter. Well, to each his own. Peter and I ate ours straight from the jar—little by little, using his old baby spoons so it would last longer. Apparently other people discovered the goodness of nutella since it is now available in the United States. Supermarkets usually stock it in the peanut butter and jelly section (it must be that picture of bread on the label). I still eat it straight from the jar, but it's terrific with ice cream. At room temperature the sauce is soft; if frozen with ice cream it becomes firm as in these Easy Nutella Ice Cream Cups.

**1 pint chocolate ice cream, softened until spreadable but not melted**
**1 scant cup nutella**
**2 pints coffee ice cream, softened until spreadable but not melted**
**8 whole toasted peeled hazelnuts (page 6)**

Have ready 8 ramekins with a 5- to 6-ounce capacity. Spread ¼ cup chocolate ice cream in the bottom of each ramekin. Drizzle 2 teaspoons nutella evenly over the chocolate ice cream. Spread ½ cup coffee ice cream in each ramekin. Smooth the top. Freeze the ramekins until the coffee ice cream is firm, about 30 minutes. Removing only 4 ramekins from the freezer at a time, spread a smooth layer of nutella over the coffee ice cream. Place a hazelnut in the center of each filled ramekin. Freeze the ramekins just until the topping is firm, about 15 minutes.

### Good Advice

Store an open jar of nutella in a cool place or in the refrigerator to prevent the oil from developing an off-flavor, but let it sit at room temperature for about two hours to soften before using it.

### Doubling the Recipe

Double the ingredients.

### To Freeze

Wrap each ramekin tightly with plastic wrap. Gently press heavy aluminum foil around each ramekin. Label with date and contents. Freeze up to 2 weeks.

### To Serve

Unwrap the ramekins and let sit at room temperature 5 to 10 minutes to soften the ice cream slightly.

# Milk Chocolate Hot Fudge Sundae

**Serves 6**

One of the most popular desserts of all time, and with good reason, is the classic hot fudge sundae. On my birthday I always go down to our local drugstore, child or husband in tow, and splurge on a sundae served in a tall old-fashioned sundae glass. One year as I was finishing up my birthday sundaes, I thought, Wouldn't this sauce be great made with milk chocolate? Definitely worth trying, I decided. It didn't take long to come up with this thick and fudgy milk chocolate sauce.

**½ cup whipping cream**
**2 tablespoons unsalted butter**
**8 ounces good quality milk chocolate, chopped**

**2 pints ice cream, for making the sundaes**

Put the cream and butter in a medium saucepan and heat over medium-low heat until the cream is hot and the butter is melted. The mixture will form tiny bubbles and measure about 175°F. on a food thermometer. Do not boil. Remove from the heat and add the milk chocolate. Let the chocolate melt in the cream for 1 minute. Gently stir the chocolate and cream together until the chocolate is completely melted and the sauce is smooth. The sauce is ready to serve, refrigerate up to 2 weeks, or freeze.

## Good Advice

- Vanilla, butter pecan, or cherry ice cream will not overpower the delicate sauce.

## Doubling the Recipe

Double the ingredients.

## To Freeze the Sauce

Pour the sauce into a plastic freezer container, leaving 1 inch of space at the top. Loosely cover and cool for 1 hour at room temperature. Press a piece of plastic wrap onto the top of the sauce and cover the container tightly. Label with date and contents. Freeze up to 2 months.

## To Serve

Defrost the sauce in the covered container overnight in the refrigerator. Pour the sauce into a small saucepan and cook over low heat, stirring frequently, until warm. If you need the sauce in a hurry and don't have time to defrost it, run some hot water over the covered container and remove the frozen sauce from the container. Warm the sauce in a heatproof container placed over, but not touching, barely simmering water, stirring occasionally. Pour a spoonful of sauce in the bottom of each serving dish, add ice cream, and top with warm sauce.

# Toffee Fudge Brownie Sundae with Warm Caramel Sauce

**Serves 12**

One rainy, rather dreary fall day my friend Deb Martin suggested that we needed a really extravagant but down-to-earth dessert to cheer up our customers. I decided that a caramel and brownie sundae would be just the right choice—and it was.

**12 Toffee Fudge Brownies (page 75)**
**1¼ cups whipping cream**
**1¼ cups sugar**
**1 teaspoon vanilla extract**
**3 pints ice cream, coffee, chocolate, or butter pecan preferred, for serving**

1. Prepare the Toffee Fudge Brownies as directed.

2. Heat the cream in a small saucepan and keep it hot, about 150°F. if measured with a food thermometer, without boiling it. Put the sugar in a medium heavy-bottomed saucepan and cook over low heat until the sugar begins to melt. Increase the heat to medium-high and cook until the sugar melts, caramelizes, and turns a dark golden color. Watch the sugar carefully and stir it occasionally with a wooden spoon to ensure it cooks evenly. Remove from the heat. Slowly and carefully add the hot cream to the hot sugar. The mixture will bubble up and can splatter so be careful. Return the saucepan to medium heat and cook the mixture, stirring with the wooden spoon, until the caramel is completely dissolved and the sauce is smooth. Stir in the vanilla. The sauce is ready to use or it can be covered and refrigerated up to 2 weeks or frozen.

### Good Advice

Since the hot caramel sauce softens the ice cream, it is not necessary to soften it before serving.

### Doubling the Recipe

Double the ingredients.

### To Freeze the Sauce

Cool the caramel sauce to lukewarm and pour it into a plastic freezer container, leaving at least 1 inch of space at the top. Press plastic wrap onto the surface of the sauce and refrigerate the sauce until it is cold. Cover the container tightly. Label with date and contents. Freeze up to 2 months.

### To Serve

If the caramel sauce is frozen, defrost it at room temperature for about 5 hours. Put the caramel sauce in a medium saucepan and warm it over low heat. The sauce should be warm and pour easily. For each serving, place a brownie in a shallow bowl. A glass bowl looks nice. Top each brownie with a scoop of ice cream and some warm caramel sauce. You will have some ice cream left over.

# Hot Caramel Sundae with Caramel Vanilla Ice Cream

Serves 6

In this upside-down sundae the caramel sauce is served under the ice cream, and there is the pleasant sensation of digging down through cold soft ice cream into hot sticky sauce. The same caramel sauce is used to flavor the ice cream.

**1½ cups whipping cream**
**1½ cups sugar**
**1 teaspoon vanilla extract**

Caramel Vanilla Ice Cream

**1½ cups whole milk**
**1½ cups whipping cream**
**5 large egg yolks**
**⅔ cup sugar**
**2 teaspoons vanilla extract**

1. Heat the cream in a small saucepan and keep it hot, about 150°F. if measured with a food thermometer, without boiling it. Put the sugar in a medium heavy-bottomed saucepan and cook over low heat until the sugar begins to melt. Increase the heat to medium-high and cook, stirring occasionally with a wooden spoon, until the sugar melts and turns a dark golden color. Watch the sugar. Remove from the heat. Slowly and carefully add the hot cream. The mixture will bubble up, so be careful. Return the saucepan to medium heat and cook, stirring with the wooden spoon, until the caramel is completely dissolved and the sauce is smooth. Stir in the vanilla. The sauce is ready to use or it can be covered and refrigerated up to 2 weeks or frozen. Set aside ¼ cup of the sauce to add to the ice cream and refrigerate or freeze it separately. Warm it until soft before using.

## Prepare the ice cream

2. Heat the milk and cream in a large saucepan just until a few bubbles form, about 150°F. if measured on a food thermometer. Do not boil. Put the egg yolks and sugar in the large bowl of an electric mixer and beat at medium speed until the sugar is dissolved and the mixture thickens slightly and lightens in color, about 45 seconds. Decrease the speed to low and slowly add the hot milk mixture. Return to the saucepan and cook over low-medium heat to 170°F., stirring constantly with a wooden spoon. Stir the mixture often where the sides and the bottom of the pan meet. The mixture will thicken slightly and leave a path on the back of a spoon when you draw your finger across it. A little steam will just begin to rise. Do not boil. Strain the hot mixture into a bowl. Stir in the vanilla and ¼ cup of the caramel sauce. Cover and refrigerate until the ice cream mixture is very cold, about

### Good Advice

Warm the caramel sauce for the ice cream just enough to be able to stir it in.

### Doubling the Recipe

Double the ingredients.

### To Freeze the Sauce

Pour the remaining warm sauce into a plastic freezer container, leaving at least 1 inch of space at the top. Press plastic wrap onto the surface of the sauce and chill thoroughly. Cover the container tightly. Label with date and contents. Freeze up to 2 months.

### To Freeze the Ice Cream

Transfer the ice cream to the chilled container. Press plastic wrap onto the surface of the ice cream and cover tightly. Label with date and contents. Freeze overnight or up to 10 days.

### To Serve

If the caramel sauce is frozen, defrost it at room temperature for about 5 hours. Warm the sauce in a medium saucepan over low heat until it is warm and soft. Let the ice cream soften at room temperature about 10 minutes before serving. Spoon about ¼ cup warm caramel sauce into the bottom of 6 footed sundae glasses or shallow glass bowls. Top the sauce with caramel vanilla ice cream and drizzle a teaspoon of caramel sauce over the top of the ice cream.

5 hours or overnight. Stir the mixture several times while it is chilling. Chill a moisture-proof carton or plastic freezer container for the ice cream. Transfer the custard to an ice cream maker and process according to the manufacturer's directions.

### Variation

Use slightly softened premium vanilla ice cream like Ben & Jerry's or Häagen-Dazs instead of the homemade ice cream.

## Espresso Brownies with Ice Cream and Hot Fudge Sauce

Serves 12

Topped with ice cream and warm Chocolate Truffle Sauce, Espresso Brownies transform a traditional brownie sundae into a sophisticated dessert.

**12 Espresso Brownies (page 78)**
**2 pints ice cream, coffee, chocolate, or vanilla preferred, for serving**
**1½ cups Chocolate Truffle Sauce (page 45), warmed to pouring consistency, for serving**

Prepare the Espresso Brownies as directed.

### Good Advice

For a less rich dessert, serve the brownies topped only with ice cream, no sauce.

### Doubling the Recipe

Double the ingredients.

### To Serve

Defrost the wrapped bars at room temperature for about 3 hours. For each serving place a brownie in an individual shallow bowl. Glass bowls look nice. Top each brownie with ice cream and warm Chocolate Truffle Sauce.

# Raspberry Rhubarb Sundae over Buttery Pound Cake

Serves 6

Rhubarb signals the beginning of spring for me. As soon as it arrives, I cook a big pot of raspberry rhubarb sauce and freeze several containers to have the sauce on hand for a refreshing fruit sundae.

Raspberry Rhubarb Sauce

**4 cups coarsely chopped fresh rhubarb stalks**
**¼ cup sugar**
**¼ cup water**
**1½ cups fresh or frozen unsweetened raspberries**

**½ Pound Cake (page 40), cooled or defrosted, for serving with the sundae**
**2 pints vanilla ice cream, for serving with the sundae**
**Sweetened whipped cream, for serving with the sundae**

Put the rhubarb, sugar, and water in a large nonreactive saucepan. Cover the pan and cook over medium heat for 10 minutes, until the mixture begins to simmer and release liquid. Remove the cover and gently stir in the raspberries. Simmer, uncovered, over medium-high heat until the rhubarb feels soft when pierced with a fork, about 10 minutes. Remove the sauce from the heat. Skim and discard any foam from the top of the sauce. Pour the sauce into a plastic freezer container, leaving 1 inch of space at the top. Cool completely. For a large quantity of sauce, divide the sauce among several containers.

## Good Advice

Fresh rhubarb should be crisp—wave a stalk in the air and it will not flop around—and the stem end firm and clean with no signs of rotting. Do not use the leaves; they are poisonous. Not all rhubarb is bright red; sometimes it is rosy pink, but raspberries will redden the sauce.

## Doubling the Recipe

Multiply the ingredients by two or three.

## To Freeze

Press plastic wrap onto the surface of the sauce and chill it in the refrigerator. The sauce will thicken as it cools. When the sauce is cold, cover the container tightly and freeze up to 3 months.

## To Serve

Defrost the sauce overnight in the refrigerator. Slice the Pound Cake into ¾-inch slices. If using a long narrow cake, cut 12 slices; if using a regular loaf cake, cut 6 slices and cut them in half. Place 2 slices on each plate, leaving a space between them. Put 2 scoops of ice cream between the slices. Stir the sauce to smooth it and top the ice cream with a generous ⅓ cup of sauce. Spoon sweetened whipped cream over each sundae.

# Ice Cream *and* Sorbet

Americans consume more ice cream than people in any other country in the world. More and more good brands of ice cream are available commercially, so I wanted all of these homemade ice creams and sorbets to be different and better than anything you could buy. Fruit flavors have an abundance of fresh fruit, chocolate flavors contain plenty of real chocolate, and any added mixtures like praline or cookie dough are homemade.

Except for the Brown Bread Crunch Ice Cream, which contains no eggs, all of the ice creams start with a cooked custard. This is a classic method for preparing an ice cream base, and cooking the custard to at least 160°F. will kill any salmonella that might be present in raw eggs. I use an instant-read food thermometer to check the temperature of the custard; this kind of thermometer doesn't have to be clipped onto the side of the pan and so won't interfere with stirring. Chill the ice cream mixture thoroughly in the refrigerator before churning it. Overnight chilling is fine and divides the job into two easy steps.

The sorbets are a mixture of sugar syrup and fresh fruit or juice and contain no fat. Properly balancing the amount of fruit and sugar syrup in the sorbets will strengthen the taste of the fruit. Harold McGee's book *The Curious Cook* has clear information on sugar and fruit proportions for sorbets. I used his charts as a preliminary measurement for my sugar syrups, then I experimented by adding more fruit to intensify the flavor. The sorbets in this chapter have just enough sugar to bring out the taste of the fruit. Oddly enough, there is a point at which too much fruit will leave a sorbet tasting flat.

I prepared the sorbets and ice creams in this chapter and the Caramel Vanilla Ice Cream (page 224) in a Simac Il Gelataio Super and a Simac Il Gelataio SC. Use any ice cream machine that is in good working order. Simply follow the manufacturer's directions and churn away. More air will be beaten into the ice cream or sorbet the longer it churns. An ice cream or sorbet with less air will have less volume and a somewhat creamier texture than one with relatively more air.

Ice cream or sorbet served rock hard has little flavor, all it does is freeze the fillings in your teeth. Let ice cream or sorbet sit at room temperature ten to fifteen minutes to soften slightly. When an ice cream scoop or spade slides easily through the ice cream or sorbet, it is ready to eat. Sorbet will not even form scoops when it is frozen hard; it will break off into irregular pieces.

Repeated softening and freezing results in an icy texture. If you plan to serve one batch of sorbet several times, it's a good idea to freeze the batch in several small containers and remove one container at time. Chilling the containers while churning and pressing plastic wrap on the surface of ice cream or sorbet are simple tricks to remember. If handled carefully, ice cream and sorbet will remain in good condition for about ten days. Ice cream actually develops flavor during its first twenty-four hours in the freezer, but after ten days the texture and flavor begin to deteriorate.

All of the ice creams are as rich or possibly richer than a premium ice cream. They deliver such flavor value for each calorie you can serve smaller portions than usual. It's a good trade-off.

# White Chocolate and Hazelnut Ice Cream

**Makes about 1 1/2 quarts**

A simple change to white chocolate and hazelnuts creates an intriguing new ice cream flavor, quite unlike the Gianduia (page 230).

**12 ounces white chocolate, chopped into ½-inch pieces, Callebaut preferred**
**1½ cups whole milk**
**1½ cups whipping cream**
**5 large egg yolks**
**⅓ cup sugar**
**2 teaspoons vanilla extract**
**1 cup toasted peeled hazelnuts (page 6)**

1. Put the chopped white chocolate in a large bowl and set aside. Heat the milk and cream in a large saucepan just until a few bubbles form, about 150°F. if measured with a food thermometer. Do not boil. Put the egg yolks and sugar in the large bowl of an electric mixer and beat at medium speed until the mixture thickens slightly and lightens in color, about 45 seconds. Decrease the speed to low and slowly add the hot milk mixture. Return the mixture to the saucepan and cook the custard over low-medium heat, stirring constantly, until the mixture reaches 170°F. measured on a food thermometer. Stir the mixture often where the sides and the bottom of the pan meet. The mixture will thicken slightly and leave a path on the back of a spoon when you draw your finger across it. A little steam will just begin to rise from the mixture. Do not boil. Strain the hot mixture into the bowl containing the chopped white chocolate. Stir until the white chocolate melts and the mixture is smooth. Add the vanilla. Cover and refrigerate until the mixture is very cold, about 5 hours or overnight. Stir the mixture several times while it is chilling.

2. Put the hazelnuts in a food processor fitted with the steel blade and process the nuts with quick on/off bursts until they are finely chopped. Add 2 cups of the cold ice cream mixture and process until the nuts are finely ground, about 30 seconds. Stir the hazelnut mixture into the ice cream mixture. Chill a moisture-proof carton or plastic freezer container for the ice cream. Transfer the ice cream mixture to an ice cream maker and process according to the manufacturer's directions.

### Good Advice

- Since white chocolate has a delicate taste that can be overwhelmed by other ingredients, the recipe contains a large amount of it.
- Use a good quality white chocolate like Callebaut.

### Doubling the Recipe

Double the ingredients.

### To Freeze

Transfer the ice cream to the chilled container. Press plastic wrap onto the surface of the ice cream and cover tightly. Label with date and contents. Freeze overnight or up to 10 days.

### To Serve

Let the ice cream soften about 10 minutes before serving. It should be soft but not melted.

# Gianduia Ice Cream

**Makes about 1 1/2 quarts**

To Italians, *gianduia* means a combination of chocolate and hazelnuts. To me, it means, "Order immediately."

I first tasted Gianduia Ice Cream at Vivoli in Florence, Italy. When we asked for directions to Vivoli the first time, we were pointed to the Via Ghibellina and told to follow the trail of discarded ice cream cups. Sure enough, we found Vivoli easily enough. The shop features about twenty flavors each day, and they will scoop several flavors into each cup, making a difficult choice a little easier. Their Gianduia Ice Cream is soft and creamy with just the right proportion of hazelnut to chocolate.

Since we do not get to Florence often, I decided I had to create my own version. Not so easy. I used plenty of chocolate and toasted hazelnuts and soon got the right ratio of hazelnuts to chocolate, but the texture eluded me. Finally, after much experimentation, I found that substituting honey for some of the sugar produced an especially smooth ice cream. "Brava, Elinor," I can hear them cheering.

**9 ounces semisweet chocolate, chopped**
**1 ounce unsweetened chocolate, chopped**
**1½ cups whole milk**
**1½ cups whipping cream**
**6 large egg yolks**
**⅔ cup sugar**
**¼ cup honey**
**2 teaspoons vanilla extract**
**¾ cup peeled and toasted hazelnuts (page 6)**

1. Put the chopped semisweet chocolate and unsweetened chocolate in a large bowl and set aside. Put the milk and cream in a large saucepan and heat until a few bubbles just begin to form, about 150°F. if measured with a food thermometer. Do not boil the mixture. Put the egg yolks and sugar in the large bowl of an electric mixer and beat at medium speed until the mixture thickens slightly and lightens in color, about 45 seconds. Mix in the honey. Decrease the speed to low and slowly add the hot milk mixture. Return the mixture to the saucepan and cook the custard over low-medium heat to 170°F. on an instant-read food thermometer, stirring constantly. Stir the mixture often where the sides and the bottom of the pan meet. The mixture will thicken slightly and leave a path on the back of a spoon when you draw your finger across it. A little steam will just begin to rise from the custard mixture. Do not let the custard boil or it will curdle. Strain the hot mixture into the bowl containing the chopped chocolate. Whisk until the chocolate melts and the mixture is smooth. Add the vanilla. Cover and refrigerate until the mixture is very cold, about 5 hours or overnight. Stir the mixture several times while it is chilling.

### Good Advice

The easiest way to grind the nuts fine is to process the hazelnuts with some of the ice cream mixture in a food processor until the mixture is smooth.

### Doubling the Recipe

Double the ingredients.

### To Freeze

Transfer the ice cream to the chilled container. Press plastic wrap onto the surface of the ice cream and cover tightly. Label with date and contents. Freeze overnight or up to 10 days.

### To Serve

Soften the ice cream for about 10 minutes until it scoops easily and has a creamy texture.

2. Put the hazelnuts in a food processor fitted with the steel blade and process the nuts with quick on/off bursts until they are finely chopped. Add 2 cups of the cold ice cream mixture and process until the nuts are finely ground, about 30 seconds. Stir the hazelnut mixture back into the rest of the ice cream mixture. Chill a moisture-proof carton or plastic freezer container to hold the ice cream. Transfer the ice cream mixture to an ice cream maker and process according to the manufacturer's directions.

# Chocolate Chip Cookie Dough Ice Cream

**Makes about 1 1/2 quarts**

In a survey I read not long ago, Chocolate Chip Cookie Dough Ice Cream was named the most popular flavor in the United States. Not too surprising, since it combines two of America's favorites.

### Good Advice

Use miniature chocolate chips, which soften as you eat the ice cream, rather than large chocolate chips, which remain hard.

### Doubling the Recipe

Double the ingredients for the ice cream mixture. Use all of the chocolate chip cookie dough for the ice cream.

#### Ice Cream Mixture

**1½ cups whole milk**
**1½ cups whipping cream**
**5 large egg yolks**
**⅔ cup sugar**
**2 teaspoons vanilla extract**

#### Chocolate Chip Cookie Dough for Ice Cream

**5 tablespoons soft unsalted butter**
**5 tablespoons (packed) light brown sugar**
**3 tablespoons granulated sugar**
**Pinch salt**
**1 teaspoon vanilla extract**
**1 tablespoon plus 1 teaspoon water**
**¾ cup unbleached all-purpose flour**
**1 cup (6 ounces) miniature semisweet chocolate chips**

*continued*

## Prepare the ice cream

1. Heat the milk and cream in a large saucepan until it is hot and a few bubbles begin to form, about 150°F. if measured with a food thermometer. Do not boil. Put the egg yolks and sugar in the large bowl of an electric mixer and beat at medium speed until the mixture thickens slightly and lightens in color, about 45 seconds. Decrease the speed to low and slowly add the hot milk mixture. Return the mixture to the saucepan and cook the custard over low-medium heat, stirring constantly, until it reaches 170°F. measured on a food thermometer. Stir the mixture often where the sides and the bottom of the pan meet. The mixture will thicken slightly and leave a path on the back of the spoon when you draw your finger across it. A little steam will just begin to rise from the custard mixture. Do not boil. Strain the hot mixture into a bowl and stir in the vanilla. Cover and refrigerate until very cold, about 5 hours or overnight. Stir the mixture several times while it is chilling.

## Prepare the cookie dough

2. Put the butter, brown sugar, sugar, and salt in the large bowl of an electric mixer. Beat on low speed until the mixture is smooth. Mix in the vanilla and water just until it is incorporated. Mix in the flour just until it is incorporated. Stir in the chocolate chips. If you are preparing only 1 recipe of ice cream, you will use only 1 cup of the cookie dough.

## Assemble the ice cream

3. Chill a moisture-proof carton or plastic freezer container that will hold the ice cream. Transfer the chilled custard to an ice cream maker and process according to the manufacturer's directions. During the last 2 minutes of churning, add 1 cup of the cookie dough, breaking the dough into pieces as you add it.

### To Freeze the Cookie Dough

Put the remaining cup of cookie dough in a plastic freezer container and press plastic wrap onto the dough. Cover the container. Label with date and contents. Refrigerate up to 3 days or freeze up to 2 months. Defrost the frozen dough in the refrigerator about 3 hours before using it.

### To Freeze the Ice Cream

Transfer the ice cream to the chilled container. Press plastic wrap onto the surface of the ice cream and cover tightly. Label with date and contents. Freeze overnight or up to 10 days.

### To Serve

Soften the ice cream for about 10 minutes until it scoops easily and has a creamy texture.

# Coffee Chocolate Chip Cookie Dough Ice Cream

Makes about 1 1/2 quarts

Coffee ice cream makes a good flavor contrast to chunks of chocolate chip cookie dough. A splash of cognac gives the ice cream an elusive but not overpowering taste of the liqueur.

**1½ cups whole milk**
**1½ cups whipping cream**
**5 large egg yolks**
**⅔ cup sugar**
**2 teaspoons vanilla extract**
**1 tablespoon plus 1 teaspoon instant decaffeinated coffee**
**1 tablespoon cognac or brandy**
**1 cup Chocolate Chip Cookie Dough for Ice Cream (page 231)**

Heat the milk and cream in a large saucepan just until a few bubbles form, about 150°F. if measured with a food thermometer. Do not boil. Put the egg yolks and sugar in the large bowl of an electric mixer and beat at medium speed until the mixture thickens slightly and lightens in color, about 45 seconds. Decrease the speed to low and slowly add the hot milk mixture. Return the mixture to the saucepan and cook the custard over low-medium heat, stirring constantly, until the mixture reaches 170°F. measured on a food thermometer. Stir the mixture often where the sides and the bottom of the pan meet. The mixture will thicken slightly and leave a path on the back of the spoon when you draw your finger across it. A little steam will just begin to rise from the custard mixture. Do not boil. Strain the hot mixture into a bowl and stir in the vanilla, instant coffee and cognac. Cover and refrigerate until very cold, about 5 hours or overnight. Stir the mixture several times while it is chilling. Chill a moisture-proof carton or plastic freezer container for the ice cream. Transfer the custard to an ice cream maker and process according to the manufacturer's directions. During the last 2 minutes of churning, add the chocolate chip cookie dough, breaking the dough into pieces as you add it.

### Good Advice

Since the cookie dough is not baked, the recipe contains no raw egg or leavening.

### Doubling the Recipe

Double the ingredients for the ice cream mixture and use two cups of the cookie dough.

### To Freeze

Transfer the ice cream to the chilled container. Press plastic wrap onto the surface of the ice cream and cover tightly. Label with date and contents. Freeze overnight or up to 10 days.

### To Serve

Let the ice cream soften about 10 minutes before serving. It should be creamy.

## Good Advice

- Use My*T*Fine brand chocolate pudding, it gives the ice cream a good chocolate pudding taste.
- Note that this dense ice cream can be frozen up to two weeks rather than ten days.

## To Freeze

Transfer the ice cream to the chilled container. Press plastic wrap onto the surface of the ice cream and cover tightly. Label with date and contents. Freeze overnight or up to 14 days.

## To Serve

Scoop the ice cream into dishes without softening it.

# Chocolate Pudding Ice Cream

**Makes about 1 quart**

Close your eyes and imagine a dark, cold, ultra-smooth chocolate pudding. That gives you an idea of the taste of this ice cream. Although Chocolate Pudding Ice Cream is no richer than other homemade ice creams, it certainly tastes as if it is. You can scoop this ice cream straight from the freezer since it remains soft even when frozen. Memories of Chocolate Pudding Ice Cream feasts at Herrell's ice cream shop in Northampton, Massachusetts, during my daughter Laura's college years inspired this recipe.

**1½ cups milk**
**1½ cups whipping cream**
**3 large eggs**
**¾ cup sugar**
**Two 3⅝-ounce packages chocolate pudding and pie filling, not instant**
**6 ounces semisweet chocolate chips or semisweet chocolate, chopped**
**2 teaspoons vanilla extract**

In a large saucepan heat the milk and cream until the mixture is hot and a few bubbles begin to form, about 150°F. if measured with an instant-read food thermometer. Do not boil. Put the eggs and sugar in the large bowl of an electric mixer and beat on medium speed for 2 minutes. Decrease the speed to low and mix in the chocolate pudding just until incorporated. Slowly pour the hot milk mixture into the egg mixture and mix to incorporate it. Pour the mixture back into the saucepan. Stirring constantly, cook over low-medium heat until the mixture thickens slightly and reaches 170°F. measured with a food thermometer. Be sure to stir often where the sides and the bottom of the pan meet. As soon as the chocolate mixture reaches 170°F., strain it into a large bowl. Stir in the semisweet chocolate and vanilla. Stir until the chocolate is completely melted and the mixture is smooth. Cover and refrigerate until very cold, about 5 hours or overnight. Stir the mixture several times while it is chilling. Chill a moisture-proof carton or plastic freezer container for the ice cream. Stir the cold mixture smooth and transfer to an ice cream maker. Process according to the manufacturer's directions.

## Good Advice

• Watch the coconut carefully while it toasts and remove it from the oven as soon as it turns golden.

• Let the ice cream soften about fifteen minutes before serving. It should be very soft when you serve it for maximum contrast with the crisp toasted coconut.

## Doubling the Recipe

Double the ingredients.

## To Freeze

Transfer the ice cream to the chilled container. Press plastic wrap onto the surface of the ice cream and cover tightly. Label with date and contents. Freeze overnight or up to 10 days.

## To Serve

Let the ice cream soften about 15 minutes before serving, until it is very soft but not melted.

# Toasted Coconut Ice Cream

**Makes about 1½ quarts**

Several years ago, my mother, my daughter, and I took a trip together to Santa Fe, New Mexico. During our stay, we discovered an informal restaurant called Pasqual's that was so good, we kept going back there to eat. After each meal we splurged on their Toasted Coconut Ice Cream. It was the ideal conclusion to the spicy southwestern dishes. As soon as I returned home, I began making my own version and reliving our Santa Fe holiday.

**1½ cups shredded sweetened coconut**
**1½ cups whole milk**
**1½ cups whipping cream**
**5 large egg yolks**
**⅔ cup sugar**
**2 teaspoons vanilla extract**
**1 tablespoon dark rum**

1. Position a rack in the middle of the oven. Preheat the oven to 300°F.

2. Spread the coconut on a baking sheet. Toast about 10 minutes, until the coconut becomes golden, stirring once. Set the coconut aside to cool thoroughly.

3. Heat the milk and cream in a large saucepan just until a few bubbles form, about 150°F. if measured on a food thermometer. Do not boil. Put the egg yolks and sugar in the large bowl of an electric mixer and beat at medium speed until the mixture thickens slightly and lightens in color, about 45 seconds. Decrease the speed to low and slowly add the hot milk mixture. Return the mixture to the saucepan and cook over low-medium heat stirring constantly, until it reaches 170°F. measured on a food thermometer. Stir the mixture often where the sides and the bottom of the pan meet. The mixture will thicken slightly and leave a path on the back of a spoon when you draw your finger across it. A little steam will just begin to rise from the custard mixture. Do not boil. Strain the hot mixture into a bowl and stir in the vanilla and rum. Cover and refrigerate until very cold, about 5 hours or overnight. Stir the mixture several times while it is chilling. Chill a moisture-proof carton or plastic freezer container for the ice cream. Transfer the custard to an ice cream maker and process according to the manufacturer's directions. Add the toasted coconut during the last 5 minutes of churning.

# Brown Bread Crunch Ice Cream

**Makes about $1^3/_4$ pints**

When my friend Helen Hall sent me this recipe, I was, frankly, skeptical about using bread crumbs in ice cream. But I trust Helen's judgment, so I tried her recipe. The ice cream mixture is simple enough, and the whole wheat bread crumbs are baked with brown sugar to form a spicy crunch. A lot of the crunch is added to the ice cream for an appealing dark golden color with sweet spicy taste.

**7 slices stale firm-textured whole wheat bread, such as Pepperidge Farm**
**1 cup (packed) light brown sugar**
**2 cups cold whipping cream**
**¼ cup granulated sugar**
**1 teaspoon vanilla**

1. Position a rack in the center of the oven. Preheat the oven to 375°F. Lightly oil a baking sheet.

2. Cut each slice of bread, including crusts, into 4 pieces. Fit a food processor with the metal blade. Starting with a few on/off pulses, process the bread in 2 batches until it forms coarse crumbs. There should be 2 cups. Spread the bread crumbs on the baking sheet. Sprinkle evenly with the brown sugar. Bake, stirring the crumbs and sugar together every 5 minutes, until the brown sugar is melted and the crumbs are well coated with the melted brown sugar, about 15 minutes. Cool thoroughly. The crumbs will crisp as they cool.

3. Put the cream, granulated sugar, and vanilla in the large bowl of an electric mixer and beat on medium speed until the cream thickens to the consistency of sour cream and lines begin to form in the cream from the motion of the beaters. Chill a moisture-proof carton or plastic freezer container for the ice cream. Transfer the custard to an ice cream maker and process just until the ice cream has the consistency of soft frozen custard, about 5 minutes less than the normal time for churning ice cream. Add the brown bread crunch during the last 5 minutes of churning.

### Good Advice

- Use stale bread for the bread crumbs. If it is fresh, toast the slices in a 300°F. oven for seven to ten minutes.
- Whip the cream just until it resembles sour cream, it should not be whipped to soft peaks.
- Churn the ice cream just to the consistency of soft frozen custard.

### Doubling the Recipe

Double the ingredients.

### To Freeze

Transfer the ice cream to the chilled container. Press a piece of plastic wrap onto the surface of the ice cream and cover tightly. Label with date and contents. Freeze up to 10 days.

### To Serve

Soften the ice cream for about 10 minutes until it scoops easily and has a creamy texture.

# Pine Nut Praline Ice Cream

**Makes about 1 1/4 quarts**

Crisp bits of pine nut praline add a new dimension to a luxurious vanilla ice cream. The praline is crushed rather than ground, so that pieces of pine nut, with all its rich, buttery flavor, remain.

**1½ cups whole milk**
**1½ cups whipping cream**
**5 large egg yolks**
**⅔ cup sugar**
**2 teaspoons vanilla extract**
**1 tablespoon dark rum**
**6 tablespoons crushed pine nut praline (page 48)**

Heat the milk and cream in a large saucepan just until a few bubbles form, about 150°F. if measured on a food thermometer. Do not boil. Put the egg yolks and sugar in the large bowl of an electric mixer and beat at medium speed until the mixture thickens slightly and lightens in color, about 45 seconds. Decrease the speed to low and slowly add the hot milk mixture. Return the mixture to the saucepan and cook the custard over low-medium heat, stirring constantly, until it reaches 170°F. measured on a food thermometer. Stir the mixture often where the sides and the bottom of the pan meet. The mixture will thicken slightly and leave a path on the back of a spoon when you draw your finger across it. A little steam will just begin to rise from the custard mixture. Do not boil. Strain the hot mixture into a bowl and stir in the vanilla and rum. Cover and refrigerate until cold, about 5 hours or overnight. Stir the mixture several times while it is chilling. Chill a moisture-proof carton or plastic freezer container for the ice cream. Transfer the custard to an ice cream maker and process according to the manufacturer's directions. Remove the pine nut praline from the freezer and add during the last 5 minutes of churning.

### Good Advice

Use nut praline prepared by either method—powdered sugar or granulated sugar—for the ice cream.

### Doubling the Recipe

Double the ingredients.

### To Freeze

Transfer the ice cream to the chilled container. Press plastic wrap onto the surface of the ice cream and cover tightly. Label with date and contents. Freeze overnight or up to 5 days. Although the ice cream will taste fine, the praline will soften after 5 days and no longer be crunchy.

### To Serve

Let the ice cream soften at room temperature about 10 minutes before serving.

# Pistachio Ice Cream

**Makes about 1 quart**

With pistachio ice cream there doesn't seem to be any in between—either you love it or you hate it. I'm on the "love it" side. Maybe the "hate its" have never tasted pistachio ice cream like this, full of pistachio nuts and never turned green with food coloring.

**¾ cup shelled pistachios nuts, roasted and unsalted**
**1½ cups whole milk**
**1½ cups whipping cream**
**5 large egg yolks**
**⅔ cup sugar**
**2 teaspoons vanilla extract**
**½ teaspoon almond extract**

1. Position a rack in the middle of the oven and preheat to 300°F.

2. Spread the pistachio nuts on a baking sheet and bake 5 minutes to freshen the nuts. Cool the nuts and rub off any loose skins. Coarsely chop the nuts and set aside.

3. Heat the milk and cream in a large saucepan just until a few bubbles form, about 150°F. if measured on a food thermometer. Do not boil. Put the egg yolks and sugar in the large bowl of an electric mixer and beat at medium speed until the mixture thickens slightly and lightens in color, about 45 seconds. Decrease the speed to low and slowly add the hot milk mixture. Return the mixture to the saucepan and cook over low-medium heat, stirring constantly, until it reaches 170°F. measured on a food thermometer. Stir the mixture often where the sides and the bottom of the pan meet. The mixture will thicken slightly and leave a path on the back of a spoon when you draw your finger across it. A little steam will just begin to rise from the mixture. Do not boil. Strain the hot mixture into a bowl and stir in the vanilla and almond extract. Cover and refrigerate until very cold, about 5 hours or overnight. Stir the mixture several times while it is chilling. Chill a moisture-proof carton or plastic freezer container for the ice cream. Transfer the custard to an ice cream maker and process according to the manufacturer's directions. Add the chopped pistachio nuts during the last 5 minutes of churning.

### Good Advice

Shelled pistachio nuts are available at specialty food shops and can be ordered by mail from G. B. Ratto (page 245). Freeze the nuts in a tightly covered plastic container for up to 1 year.

### Doubling the Recipe

Double the ingredients.

### To Freeze

Transfer the ice cream to the chilled container. Press plastic wrap onto the surface of the ice cream and cover tightly. Label with date and contents. Freeze overnight or up to 10 days.

### To Serve

Let the ice cream soften about 10 minutes before serving.

## Good Advice

- Taste one of the peaches to check that it has a good peach flavor. The ice cream will be only as good as the peaches.
- You will need about six large peaches.

## Doubling the Recipe

Double the ingredients.

## To Freeze

Transfer the ice cream to the chilled container. Press plastic wrap onto the surface of the ice cream and cover tightly. Label with date and contents. Freeze overnight or up to 10 days.

## To Serve

Let the ice cream soften about 10 minutes before serving.

# Summer Peach Ice Cream

**Makes about 2 quarts**

The secret of good peach ice cream is simple—peaches, lots of peaches. When sweet, juicy peaches reach their peak in summer, it's prime time for peach ice cream. This usually coincides with the most sweltering heat wave of the year; the ice cream offers some refreshing heat relief.

**1 cup whole milk**
**1 cup whipping cream**
**3 large egg yolks**
**½ cup plus 1 tablespoon sugar**
**2 teaspoons vanilla extract**
**1 tablespoon amaretto**
**3 cups peeled and sliced, ripe peaches (page 95)**

1. Heat the milk and cream in a large saucepan just until a few bubbles form, about 150°F. if measured on a food thermometer. Do not boil. Put the egg yolks and sugar in the large bowl of an electric mixer and beat at medium speed until the mixture thickens slightly and lightens in color, about 45 seconds. Decrease the speed to low and slowly add the hot milk mixture. Return the mixture to the saucepan and cook over low-medium heat, stirring constantly, until the mixture reaches 170°F. measured on a food thermometer. Stir the mixture often where the sides and the bottom of the pan meet. The mixture will thicken slightly and leave a path on the back of a spoon when you draw your finger across it. A little steam will just begin to rise from the mixture. Do not boil. Strain the hot mixture into a bowl and stir in the vanilla and amaretto. Cover and refrigerate until very cold, about 5 hours or overnight. Stir the mixture several times while it is chilling.

2. Put the peach slices in the workbowl of a food processor fitted with a metal blade and process until the peaches form a puree. Mix the pureed peaches into the chilled custard mixture. Transfer the custard to an ice cream maker and process according to the manufacturer's directions. Chill a moisture-proof carton or plastic freezer container for the ice cream.

# Red Raspberry Ice Cream

**Make about 1½ quarts**

If someone asked me to choose the most elegant fruit, I'd say raspberries. And if someone asked me to choose the most elegant ice cream, my answer would be this rich vanilla ice cream churned with raspberry puree.

**1½ cups whole milk**
**1½ cups whipping cream**
**5 large egg yolks**
**¾ cup plus 2 teaspoons sugar**
**1 teaspoon vanilla extract**
**1½ to 2 cups fresh or defrosted frozen unsweetened raspberries**

1. Put the milk and cream in a large saucepan and heat the mixture over medium heat until it is hot and a few bubbles just begin to form, about 150°F. if measured with a food thermometer. Do not boil. Put the egg yolks and sugar in the large bowl of an electric mixer and beat at medium speed until the mixture thickens slightly and lightens in color, about 45 seconds. Decrease the speed to low and slowly add the hot milk mixture. Return the mixture to the saucepan and cook the custard over low-medium heat, stirring constantly, until it reaches 170°F. measured on a food thermometer. Stir the mixture often where the sides and the bottom of the pan meet. The mixture will thicken slightly and leave a path on the back of a spoon when you draw your finger across it. A little steam will begin to rise from the custard. Do not boil. Strain the hot mixture into a bowl and stir in the vanilla. Cover and refrigerate until very cold, about 5 hours or overnight. Stir the mixture several times while it chills.

2. Place a strainer over a small bowl and put 1½ cups of the raspberries in the strainer. Use the back of a large spoon to press the raspberry pulp and juice through the strainer. If necessary, strain more raspberries to make ½ cup of puree. There may be a few stray seeds in the puree which you can remove by straining it again. Or leave them in the puree as I do. A few seeds remind me of the whole raspberries and seem more natural to me. Press plastic wrap onto the surface of the puree and refrigerate up to 1 week.

3. Mix the raspberry puree into the chilled custard mixture. Transfer the custard to an ice cream maker and process according to the manufacturer's directions. Chill a moisture-proof carton or plastic freezer container for the ice cream.

### Good Advice

Frozen unsweetened raspberries give off more liquid than fresh raspberries; you'll probably need less of them to make the amount of raspberry puree needed for the ice cream.

### Doubling the Recipe

Double the ingredients.

### To Freeze

Transfer the ice cream to the chilled container. Press plastic wrap onto the surface of the ice cream and cover tightly. Label with date and contents. Freeze overnight or up to 10 days.

### To Serve

Let the ice cream soften at room temperature about 10 minutes before serving.

# Pink Grapefruit Sorbet

**Makes about 1 pint**

Grapefruit is one of the few fruits that are at their peak in the winter months, but few desserts cry out for fresh grapefruit. An exception is this pink grapefruit sorbet. It makes a refreshing conclusion to a hearty winter meal.

**½ cup water**
**⅓ cup sugar**
**1½ cups fresh pink grapefruit juice, including any pulp (2 to 3 grapefruit)**
**1 tablespoon vodka**

Put the water and sugar in a small saucepan and heat, stirring occasionally, until the sugar is dissolved and the mixture just begins to boil. Pour into a medium bowl and stir in the grapefruit juice. Cover and refrigerate until the mixture is cold, about 3 hours or overnight. Stir the vodka into the grapefruit mixture and transfer it to an ice cream maker. Process according to manufacturer's instructions. Chill a moisture-proof carton or plastic freezer container for the sorbet.

## Good Advice

The sorbet will be either a pale pink or a creamy color, depending on how pink the grapefruit. White grapefruit can be substituted, but I find pink grapefruit usually sweeter than the white.

## Doubling the Recipe

Double or triple the ingredients.

## To Freeze

Transfer the sorbet to the cold container. Press plastic wrap onto the surface of the sorbet and cover tightly. Label with date and contents. Freeze overnight or up to 10 days.

## To Serve

Let the sorbet soften at room temperature about 10 minutes before serving.

# Mighty Orange Sorbet

**Makes about 1 quart**

The intense orange flavor of this sorbet was a happy surprise. My husband, Jeff, who is a sorbet lover, asked me to make a lime and orange sorbet. To our amazement, the sorbet did not taste like a combination of the two fruits. Instead, the lime juice intensified the orange flavor, giving up its own personality. This is one mighty orange dessert.

**2 cups water**
**¾ cup plus 2 tablespoons sugar**
**1 cup fresh orange juice (3 to 4 oranges)**
**½ cup fresh lime juice (4 to 5 limes)**
**2 tablespoons vodka**

Put the water and sugar in a small saucepan and cook over medium heat, stirring occasionally, until the sugar is dissolved and the mixture just begins to boil. Pour the sugar syrup into a medium bowl. Stir in the orange juice and lime juice. Cover and refrigerate until the mixture is cold, about 3 hours or overnight. Chill a moisture-proof carton or plastic freezer container for the sorbet. Stir the vodka into the juice mixture and transfer to an ice cream maker. Process according to manufacturer's instructions.

### Good Advice

Vodka doesn't change the taste of the sorbet—it keeps the frozen sorbet softer by lowering its freezing temperature.

### Doubling the Recipe

Double the ingredients.

### To Freeze

Transfer the sorbet to the chilled container. Press plastic wrap onto the surface of the sorbet and cover tightly. Label with date and contents. Freeze overnight or up to 10 days.

### To Serve

Let the sorbet soften at room temperature about 10 minutes before serving.

# Marvelous Mango Sorbet

**Makes about 1 pint**

Mango sorbet is a sunny yellow-orange color, as bright as the tropical sunshine where mangoes grow. The dense pulp of the fruit gives sorbet a rich flavor and a satin-smooth texture.

**¾ cup water**
**⅓ cup sugar**
**3 to 4 ripe mangoes**
**4 tablespoons fresh lemon juice**
**4 tablespoons fresh orange juice**

Put the water and sugar in a small saucepan and cook over medium heat, stirring occasionally, until the sugar is dissolved and the mixture just begins to boil. Pour the sugar syrup into a small bowl. Cover and refrigerate the syrup until it is chilled thoroughly, about 3 hours. The syrup can be prepared up to 1 week ahead and stored in the refrigerator. Peel the mangoes and cut the fruit away from the pit. Put the fruit in a food processor fitted with a steel blade and process to a puree. Strain the mango puree into a large bowl. You should have 1½ cups of puree. Stir the lemon juice, orange juice, and ⅔ cup of the cold sugar syrup into the puree. Taste and add up to 1 tablespoon of sugar syrup. Transfer the sorbet mixture to an ice cream maker. Process according to the manufacturer's instructions. Chill a moisture-proof carton or plastic freezer container for the sorbet.

### Good Advice

- Mangoes vary in sweetness. Taste the sorbet mixture before churning it and add up to 1 tablespoon more of sugar syrup if needed; you will have enough.
- Do not add vodka to this sorbet; the consistency is fine without it.

### Doubling the Recipe

Double the ingredients.

### To Freeze

Transfer the sorbet to the cold container. Press plastic wrap onto the surface of the sorbet. Cover tightly and freeze overnight or up to 10 days.

### To Serve

Let the sorbet soften at room temperature about 10 minutes before serving.

# Banana Sorbet

**Makes about 1½ pints**

When I'm on a diet but want something rich and satisfying for dessert, I make this banana sorbet. One and a half pints of sorbet contain only two tablespoons of sugar and a teaspoon of vodka. Most of the calories come from the bananas.

**½ cup water**
**2 tablespoons sugar**
**3 medium bananas**
**2 tablespoons lemon juice**
**3 tablespoons orange juice**
**1 teaspoon vodka**

Put the water and sugar in a small saucepan and cook over medium heat, stirring occasionally, until the sugar is dissolved and the mixture just begins to boil. Pour the sugar syrup into a small bowl. Cover and refrigerate until chilled thoroughly, about 3 hours. The syrup can be prepared up to 1 week ahead and stored in the refrigerator. Put the bananas in a food processor fitted with a steel blade and process to a puree. With the machine running, add the lemon juice, orange juice, and chilled sugar syrup, and process for about 15 seconds until the mixture is smooth. Immediately transfer the sorbet mixture to an ice cream maker. Process according to the manufacturer's instructions. After the sorbet has churned for 10 minutes, add the vodka and complete the churning. Chill a moisture-proof carton or plastic freezer container for the sorbet.

### Good Advice

Have the sugar syrup chilled before starting the banana puree so that the sorbet can be churned right away. If it is not, the bananas will darken it.

### Doubling the Recipe

Double the ingredients.

### To Freeze

Transfer the sorbet to the chilled container. Press plastic wrap onto the surface of the sorbet. Cover tightly and freeze overnight or up to 10 days.

### To Serve

Let the sorbet soften at room temperature about 10 minutes before serving.

# Mail Order Sources

Hadley Fruit Orchards
P.O. Box 495
Cabazon, CA 92230
(800) 854-5655

Excellent quality dried fruits and nuts.

King Arthur Flour Baker's Catalogue
P. O. Box 876
Norwich, VT 05055
(800) 827-6836
Fax: (802) 649-5359

Baking ingredients and equipment.

Maid of Scandinavia
3244 Raleigh Ave.
Minneapolis, MN 55416
(800) 328-6722
Fax: (612) 927-6215

Baking equipment including cardboard cake circles, pastry bags, and pastry tips.

Penzey's Spice House Ltd.
P. O. Box 1448
Waukesha, WI 53187
(414) 574-0277
Fax: (414) 574-0278

Fresh spices and dried herbs. Source for ground extra-fancy China Tunghing cassia cinnamon, a sweet cinnamon of high quality.

G. B. Ratto and Co.
821 Washington St.
Oakland, CA 94607
(510) 832-6503

Ingredients include Guittard and Callebaut chocolate and Nutella.

Williams-Sonoma
P.O. Box 7456
San Francisco, CA 94120-7456
(800) 541-2233

Baking equipment and ingredients.

Zingerman's
422 Detroit St.
Ann Arbor, MI 48104
(313) 663-3400
Fax: (313) 769-1235

Callebaut chocolate.

# Bibliography


Bradley, Hassell, and Carole Sundberg. *Keeping Food Safe: The Complete Guide to Safeguarding Your Family's Health While Handling, Preparing, Preserving, Freezing and Storing Food at Home*. New York: Doubleday and Company, 1975.

Bridge, Fred, and Jean F. Tibbetts. *The Well-Tooled Kitchen*. New York: William Morrow and Company, Inc., 1991.

Cox, Beverly. *Cooking Techniques*. Massachusetts: Little, Brown and Company, 1981.

Essipoff, Marie. *Making the Most of Your Food Freezer*. New York: Holt, Rinehart and Company, 1954.

Desrosier, Norman W., and Donald K. Tressler. *Fundamentals of Food Freezing*. Connecticut: Avi Publishing Company, Inc., 1977.

Fabian, F. W. *Home Food Preservation*. Connecticut: Avi Publishing Company, Inc., 1943.

Gates, June. *Basic Foods*. New York: Holt, Rinehart, and Winston, 1976.

Gortner, Willis, Frederick Erdman, and Nancy Masterman. *Principles of Food Freezing*. New York: John Wilson and Sons, Inc., 1948.

Herbst, Sharon Tyler. *Food Lover's Companion*. New York: Barron, 1990.

Kirk, Raymond E., and Donald Othmer. *Encyclopedia of Chemical Technology*, Fourth Edition, Volumes VI and III. New York: John Wiley and Sons, Inc., 1992.

McGee, Harold. *The Curious Cook*. California: North Point Press, 1990.

McGee, Harold. *On Food and Cooking*. New York: Macmillan Publishing Company, 1984.

Simpson, Jean. *The Frozen Food Cookbook*. Connecticut: Avi Publishing Company, Inc., 1962.

Sultan, William. *Practical Baking*. Third Edition. Connecticut: Avi Publishing Company, Inc., 1983.

Tressler, Donald K. *Some Aspects of Food Refrigeration and Freezing*. Washington, D.C.: Agriculture Organization of the United Nations, 1950.

Handbooks

*The Story of Chocolate*, The Chocolate Manufacturers Association of the U.S.A., McLean, Virginia

*Sugar's Functional Roles in Cooking and Food Preparation*, The Sugar Association, Inc., Washington, D.C.

# Index

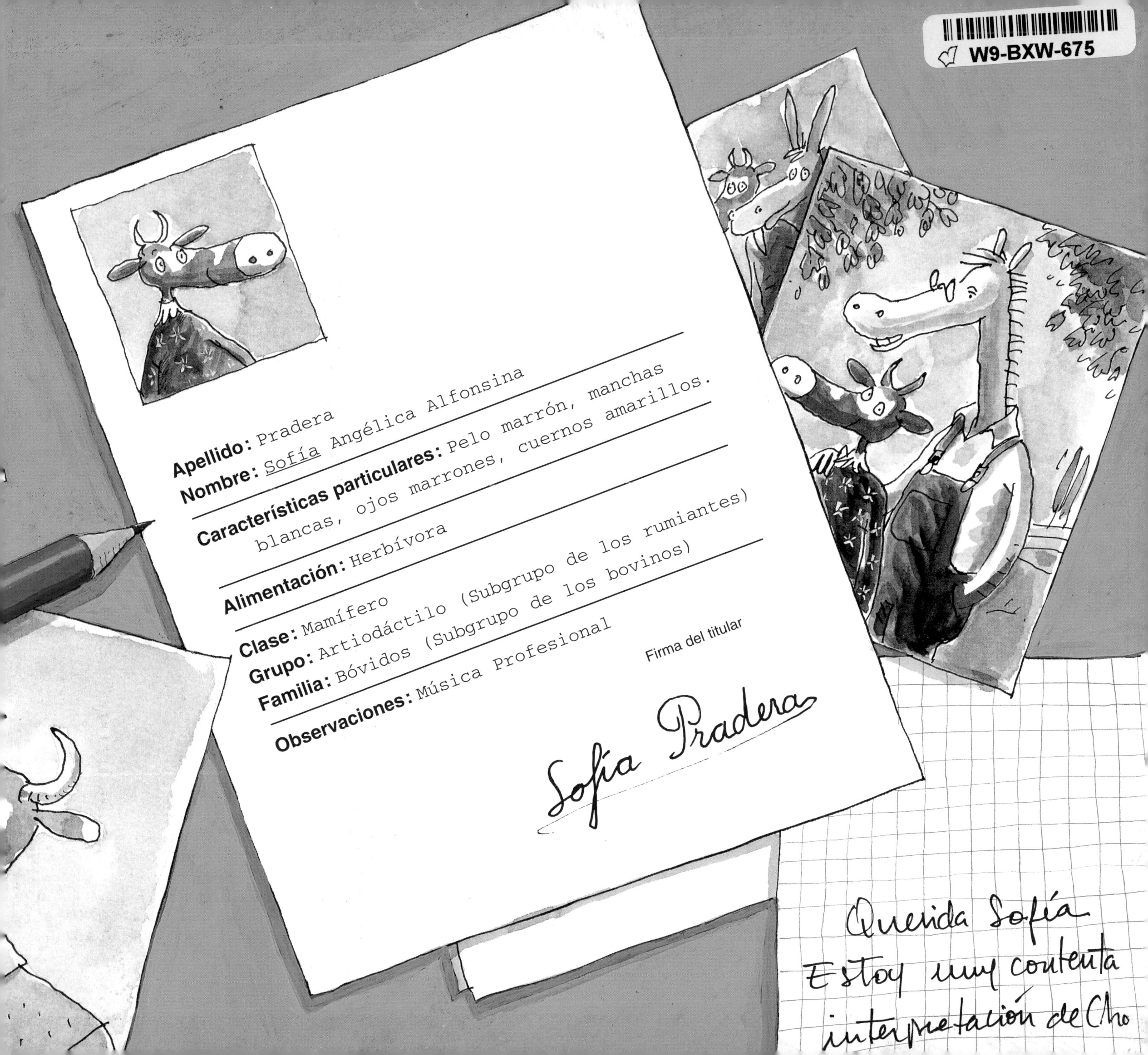
W9-BXW-675
Apellido: Pradera
Nombre: Sofía Angélica Alfonsina
Características particulares: Pelo marrón, manchas blancas, ojos marrones, cuernos amarillos.
Alimentación: Herbívora
Clase: Mamífero
Grupo: Artiodáctilo (Subgrupo de los rumiantes)
Familia: Bóvidos (Subgrupo de los bovinos)
Observaciones: Música Profesional
Firma del titular
Sofía Pradera
Querida Sofía
Estoy muy contenta
interpretación de Cho

*A mi hermano Éric*

Traducción al español: Julia Vinent

Ronda del General Mitre 95, 08022 Barcelona
e-mail: corimbo@retemail.es
www.corimbo.es
Título de la edicion original: «Sophie la vache musicienne»
1ª edición, noviembre 2001

Impreso en Francia por Pollina s.a., 85400 Luçon

Geoffroy de Pennart

# Sofía, la vaca que amaba la música

Editorial Corimbo
Barcelona

Sofía vive en el campo. Adora la música. Le gusta mucho cantar y, cuando da un concierto, su familia y sus amigos quedan encantados.

Un día, se convoca un importante concurso de música.
Todas las orquestas del país están invitadas a participar.

«Quiero probar suerte», dice Sofía a sus amigos.
«A lo mejor encuentro trabajo en una orquesta.»
«¿Quieres ir a la ciudad?», pregunta su madre, preocupada.
«¡Quieres dejarnos!», exclama su padre.
«¿Y nuestros conciertos nocturnos?», comentan apenados sus amigos.

«Escuchad», dice Jorge, el viejo caballo,
«aunque estamos todos un poco asustados,
Sofía tiene razón: debe intentarlo, tiene talento y lo conseguirá.»

Jorge los ha convencido.
El día de su partida, todos acompañan a Sofía a la estación…

... ¡Por fin, la gran ciudad!

Sofía compra un periódico
y un plano de la ciudad,
se sienta en la terraza de un café
y lee las ofertas de trabajo:
Muchas orquestas buscan músicos.
«A ver, a ver. Mm, éste,
*La Gran Orquesta de la Sonrisa Rutilante*.
Está muy cerca de aquí.
¡Qué nombre tan extraño! Bueno,
vamos allá…»

« ¿Viene por el trabajo? En principio,
no contratamos herbívoros, pero pase, pase … »

Sofía huye a toda velocidad.
«Tengo que prestar más atención
al nombre de las orquestas», piensa.
«¡Oh! *Los Herbívoros Melómanos*.
Yo soy herbívora, vamos pues…»

«Si viene por la vacante
lo siento, querida… ¡buscamos a alguien de más peso!»

«Qué tendrá que ver el peso
con la música», exclama Sofía.
«¡Mm! *Armonía Real de los Rumiantes*.
Yo rumio, vamos pues...»

« ¿Viene por la vacante?
Lo siento, querida… ¡temo que no esté a la altura! »

«Qué tendrá que ver la talla
con la música», se indigna Sofía.
«¡Ah! *Círculo Musical de los Animales con Cuernos*.
Yo tengo cuernos, vamos pues…»

« ¿Viene usted por la vacante?
Lo siento, querida, hay cuernos y cuernos… »

«Qué tendrán que ver los cuernos
con la música»,
se enfada Sofía.
«*Conjunto Orquestal Bovino*.
Yo soy bovina, vamos pues…»

«¡Bah! Nada de vacas marrones en este conjunto.»

«Qué tendrá que ver el color
con la música», dice, encolerizada, Sofía.
«¡Ah! *Los Bóvidos Virtuosos.*
Yo soy un bóvido, vamos pues…»

« ¿Viene usted por la vacante? Lo sieeento, queriiida, pero creo quc no es usted suficientemeeente elegante para nuestra orquesssta. »

«Vaya grupo de pijas»,
dice Sofía, furiosa.
«¡Pero qué tendrá que ver
la elegancia con la música!»
Vuelve a consultar su periódico.
«Ah, *Gran Orquesta de las Vacas Locas*.
Yo soy vaca y estoy loca… de rabia. ¡Vamos pues!»

« ¿Viene usted por la vacante ? Entre, entre, cuantos más seamos,
más nos reiremos ... »
« Oh, bueno ... Creo ... que me he equivocado de dirección », balbucea Sofía.

Sofía está desanimada.
*Orquesta Real Canina*, *Los Gatos Ronroneantes*,
para qué continuar…
«No me queda más opción que volver a casa.»

Triste, se sienta en la terraza del café de la estación.
«¿Y bien, señorita, no van bien las cosas?», se interesa el camarero.

Sofía le cuenta sus desgracias.
«¡Oh!, no me extraña nada, señorita. Estas orquestas no valen nada,
no aman verdaderamente la música. Yo mismo, que soy músico,
he pasado por eso: tenía el pelo o muy largo o muy corto;
tenía las orejas caídas, el morro demasiado puntiagudo;
no tenía la altura, ni el color, ni el pedigrí adecuados...»

« Entonces, ¿por qué no formamos una orquesta nosotros? ¡No contrataremos a nadie si no es por su talento! Permita que me presente: soy Sofía. »
« ¡Chóquela, señorita! Soy Thelonius. »
« ¡Muy bien Thelonius! Y llámeme Sofía. »

**LA ARMONÍA REAL DE LOS RUMIANTES** ofrece una plaza de cantante. Los candidatos pueden presentarse hoy en la avenida de Los Mustang, 93.

**EL CÍRCULO MUSICAL DE LOS ANIMALES CON CUERNOS** contrata instrumentistas. Audiciones en el local de la orquesta, calle Sírex, 23.

**CONJUNTO ORQUESTAL BOVINO** contrata músicos y músicas. Plaza de Los Diablos s/n.

**LOS HERBÍVOROS MELÓMANOS** buscan cantante. Presentarse en calle Pequeniques, 36.

Con intención de crear una orquesta para participar en el concurso, **SOFÍA Y THELONIUS** buscan buenos músicos. Todas las candidaturas serán examinadas. Audiciones hoy, a partir de las 10 h. en casa de Thelonius. Calle Nino Bravo, 2.

**LA GRAN ORQUESTA DE LA SONRISA RUTILANTE** contrata músicos. Dirigirse a la señora Dientes, avenida Tequila, 2.

**LA GRAN ORQUESTA DE LAS VACAS LOCAS** está loca por escucharte hoy en el 77 de la calle Parchís.

**ORQUESTA REAL CANINA** Los músicos que lo deseen pueden optar a una plaza presentándose en la calle Carlos Cano, 8.

**LOS BÓVIDOS VIRTUOSOS** buscan músicos. Imprescindible buena presencia. Calle Tarrés, 1.

Sofía y Thelonius han puesto un anuncio en el periódico,

y los candidatos hacen cola.

Ambos se toman su tiempo para escucharlos con mucha atención.
Al cabo de un rato han contratado…

... a cuatro excelentes músicos.

Sofía bautiza el grupo *Los Amigos de la Música*. Y, por supuesto,

ganan el concurso.